5 $\frac{00}{}$

JOHN FORSYTH
Political Tactician

JOHN FORSYTH
Political Tactician

BY
ALVIN LAROY DUCKETT

UNIVERSITY OF GEORGIA PRESS

To

FLETCHER M. GREEN

for his scholarly advice
and genuine friendship

COPYRIGHT © 1962 BY UNIVERSITY OF GEORGIA PRESS
LIBRARY OF CONGRESS CATALOGUE CARD NUMBER: 62-12497
PUBLICATION OF THIS BOOK WAS AIDED BY A GRANT FROM THE FORD FOUNDATION
PRINTED IN THE UNITED STATES OF AMERICA BY
FOOTE & DAVIES, INC., ATLANTA

Contents

	PREFACE	vii
I	THE CURTAIN RISES	1
II	THE HALLS OF CONGRESS	12
III	MISSION TO MADRID	42
IV	LAND OF THE DONS	65
V	HIS EXCELLENCY, THE GOVERNOR	81
VI	CREEKS AND CHEROKEES	105
VII	STAUNCH DEFENDER OF JACKSON	128
VIII	TARIFF AND NULLIFICATION	150
IX	AFFAIRS OF STATE	167
X	DIPLOMACY: SOUTHWEST AND NORTHEAST	194
XI	THE CURTAIN FALLS	213
	NOTES	223
	BIBLIOGRAPHY	244
	INDEX	255

ALVIN LAROY DUCKETT was born in Greenwood, South Carolina, in 1908. A graduate of The Citadel at Charleston, South Carolina, he received his M.A. and Ph.D. degrees from the University of North Carolina.

After teaching history in the high schools of Clinton and Rock Hill, South Carolina, he served for more than five years with the U. S. Army prior to and during World War II, being separated from active duty with the rank of lieutenant colonel. He taught history at Washington and Lee University and since 1950 has been a member of the History and Government Department at Winthrop College, the South Carolina College for Women, in Rock Hill.

Dr. Duckett is a member of the Southern Historical Association, the South Carolina Historical Association, and Phi Alpha Theta.

Preface

AMERICAN history is replete with varied political patterns.
Interwoven into each pattern are the contributions of certain
individuals without which the course of events would have been
processed into a different channel or else modified into a vague
resemblance of accepted interpretation. It has been said that
history is influenced by the deeds of great men and women. An
objection to the statement is that the word "great" is superfluous.
A ranking official of the national government may not be considered among the highest echelon of historical figures, yet his
activities cannot be disregarded in appraising the American scene.
The same is true when that individual's career is associated with
state and local politics.

The first half of the nineteenth century was a tumultuous and
kaleidoscopic era. It was such a complex age that, at the present
time, an adequate textbook on the period alone is difficult to
locate whereas competent volumes concerning colonial, recent, or
other divisions of American history are comparatively abundant.
It was a colorful period in which the Jacksons, the Calhouns, and
the Clays dominated the national stage. Nevertheless, the Forsyths
gave additional depth to the parade of events.

The situation in Georgia during those fifty years was a reflection of the over-all picture. Within the smaller arena, the Forsyths
tended to play a more prominent role. John Forsyth emerged as
a controversial figure and, as such, was a product of his time.
Despite his long service with the federal government and his
limited presence in Georgia, he managed to contribute to the
welfare of his state.

Publication of a book is dependent upon the efforts of many individuals. This work is no exception. I am indebted to numerous associates for their assistance and guidance, for their material and moral support. It is unfortunate that limited space does not permit an identification of each person. For lack of a better method of acknowledging my appreciation, I wish to cite the staffs of the following: the Library of Congress, the National Archives, the Princeton University Library, the University of Georgia Library, the Emory University Library, the Washington Memorial Library of Macon, the University of North Carolina Library, the Duke University Library, and the Winthrop College Library.

There are certain individuals for whom special recognition must be accorded. Fletcher M. Green of the University of North Carolina suggested the study and offered constructive criticism. Ralph Betts Flanders of New York University directed attention to the Princeton University collection of Forsyth papers. Mrs. Mary G. Bryan, Georgia Department of Archives and History, Mrs. Lilla Mills Hawes, Georgia Historical Society, and Percy Powell, Manuscript Division of the Library of Congress, rendered courteous and valuable service. Mary Elizabeth Massey of the Winthrop College faculty read the manuscript and assisted with the index. Mrs. Eva Anderson, Mrs. Jean Roper James, and Kathryn Davis were proficient typists. To all, I am deeply grateful.

ALVIN L. DUCKETT

Winthrop College
Rock Hill, S. C.

I

The Curtain Rises

JOHN FORSYTH, long identified with the State of Georgia, was, as a matter of fact, an adopted son of that state. While a child, he came with his parents to Georgia, and he retained a legal residence there for the remainder of his life; but he was born in Virginia. His ancestry was Scottish. His paternal great-great-grandfather was James Forsyth, first of the lineage known to have settled in America. James emigrated from Scotland about 1680 and located in Virginia, where he was granted land in Amelia County in 1688. Among James's descendants in Scotland was a son James, who in turn had a son named Matthew.[1] The latter, a physician in the Royal Navy, became implicated in the Irish political disturbances and decided to change his residence to America. He and his family settled in Chester, New Hampshire, where they were well received.[2]

Robert Forsyth, the younger son of Matthew, and John's father, was born in Scotland in 1754. He came with his father to New England, but, before 1774, moved to Fredericksburg, Virginia. Upon the outbreak of the American Revolution in 1776, Robert joined the Continental Army and served three years, part of the time as a captain in Colonel Henry ("Light-Horse Harry") Lee's Battalion of Light Dragoons. Subsequently, Robert attained the rank of major of Virginia state militia. For his services, the state of Virginia later awarded his heirs 5,333-1/3 acres of land in the Military District of Ohio.[3]

After 1779, Major Robert Forsyth held an extremely demanding position. Whether as Deputy Commissary General of Purchases for the Southern Army or as Deputy Commissary for Virginia Purchases, his problem was to obtain supplies of beef,

salt, flour, rum, other foodstuffs, and the like for the use of the
army. The requisitions upon the states by the Continental
Congress were not always met, and as a result there were continual complaints. On one occasion, Major Forsyth wrote to Governor Benjamin Harrison of Virginia stating that the agreement
to sell flour in order to purchase supplies for the prisoners at
Winchester had not been complied with; no flour had been de-
posited for sale, and one thousand barrels for that purpose were
necessary immediately. He also repeated a request that salt be
supplied in order to cure the meat on hand.[4] In 1782, Colonel
Christopher Febiger noted that the meat was of such inferior
quality that the troops refused to eat it, and indeed went so far
as to express their opinion of it in a riot, which had to be
suppressed. He stated: "I have wrote [sic] to Major Forsyth.
he has no Resource in the world but the Carrion from Richmond
or Manchester."[5] On another occasion, this same officer complained that the people were reluctant to sell their bacon except
for sound money. He was alarmed and wrote to Major Forsyth,
who replied that he had neither money nor provisions.

Robert Forsyth returned to Fredericksburg at the close of the
American Revolution. He now had a family to consider. He had
married Mrs. Fanny Johnston Houston, a young widow of a
prominent Virginia family. She was a sister of Judge Peter
Johnston of Fredericksburg and aunt of Joseph Eggleston Johnston, who was to become a general in the Confederate Army.
Robert and Fanny Forsyth were blessed with two sons, the older
being Robert Moriah, born in 1778.[6] The second boy was John
Forsyth, who was born in Fredericksburg, Virginia, on October
22, 1780.[7]

Major Forsyth's stay in Fredericksburg after the war was brief.
Little is known of his activities during this period other than
that he became a member of the Virginia Order of the Cin-
cinnati in 1783. The following year, he and his family moved to
Charleston, South Carolina, where they lived for only a short
time. In 1785, they moved to Richmond County, Georgia, and
established a residence in Augusta, where Robert spent the remainder of his life.[8] The new home was near the land in Wilkes
County which was later granted to the major by Georgia in
recognition of his services during the war.

Almost immediately, Major Forsyth became a prominent personage in the locality. As a member of the Board of Commissioners for the town of Augusta in 1786, he took an active part

in the life of the community. The Board's functions were both numerous and varied. It supervised the public sale of lots and made agreements for the construction of a church. In 1787 it appointed Charles Francis Chevalier as French tutor in the Richmond Academy (in Augusta). The commissioners were responsible for the repair of the roads. On one occasion, they issued a warning that all responsible persons, and their slaves, were expected to work six days on a road leading from Augusta; all who refused were to be fined ten shillings per day by the Superior Court.[9]

The father of John Forsyth was also engaged in other community enterprises. In 1790, Richmond County had neither a courthouse nor a jail, and Robert was selected as a member of a commission to supply these needs. The commissioners asked the citizens of Augusta for private contributions, explaining that Augusta, as the commercial center of the state and a growing town, needed restraints upon crime. They predicted that, as a result of the convening of courts and the imprisonment of criminals, "society will be improved and regulated; government will be obeyed and respected; and the commerce between the merchant and planter protected."[10] The appeal was successful, construction was started, and by 1792 the commissioners were able to request that all accounts toward the project be rendered for settlement. Another civil function performed by Major Forsyth was that of assessor; as such, he received the returns of taxable property from the inhabitants of Augusta and vicinity. He also acted as a justice of the peace, as an executor of the estate of one John Bacon of Richmond County, and as a trustee of Richmond Academy.[11] In addition, he was a member of the Masonic Order, serving as Master of the Lodge Columbia, and at the time of his death he was Deputy Grand Master for the State of Georgia.

As a means of livelihood, Robert Forsyth entered into a business partnership with John Meals. In addition to operating general stores, they were interested in real estate. Forsyth severed relations with Meals late in 1786 and engaged in farming.[12]

With the organization of the federal government, Major Forsyth was designated a law-enforcement official. President George Washington submitted his name to the Senate of the United States on September 24, 1789, for the position of Marshal for the District of Georgia. The Senate confirmed the appointment two days later.[13] The first to hold this office, Robert had duties that were not confined entirely to the apprehension of criminals. He conducted public sales of those slaves who, considered the property of their owners, had been "seized under execution."[14] Also, it became his responsibility to direct the taking of the first United States census in the District of Georgia.[15]

Robert Forsyth was killed while performing a duty connected with his office. The misfortune occurred on January 11, 1794, when he went to the home of a Mrs. Dixon, in Augusta, for the purpose of serving processes on two brothers, Beverly and William Allen, the former described as a Methodist minister from South Carolina. Seeing Beverly engaged in business conversation with several gentlemen and not wishing to cause embarrassment, the Marshal asked him to step outside. Instead of following Forsyth, the Reverend Mr. Allen went into another room, where he was joined by his brother, who, in the meantime, had been served with a writ. When Major Forsyth, accompanied by Deputy Marshals Richards and Randolph, proceeded upstairs and advanced toward the room where the Allens had withdrawn, Beverly fired a pistol through the opening of the door. The ball struck Forsyth in the head, killing him instantly. Allen was immediately arrested and placed in prison. The coroner's inquest returned a verdict of willful murder.[16]

William Allen was indicted for murder and arraigned; upon entering a plea of not guilty, he was released. His brother Beverly remained in the Augusta jail until the night of February 26, when, through the alleged connivance of a guard, he escaped. Governor George Mathews of Georgia offered a reward of £75 for the apprehension of the criminal, and to this amount was added $480, raised by the citizens of Augusta through popular subscription. Subsequently, Beverly Allen was arrested in Elbert County and confined to the jail there, from which he was rescued by a group of armed men led by his brother William.[17] Thereafter, the murderer fled to Texas; he was never captured and punished for his crime.

Funeral services were conducted for Major Forsyth on the second day after his death. Minute guns were fired from the home of the deceased while the body was being taken to Saint Paul's Church. Included in the numerous procession were artillery and infantry companies, prominent families, and members of the Lodge Columbia in Masonic regalia. The remains were interred in the cemetery of Saint Paul's Church, Augusta, where a monument was erected to his memory.[18] Thus ended, at the age of forty years, the life of a man whose character and ability won the esteem of his contemporaries. As a gesture designed to show appreciation for the services rendered by Marshal Forsyth, the Congress of the United States turned its attention toward making some provision for his widow and orphans. In March, 1794, Senator James Jackson of Georgia introduced a measure to provide compensation which, though passed in the Senate, was defeated in the House of Representatives by the narrow margin of 40 to 37. Within a few days, Representative Abraham Baldwin of Georgia introduced a bill with a slightly different title, but with the same intention. This measure, which appropriated a sum of $2,000 for the education and support of the Forsyth family, was passed in both houses of Congress with only slight amendments.[19]

John Forsyth was thirteen years old at the time of his father's death. Little is known of his boyhood. His early education was acquired at an academy in Wilkes County, Georgia, where he studied the classics under the talented and gigantic John Springer, a Presbyterian minister reputed to weigh over four hundred pounds. The school was one of note, which boys from Augusta frequently attended. It was located at Walnut Hill, on the Mallorysville Road, about four miles from Washington, Georgia. Among the students who enrolled at the Springer academy were Jesse Mercer, later to become an outstanding Baptist minister, and William Harris Crawford, a future United States Senator and Secretary of the Treasury under President James Monroe.[20]

In 1795, John Forsyth entered Princeton College and was one of eighteen graduating in 1799. The Master's degree was conferred on him three years later, according to the custom at the New Jersey school for those graduates engaged in literary or professional pursuits. After leaving college, Forsyth returned to Augusta and began the study of law in the office of the eminent attorney John Y. Noel. He was admitted to the bar in 1802 and commenced his practice immediately thereafter.

It was while John was enrolled as a student at Princeton that his only brother died. Robert Moriah Forsyth, after his graduation with high honors in 1796, had remained at Princeton College in the capacity of tutor for one year. Afterward, he had become a law student in Savannah, where his death occurred on July 26, 1797. He was regarded as a modest, friendly, and accomplished youth.[21]

On May 12, 1802, John Forsyth was married to Clara Meigs,

the oldest daughter of Josiah Meigs, first president of Franklin College in Athens, Georgia.[22] In writing to Julia Austin of New Haven, Connecticut, Clara imparted the following information:

. . . I must own that I have grown a little proud *or so,* but my pride is laudable and becoming, for who is there that would not be proud of a good, handsome and genteel husband, such a one as your friend Clara had the good fortune of catching. I had been in Georgia but a fortnight, before I saw him, he was introduced, and one might soon & easily perceive that Cupid had been busy with each of our hearts, I engaged myself to him conditionally. He left me to wait on his mother & sister . . . [for] eight months—like so many years to me. I found that absence serv'd only to increase my affection, insomuch that I refused two or three rich & clever fellows for him. (vanity enough say you) . . . he returned, and shortly after we were joined in the holy bonds of Matrimony, and thus your wild friend Clara Meigs has been converted into that sober thing called a Wife. . . .[23]

In the years that followed, six girls and two boys were born of the marriage. Julia, born in 1803, married Alfred Iverson, future United States Senator from Georgia and judge on the Georgia Supreme Court. The second child, Mary Athenia, was born in 1807. She married Arthur Shaaff of Georgetown, District of Columbia, and Annapolis, Maryland, despite her father's vigorous objections on the grounds that the young man was not able financially to support a wife.[24] They were married on September 16, 1825. The third daughter, Clara, was born in 1810 and married Lieutenant Murray Mason of the United States Navy on December 7, 1837. John, Junior, born in Augusta in 1812, was graduated from Princeton College in 1832, and later became United States Minister to Mexico, mayor of Mobile, Alabama, and editor of the Mobile *Register.* His wife was Margaret, daughter of Latham Hull of Augusta. Virginia, born in 1818, married George Hargraves. The twins, Rosa and Anna, were born in 1823. Rosa became the wife of William P. Aubrey of Baltimore, subsequently of Cartersville, Georgia; Anna never married. The youngest of the Forsyth family was Robert, born in Augusta in 1826. He was to be Confederate commander of Mobile Bay fortifications. He married Julia, another of Latham Hull's daughters.

As a young lawyer, John Forsyth's life was filled with many problems and vicissitudes. Although he enthusiastically entered into the practice of his profession, it entailed much travel and the income was slight. When his duties required attendance at any one of the courts in Georgia, his wife in the early years often accompanied him.[25] The Forsyths were not destitute by any means, as evidenced by the fact that they were in a position to offer a prospective guest such things as beef, bacon, hens, turkey, eggs, brandy, wine, and cigars. Yet John's statement, "I do not live precisely in the Style I wish," indicates that he was ambitious to improve his fortunes.[26] Although both John and his mother were property owners, there were times when they were financially embarrassed. While carrying on negotiations to secure payment on a judgment held by his mother in 1802, John insisted that "nothing but the most urgent necessity could induce me to make a demand for the whole or any part of it at this time."[27] In 1803, real estate owned by each was advertised for sale in order to satisfy the taxes of the preceding year.

As a landowner, John Forsyth sometimes became involved in disputes over property rights. Such a controversy occurred in 1807 with Thomas Galphin of Barnwell County, South Carolina, who warned the public that he had a valid claim to certain tracts of land which were being advertised for sale by Forsyth. Forsyth disputed the claim. In the course of the acrimonious exchange of words over the matter, he asserted that his adversary had been the instigator of a falsehood, and that

the blush of shame and indignation, would burn my cheek, could I believe, that any honest man should doubt my veracity on the base assertion of any individual, much less the unsupported declaration of Thomas Galphin.[28]

Galphin replied, "you are not only disposed to descend to scurrility but false statements, rather than content yourself with giving facts as they really are."[29] Seemingly, life was never dull where the young Georgia lawyer was concerned.

Following his marriage, John and his family lived in Augusta until the spring of 1804, after which they moved to Louisville, at that time the Georgia capital, where they resided for several years. During this period, Clara, while finding no fault with her husband, became lonely and unhappy. The birth of Julia had made it impractical for her to travel with John when he attended court and she complained of having no companions. Although admitting that living conditions were better than in Augusta, she referred to Louisville as an "odious hole of scandal."[30] Her attitude was not improved by a serious illness of fever which she suffered in the latter part of 1804. In September, she wrote her brother in New York that she had "taken enough medicine to kill a horse & am still taking it," and that her condition had required the constant attendance of a physician for several days. She was anxious to see her friends in the North and "wanted to fly from this detestable climate and still more from that hole of dullness & insipidity Louisville."[31] In December, she added that she had been ill for four months, twice on the verge of death, but that her health was improving since her temporary removal to the Meigs home in Athens. Again she voiced her desire for participation in the social activities of the North, and complained that "nature never formed me to associate alone with trees & their stumps . . . ."[32] Her hatred for Georgia was so pronounced that John promised to exert every effort to establish a residence in the North at some future date. Clara returned to Louisville, where she regained her strength; but John's anxiety was increased over the delicate condition of his daughter Julia. In 1806, he reiterated his desire to move to the North, but rather disconsolately remarked: "But we must not repine. Providence has cast our lot & here we must endeavour honorably to act our part."[33]

John Forsyth's domestic life was further complicated by differences between his wife on the one hand and his mother and half sister, Mrs. Sarah Armstrong, on the other. At first, Clara had a kind and affectionate regard for John's relatives, but quarrels developed after Fanny and her daughter began to live with the young lawyer's family in Louisville. The quarrels became so serious that John eventually had to assert his authority as the head of the family. Clara described the situation as follows:

. . . all my enjoyment in the society of his relations is done away— they have quarrelled with me most bitterly—Mrs. A.[rmstrong] in the old way of malice—and his Mother has twice as good as turned me out of the house—indeed I should have taken myself off, but that my husband commanded me to keep my place as his wife—his poor mother I still feel regard for & pity with sincerity the infirmities of her mind—which has been made a wreck by great misfortunes. . . .[34]

The qualities of tactfulness and adroitness which are so often associated with John Forsyth must have been exercised frequently during such family disagreements.

In spite of hardships and perplexities of these early years, Forsyth made progress. His natural ability began to assert itself to such an extent that the young lawyer came to be recognized

as a distinguished and useful member of society. His oratorical
ability created a demand for his services and he obliged by deliv-
ering public addresses on various occasions. The Georgia legislature honored him with an appointment as a trustee of Richmond
Academy.[35] In 1805 and again in 1808, he served as a judge for
the elocutionary contests which were a part of the commencement exercises at Franklin College. John Forsyth was attracting
attention and systematically making a name for himself at the
same time.

Forsyth first held public office in 1808, being elected attorney
general of Georgia by both houses of the legislature, meeting in
joint session. The margin of victory was small. On the first
ballot, the leading candidate was John Hamill with forty-four
votes, followed by Forsyth with thirty-one, and James St. John
with thirteen. Since no one had a majority, the legislators proceeded to cast a second ballot, in which Forsyth received forty-five
votes and Hamill forty-three. Having thus been elected, Forsyth
was administered the oath of office on May 19, 1808.[36] Two years
later, at the expiration of his first term, he offered himself for
re-election and was returned to office by the Georgia General
Assembly. He held the position until his resignation on April
19, 1811.

As attorney general, John Forsyth was required to match wits
with the foremost lawyers of the state. He was equal to the task
and acquitted himself with distinction in legal contests. His
efforts were particularly outstanding in the cases involving the
fraudulent sale of fractional land. In 1803 Georgia had adopted
a new land policy with respect to the territory west of the Oconee
River which had been ceded to the state by the Indians. The
system provided that the land, surveyed and divided into tracts
of 2021/2 acres each, was to be offered to the state's citizens,
under varied stipulations, through lotteries. With the division of
the area into lots of uniform size, there remained scattered sections, each with acreage less than the required amount. These
remnants were known as fractions and were reserved for sale by
the state.[37] During Forsyth's tenure as attorney general, the land
commissioners were accused of employing fraudulent methods in
the disposition of the fractional tracts. The trials which followed
were attended by much agitation and rancorous feeling. Forsyth,
representing the state, prosecuted with such vigor and determination that he obtained full convictions, thereby winning the
general appreciation and confidence of his fellow Georgians.[38]

Having established a reputation for himself, and being an ambitious and able young politician who wished to live in the North, it was only logical that in 1810 John Forsyth should announce his candidacy for a seat in the United States House of Representatives. The campaign which followed was conducted in a bitter manner throughout the entire state, the election being by general ticket. Forsyth was accused of having belonged to the Federalist party. He labored to repudiate the charge, declaring himself to be a member of the Republican party and a staunch supporter of the Madison administration.

In reply to his assertions, it was quickly pointed out that he did not deny having been a Federalist in the past, but that he was merely admitting his loyalty to the existing administration. He was accused specifically of having eulogized John Adams at the beginning of the Jefferson administration and of having criticized Thomas Jefferson in a public address delivered in Saint Paul's Church. It was claimed that his recent conversion to Republicanism was only a scheme to advance his political fortunes.[39]

Forsyth's father-in-law, Josiah Meigs, came to the support of the attorney general. Meigs, a recognized Republican, issued a public denial to reports being circulated that he would oppose the election of his son-in-law, whom he felt to be well qualified for a seat in Congress. Meigs, who made no mention of the fact that John might have been a Federalist at one time, declared:

If I did not believe Mr. Forsyth to be a republican, and a friend to the present and late administration, I should be so far a *Brutus,* as to withhold my suffrage, even were he more nearly connected with me than he now is.[40]

In spite of every effort, Forsyth did not obtain enough votes to win the coveted seat. When the ballots were counted, he stood sixth in the group of seven. The four candidates who had been designated previously as Republicans polled the highest number of votes and were duly declared elected. The question of Forsyth's affiliation with the Federalists was to plague him again when he sought the governorship in 1827, but with different results. The truth of the matter seems to be that, early in his career, Forsyth had favored the Federalist views, but had been converted to the Republican ideas by 1810. In a subsequent year the Milledgeville *Georgia Journal* asserted that Forsyth and his friends had never attempted to deny his early Federalist tendencies.[41] Henry Stuart Foote later remembered him as "for some years a zealous and devoted Federalist."[42]

By the time of the elections in 1812, Congress had fixed a ratio of one member in the House of Representatives for every 35,000 residents of a state. This entitled Georgia to six representatives instead of four, beginning with the Thirteenth Congress. When Howell Cobb resigned his seat in the House before the end of his term, there was a vacancy for the remainder of the Twelfth Congress. John Forsyth offered himself as a candidate for both the short and long terms. Evidently the attacks against him were not so numerous as in the previous campaign, although the Athens *Georgia Express* did announce its intention of publicly identifying the Republican candidates in order that the voters "may not (as many honest Democrats were at the last Congressional Elections) be again imposed on by the misrepresentations of designing men."[43]

The elections for all the congressional officers were held on October 5, 1812. Forsyth took an early lead in the contest for Cobb's seat, but the final tabulation showed that William Barnett was the winner by a margin of less than a hundred votes —5,428 to 5,344. In the election for members to the Thirteenth Congress, Forsyth won a seat, placing sixth among the victorious candidates. Although the election results were officially proclaimed on October 27, 1812, he faced the prospect of waiting until December of the following year before being able to participate in the councils of his country. However, the ordinary procedure was disrupted by the critical state of affairs concerning the War of 1812 and, when a special session of Congress required his attendance in Washington, Forsyth, accompanied by Representative-elect Thomas Telfair, left Augusta on May 10, 1813.[44] John Forsyth's long service with the national government was entering its initial stage.

II

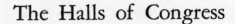

The Halls of Congress

AT THE TIME John Forsyth entered Congress he was a handsome man with genteel personality and exceptional ability. In appearance, he was well-proportioned and graceful with a height of approximately five feet eight inches. He had blue and expressive eyes, a Roman nose, light and glossy hair, and a fair complexion. His classical features were marred only by a scar on the neck, the result of a severe sword wound received when, as a young man, he fought a duel with a Colonel Williams. Forsyth's personal letters show a keen sense of humor and a deep affection for his family, while his public communications, written in a vigorous style, indicate a high degree of statesmanship. Ordinarily, he was even-tempered, tactful, and polite.

Forsyth came to be especially noted for his talents as an orator and a debater; many of his contemporaries agreed that there were few who could excel him in debate. His voice was clear, harmonious, and well modulated. His words were carefully selected and his delivery was fluent. He used few gestures, but created a profound impression upon his listeners through his method of resorting to an undertone when he wished to emphasize a particular passage. He was commonly regarded as an astute and resourceful speaker whose "keenest shafts were dipped in rose water. . . ."[1]

John Forsyth was a gentleman who "inclined to fashionable life and its heartless formalities."[2] With his courteous manners and amiable disposition, he was habitually the graceful host or the delightful guest. He was always at ease within the social circle, and the city of Washington proved a natural environment for the exercise of his social talents. He had been in the national capital less than a year when Mrs. Samuel Harrison Smith, the former Margaret Bayard, wrote the following pertinent remarks to her sister:

. . . Mr. Forsythe [sic], the universal favorite of the wise men, & fashionable women . . . promises to be one of our most distinguish'd men, he is now allow'd to be the greatest orator on the floor of congress—You may perhaps recollect him & his brother at Princeton, I knew him there & we have lately renew'd our acquaintance. He is a young man of genius, fine taste, a most animated, engaging, prepossessing countenance—Most attractive manners. . . . I am afraid he will be spoiled—he is so much carress'd [sic] & admired, particularly by the girls, who think because he is a married man; they need not conceal the pleasure his charming conversation affords.[3]

During the following years, Forsyth's enjoyment of social affairs was not confined to those of Washington. He frequently visited with Nicholas Biddle in Andalusia and in Philadelphia, where he found entertainment at dinner and dancing parties, at the theater, in playing chess, in listening to good music, and in the companionship of his host. John admitted that the Pennsylvania city had a strange fascination for him which he could not explain unless, in addition to Biddle's friendship, it was due to "the recollection of a thousand follies I have committed & some bitter feelings I have endured in it."[4] In 1818, he considered opening a law office in Philadelphia and made inquiries as to whether such a practice, in the beginning, would yield a yearly income of $4,000 or $5,000.

Forsyth and Biddle, a Princeton graduate of 1801, carried on an extensive correspondence for several years. They exchanged comments on political, personal, and social affairs, including bits of idle gossip. As a token of remembrance, Nicholas once sent John a pair of expensive gold spectacles with the hope that the latter "should view everything in the same light that I do . . . ."[5] Forsyth expressed his appreciation for the kind gift and humorously remarked:

I am not sure, that it is advantageous to view things thro precisely the same medium that you do, & yet I know none whose views & tastes too, I would be more willing to adopt than yours, were I disposed to surrender my own.[6]

After Forsyth became a strong supporter of the Jackson administration, the political convictions of the two old friends varied more than before, the result being that their exchange of letters

grew less frequent and, in those letters which they did write
there was a noticeable lack of that warmth and cordiality which
characterized their earlier correspondence.

Clara Forsyth's perennial desire for residence away from
Georgia was satisfied by her husband's election to Congress,
although the family did not move immediately. With John sometimes absent from his family for as long as seven or eight months
during his early congressional career, his wife and children remained at their home in Summerville, a village on a hill over-
looking Augusta.[7] But by 1818 the Forsyth family appears to
have been settled in the nation's capital. As early as February of
that year, Clara wrote a letter from Washington to her sister-in-
law in New York. In May, John, also writing from Washington,
confided to Biddle that, because of Clara's indisposition with
rheumatism in her shoulder and face, he had been solely responsible for buying furniture and moving household effects. In the
same letter he stated that Mrs. Forsyth wished to be remembered
to Mrs. Biddle. A later communication in 1818 revealed the
presence of three or four of his children who were, at the time,
jarring the table upon which their father was attempting to
write.

After Forsyth's family came to live in Washington, he still
maintained his legal residence in Summerville, and was obliged
to return to Georgia at intervals, particularly during the pre-
election periods, in order to associate with his constituents. Trips
to and from the South entailed a certain amount of time and
fortitude, for traveling was not easy in John Forsyth's day. A
description of one journey illustrates the arduous conditions and
the difficult problems which he encountered. On May 5, 1818, he
left Washington for Philadelphia and, traveling by boat from
the latter city, sailed through the Virginia Capes. Thanks to
favorable winds, the first third of the distance was accomplished
in three days; but, thereafter, storms and the succeeding calm
caused the vessel to slacken its speed. At the same time, the
rolling motion of the ship caused considerable discomfort to its
passengers. After eighteen days at sea, Forsyth arrived in Charleston, which he found to be hot and dusty. He remained there
for three days, in the company of friends. Then, traveling the
overland route, Forsyth and his companion, Joel Roberts Poinsett,
were required to spend their nights in the homes of strangers
where, on at least one occasion, their host felt compelled to
apologize for the quality of food served at supper. After arriving

at his destination, John was so discontented with Augusta that he was prompted to speak of it as "this dry dusty dull & wearisome City."[8]

Forsyth's sojourn in Georgia was brief. His original plans for return to Washington called for a retracing of his route; but, as the time for departure neared he was confronted with obstacles in his efforts to reach the coast. First, the stage service between Augusta and Charleston was discontinued because of the death of the owner of the line. Then, after John had secured a horse and gig as a means of transportation to the South Carolina seaport, the animal ran "thro a livery Stable with the gig at his Heels & [Richard Henry] Wilde & myself unluckily in it."[9] Although the two occupants merely sustained bruises, the vehicle was wrecked. Forsyth considered taking an alternate route to Savannah, but discarded that idea because of a possible delay of ten or fifteen days in "that unhealthy & uncomfortable City" while waiting for a vessel to sail. Consequently, he traveled the long and tedious stage route direct from Augusta to Washington, arriving in the latter city on July 28, 1818.

The first phase of John Forsyth's congressional career may be considered as extending from 1813 to 1827, with an interruption from 1819 to 1823 when he served as United States Minister to Spain. During these years, his exceptional talents and devotion to duty made an impression upon his constituents, who, generally convinced that he was representing their interests in a satisfactory manner, continued to reward him with their votes at the polls. Whereas in 1812 he had been last among the popularly elected members, in 1814 he led the ticket of Georgia's representatives to the Fourteenth Congress.

The 1816 elections were affected by the passage of the Compensation Act, a measure which included the provision that members of Congress were to receive an annual salary of $1,500 in place of the existing per diem payments. The popular reaction to the act was overwhelmingly hostile; it was denounced by newspapers, grand juries, state legislatures, town meetings, and county conventions throughout the United States as an extravagant use of the public monies. There was general prediction that there would be many new members elected to the Fifteenth Congress.[10] The ire of the voters was so aroused that, in the ensuing elections, half of the senators and two-thirds of the representatives failed to retain their seats. Unfortunately, the constituents mistakenly condemned the innocent along with the guilty parties; half of those who opposed the bill, together with four-fifths of those who favored the measure, were replaced.[11]

The entire Georgia delegation in the House voted against the hated measure, but John Forsyth was the only one who managed to salvage enough ballots for re-election, and his position on the ticket was sixth. In 1818, only six candidates offered for election to the House and the number of ballots cast was small. Nevertheless, Forsyth polled more votes than any of the other five, all of whom were elected.

Although Forsyth was elected to the House of Representatives in the Sixteenth Congress, he was anxious for promotion to the Senate. Despite William Harris Crawford's doubts that he would be successful, and his own apprehensions, he addressed a letter to the Georgia legislature, which body was responsible for the selection. Forsyth reminded the members of the General Assembly that the term of Senator Charles Tait would expire on March 4, 1819, and offered himself for the position. He hoped that his candidacy would not be misinterpreted as "a desertion of the people, to whom I am bound by the strongest ties of gratitude, affection, and respect."[12] In apologizing for not following the usual custom of personal solicitation, he called attention to the fact that his desire faithfully to perform his present duties, without absenting himself from Washington, afforded a more effectual recommendation than an application in person.

Regardless of his arguments, Forsyth did not receive the appointment he had requested. The regular term was conferred upon John Elliott. However, a vacancy was created when George Michael Troup resigned his seat in the Senate on September 23, 1818, and the place was awarded to Forsyth. The turn of events proved to be a great disappointment to Forsyth, who did not wish to leave the House during its existing session. He wanted to refuse the Senate appointment, but was afraid to do so lest such a move be construed as an act of resentment against the legislature for not granting his request for the full six-year term. Actually, such an interpretation would have been correct; his chagrin was so acute that he resolved to quit the Senate when the first favorable opportunity presented itself. However, on November 23, 1818, he took his seat in the Senate, where shortly thereafter he described himself as "a creature out of its proper element."[13]

Forsyth's determination to leave the Senate soon became an actuality. He had served less than three months when he tendered his resignation in order to accept the appointment as Minister to Spain. After several years of foreign service in Madrid, he re-entered the Congress of the United States. In 1822, even while he was performing his ministerial duties in Spain, his Georgia constituents elected him to the House of Representatives for a term beginning in March of the following year. His popularity had not declined, for, of the seven candidates obtaining seats, he polled the highest number of votes. In 1824, with only seven Georgia candidates seeking seats in the House and all being elected, Forsyth again headed the ticket.

Beginning in 1826, the method of selecting members to the House of Representatives was changed from the old plan of election by general ticket to election by districts. John Forsyth offered for re-election in the Second Congressional District, composed of Burke, Jefferson, Richmond, Columbia, Lincoln, Wilkes, and Taliaferro counties. He was elected without opposition. However, he did not complete this term, for he resigned on October 13, 1827, in order to accept the governorship of Georgia, succeeding George M. Troup, who had declined re-election.

John Forsyth's congressional career was launched amidst the tempestuous times occasioned by the War of 1812. Less than two months after his arrival in Washington, the inhabitants of the city were panic-stricken by reports that British vessels were in the Potomac River. According to family tradition, Forsyth was one of the volunteers who, with the Secretary of War, hastened to Fort Washington in defense of the nation's capital.[14] Fortunately, the enemy ships sailed away without making an attack. When the British did capture and partially burn the city in August, 1814, Congress was not in session; therefore it is not likely that Forsyth was present. By October, however, he was in the city, where he described the damaged public buildings in terms of "ruined Edifices . . . crumbled Columns and blackened Arches . . . ."[15]

The possibility that the British seizure might be repeated prompted the Thirteenth Congress to consider moving the seat of government from Washington. While privately admitting that Philadelphia would be chosen if a move should be made, Forsyth was opposed to any change. Taking the position that the approaching winter season would be ample security against enemy operations, he spoke and voted against the resolution, which was defeated in the House by a vote of 83 to 74. The close of the war found him in Washington, where he was impressed with the illumination of the city in celebration of the news of Andrew Jackson's victory at New Orleans.[16]

Forsyth began his congressional career on May 24, 1813, when he appeared and took his seat in the House of Representatives of the Thirteenth Congress. During his first session, which ended on the second of August, he participated in no debates; instead he silently observed the intricacies of legislative procedure, intent upon preparing himself for his future duties in the halls of Congress.

The silence maintained by Forsyth in the special session of the Thirteenth Congress was not to be continued in succeeding meetings. His activities during the Madison and Monroe administrations brought him recognition as an exponent of broad nationalism. This identification was changed during the presidency of John Quincy Adams, when he tended toward state rights principles, particularly with respect to the Indian situation in Georgia. Although he was destined to be a leader of the opposition during the presidency of Adams, Forsyth's stand during the terms of Madison and Monroe was with the administration. During the war and the post-bellum period, he was a strong supporter of the policies advocated by the two Virginians.

Forsyth's endorsement of aggressive war measures was emphasized in a speech supporting the Loan Bill, which he delivered in February, 1814. This measure, considered by the administration as essential to the prosecution of the war, had just been reported by the Ways and Means Committee. It authorized a loan of $25,000,000. The Federalists were violently opposed to the bill, their chief contentions being that the war with Great Britain was not justifiable and that the poor state of the public credit rendered the raising of a loan impossible. Forsyth's rebuttal to the arguments of the opposition members was so forceful and effective that the Washington *National Intelligencer* singled him out for special commendation.[17]

Forsyth began his speech by reminding the opposition that no amount of energy on the part of the minority could prevent the passage of any bill designed to bring the war to a successful conclusion. He called attention to the obstuctive tactics employed by the Federalists since the commencement of the war, the causes of which he entered into. He upheld the administration in its determination to continue the war in spite of British overtures, and declared that the administration was not attempting to prolong the conflict unnecessarily, "but with regard to our own citizens, whether native or naturalized, their security must be stipulated, or we quit the field with a wound incurable, for it affixes a stigma on the national honor."[18]

Forsyth's concluding remarks were directed against the unpatriotic efforts of the opposition. Maintaining that the chief object of the Federalist attack on the Loan Bill was to embarrass the administration, he refuted the argument that the people were unable financially to support a loan.

While praising the value of having an opposition group in any free governmental system, the Georgian condemned the Federalists for their unethical and vicious assaults upon the administration. He declared that in their anxiety to influence public opinion and to gain control of the government, they had used methods beyond the limits of constitutional and moral propriety.[19]

Subsequent to the debate on the Loan Bill, Forsyth had numerous opportunities to show his support for the administration. In February, 1816, he upheld President Madison's appointment of Peter Buell Porter, former New York representative, as one of the commissioners to determine the boundary from the St. Lawrence River to the Lake of the Woods.[20]

In December, 1817, Forsyth defended President Monroe when Representative John Rhea of Tennessee offered a motion that the President be asked to explain to the House his action in a certain incident when some American adventurers had attacked and taken possession of two Spanish-inhabited areas—Amelia Island and Galveston. The Georgian declared that he personally had no doubt but that the President had acted in a legitimate manner.[21]

He took a similar stand when Thomas Bolling Robertson, representative from Louisiana, offered a resolution that the President be requested to present to the House any available and proper information pertaining to the independence and political condition of the Spanish American countries. Forsyth stated that he did not oppose an inquiry on the subject, for he was aware of the interest of the people of the United States; but he questioned the terminology of Robertson's motion as being too extensive in its demand upon the Executive. He presumed that the President had already communicated all the facts which it was necessary for Congress to know. However, in order to allow Monroe to exercise his own judgment, Forsyth suggested that the resolution be amended so as to permit the Executive to withhold such information as might be incompatible with the public interest. As modified, the resolution received House approval.²²

The disturbances between Spain and her South American colonies provided Forsyth with further opportunities to demonstrate his strong support of the administration. He became vitally interested in the efforts of the Spanish American provinces to win their independence and was an avid reader of the available documents on the subject.²³ President Monroe was adamant in his insistence on strict neutrality by the United States;²⁴ and Forsyth, firm in his belief that intervention in behalf of the patriots would mean risking war with Spain, did not hesitate to endorse the President's policy. Consequently, the Georgia representative looked with disfavor upon the activities of Henry Clay of Kentucky, who was a vociferous champion of South American independence.

Clay, in March, 1818, made a move which was designed to aid in promoting recognition of the Spanish American states by the United States. After proposing that the general appropriation bill be amended so as to include $18,000 for an outfit and a year's salary of a minister to Buenos Aires, he delivered a lengthy speech in support of his motion. Forsyth considered the provision obnoxious and replied to Clay in positive terms. He told the House that the motion was an encroachment upon the rights of the President and the Senate in their management of foreign affairs. He pointed out that approval of the resolution would tend to confirm Spain's charges that the United States was responsible for the Spanish American disturbances and that her attitude constituted a threat to the colonial possessions of other European nations.

Forsyth claimed that there was no commercial advantage to be obtained from recognition, since there was already free intercourse between the United States and the South American countries. He believed that recognition would heighten danger of war with Spain, and moreover, if war came, the conflict would permit a neutral England to increase her commerce at the expense of the United States. In the political realm, the Georgian was opposed to the recognition of a government which had not demonstrated its ability to maintain its freedom and independence. Answering the statement that the United States should be the first to recognize a sister republic, Forsyth declared that the government of La Plata had the framework and names of free and liberal institutions, but that in reality it was a military despotism. After several days of discussion, Clay's amendment was put to a vote and defeated, 115 to 45. Commenting on the result, Forsyth hoped that the Kentuckian would "derive benefit from this lesson and abandon the idea of forcing into being new parties to distract the nation."[25]

In March, 1818, during the House discussion of an appropriation bill, Henry Clay inquired into the proposed allocation of $30,000 which had been requested by the President to compensate three commissioners sent to South America. The three men, Caesar Augustus Rodney, John Graham, and Theodorick Bland, had been appointed without diplomatic rank and dispatched to the southern continent for the purpose of obtaining information about the actual state of affairs in the Spanish American countries. In Clay's opinion, the mission could accomplish little of value and did not warrant the expenditure of public funds. He protested that the President had violated the Constitution by making the appointments without the consent of the Senate. Disagreeing with the Kentucky representative, Forsyth maintained that the desired information could be acquired in only one of two ways, either through the newspapers or by special agents appointed for the purpose. Since the first source was vague and unreliable, the President had made the logical decision of resorting to the second method and, as a result, could expect more authentic reports concerning the political conditions in South America. The Georgian assured the House that Monroe had committed no violation of the Constitution, for the appointments had been made during a recess of the Senate. As to whether the President had submitted the names since the Senate convened, Forsyth was without knowledge, but "he presumed what ought to be done would be done, and he was disposed to leave the subject to the Executive and to the Senate, to whom it more properly belonged."[26]

As a result of the distressing financial conditions in the United States during and after the War of 1812, John Forsyth turned his attention to banking and currency legislation, once again demonstrating his support of the administration. In November, 1814, a bill relative to the establishment of a second national bank was introduced in the House. The measure was based upon the recommendations of Secretary of the Treasury Alexander James Dallas, and provided for a bank with a capital of $50,000,000 of which $6,000,000 would be in specie and the remainder in government stock issued during the War of 1812. Of the total capital, $20,000,000 was to be subscribed by the government and the remaining three-fifths by companies, corporations, or individuals. Once in operation, the bank was to grant a loan of $30,000,000 to the United States. The government stock could not be sold by the bank, and the President of the United States was to be given the power of suspending payments when in his opinion the situation demanded such action.

Forsyth favored the Dallas bill and became one of the House leaders opposed to a substitute measure proposed by John Caldwell Calhoun. In defending the provision of the Treasury bill requiring government subscription of two-fifths of the bank capital, Forsyth contended that there was no conceivable evidence that the bank would be injured because the government was a stockholder; indeed a similar association with the first bank of the United States furnished sufficient proof that the government would derive definite benefits from the arrangement. Yet, in spite of his best efforts, the Georgian could not prevent a complete revision of the Dallas bill. As was to be expected, the revised bill thereafter received his continued opposition, from the time it was first debated in the House until it was refused a third reading and thus rejected. Although Forsyth voted against the revised measure, he immediately made a motion for reconsideration in order that the bill might be recommitted, his explanation being that he wanted to keep the bank question before the House. For some inexplicable reason, he soon withdrew his motion, with a hint that he might possibly renew it at a future date.

When the Senate bill for the establishment of a national bank appeared in the House, Forsyth became active in the debates and quarrels which ensued. He voted for the Senate bill, which was defeated by the deciding ballot of Speaker Langdon Cheves. However, the measure was reconsidered, sent to a select committee, and eventually accepted by the House, only to be vetoed by President Madison. Before Congress could pass a new bill for the establishment of a national bank, news that the war had ended gave an opportunity to postpone indefinitely the entire matter. Forsyth opposed the postponement, contending that the members of Congress, through their lengthy discussions, were so thoroughly familiar with the problem that they should be able to solve their differences and reach an agreement satisfactory to all parties. He attempted to have the bill referred to a select committee, but failed when the House voted for postponement by the narrow margin of 74 to 73.

The first session of the Fourteenth Congress, prompted by a suggestion contained in President Madison's annual message of December 5, 1815, lost little time in renewing efforts to charter a second national bank. A select committee, headed by John C. Calhoun, soon reported a bill based on ideas submitted by Secretary of the Treasury Dallas. The proposed bank, to be chartered for twenty years, was to have a capital of $35,000,000, of which one-fifth was to be subscribed by the national government. The parent bank, to be situated in Philadelphia, was to be empowered to establish branch banks in the states and to issue notes receivable in all payments to the United States. It was obligated to pay a bonus of $1,500,000 for its charter and to receive, transfer, and distribute the public funds. The bank was to be governed by twenty-five directors, of which five were to be appointed by the President of the United States, with the advice and consent of the Senate.

During the discussions following introduction of the bill, John Forsyth, John C. Calhoun, and Henry Clay were among those who spoke in favor of the measure, while Daniel Webster was one of the opposition speakers. The Georgia representative was particularly outspoken when an attempt was made to omit the clause providing for governmental selection of five of the bank directors. In denying the charge that he was merely a spokesman for the administration, Forsyth referred to his fruitless efforts respecting the bank bill in the preceding Congress and stated that, far from being influenced solely by the administration, he had been acting in the firm belief that a national bank was absolutely necessary. He emphasized, however, that his recommendations were directed toward the creation of a particular type of bank, one in which the government of the United States would be an active participant. He reasoned that it was only natural for private financiers to object to governmental participation in their banking affairs; but, despite their censure of a new principle, there would be no difficulty in obtaining a complete subscription of the bank capital. Forsyth questioned that the five directors might be purely political appointees; instead, he regarded the President and Senate as being in a better position than individual stockholders to choose qualified persons. On May 14, 1816, the bill came to a final vote in the House, where Forsyth had the satisfaction of seeing the measure passed by a

count of 80 to 71. Eventually, it was approved by the Senate
and became law with President Madison's signature on April
10, 1816.

John Forsyth's interest in banking and currency legislation did
not end with the successful passage of the bill establishing the
second bank of the United States. After the bank started operations, he was vigilant in his observations of its activities. When, in
January, 1817, he thought he detected an infraction of the bank's
charter, he proposed that the House conduct an investigation into
the matter. According to the provisions of the charter, the sub-
scriptions were to be paid in three installments over a twelve-
month period. The cost of a share amounted to $100, of which
at least $5 of the first installment and $10 of each of the other
two were to be paid in specie. Forsyth proposed that the Committee on the National Currency be instructed to inquire whether
the bank officials were permitting an evasion or postponement
of payment with respect to the specie portion of the second in-
stallment; and, if they were, the Georgia congressman moved
that measures be taken to provide for the enforcement of the
pertinent provision. Forsyth declared that he had been furnished
with information which indicated that the bank was receiving
certain notes in lieu of specie payments. He asserted that, regardless of the circumstances responsible for such an arrangement,
the authorization by the bank officials was a violation of the
charter; and, if they were successful in evading one provision,
there was no guarantee that they would abide by the other
articles.

In April, 1818, the House of Representatives considered a
motion to authorize the appointment of a vice-president of the
Bank of the United States, whose primary function would be the
signing of bank bills, which would permit a greater amount of
bank paper to be placed in circulation. Forsyth favored the
measure, contending that under the existing arrangement bank
officials found it was physically impossible properly to attend to
all of their assigned duties and still comply with the institution's
obligation of supplying the country with a sufficient currency for
business purposes. He added that, in the ordinary course of business, many of the distributed notes were returned to the bank
and not reissued. Forsyth mentioned the possibility that the bank,
acting within its chartered rights, might obtain its objective
through the employment of a method different from the one
being discussed. He explained as follows:

The bank is authorized to trade in bills of exchange, and trades in bills with each of its branches. The directors then have nothing to do but make an order directing the president and cashier of each branch to draw on them small bills, payable to the bearer, and the object is effected.[27]

This idea of issuing branch drafts, first suggested by Forsyth, was remembered by Bank President Nicholas Biddle and more than likely was responsible for the latter's adoption of the plan in 1826.[28]

During the early phase of John Forsyth's congressional career, the House of Representatives did not have the complete confidence and esteem of the populace of the United States. Because of its large membership and frequent replacements, the body was considered lacking in responsibility and efficiency.[29] Many of the legislators were acutely aware of the popular impression. Richard Henry Wilde of Georgia told his colleagues that the people were transferring their affections to the executive department, and thus causing the House to lose that prestige and power contemplated by the fathers of the Constitution. Convinced that the House was no longer the nation's favorite, John C. Calhoun declared that it was the duty of every member to defend its character. Both before and after Calhoun's appeal, Forsyth, recognizing the situation, was vigilant and energetic in his efforts to sustain the integrity and competence of the House.

Forsyth's opposition to the passage of the Compensation bill in 1816, and his interest in securing its repeal when Congress met in 1817, indicate his desire to defend the House from malicious attacks. In urging the repeal, the Georgian stated that he thought the popular reaction to the Compensation Act had been entirely too extreme in its application. He had never opposed the bill on account of the increased compensation, which was nominal, but because the reasons advanced for passage had been improper and irrelevant. Forsyth said that one particular argument which certainly warranted inquiry and public disapproval had been that the payment of a specified amount in lieu of a per diem allowance would tend to curtail the sessions and so expedite public business. This reason, as interpreted by the populace, seemed to indicate that under the per diem plan "a sufficient number of the members of the House were governed by the most despicable petty pecuniary motives to prolong the sessions of Congress . . . ."[30] Forsyth admitted that he personally did not believe such an allegation, but it had influenced the people in their violent protest against the act. Furthermore, he asserted, a brief session of Congress under the present act would invite the criticism that the annual compensation of members had caused a neglect of parliamentary duties. As Forsyth predicted, the bill to repeal the Compensation Act was passed in the House and eventually on February 6, 1817, was signed into law.

In the capacity as guardian of the House's reputation, Forsyth took an active part in the case involving Colonel John Anderson. In January, 1818, Lewis Williams of North Carolina, chairman of the Committee on Claims, revealed to the House that Colonel Anderson had offered him a bribe of $500 for the favorable consideration of certain claims. Immediately, Forsyth moved that the Speaker issue a warrant for Anderson's arrest and that Anderson be held in custody pending further action by the House. His motion received a favorable vote and the warrant was issued.

When the House received word of the culprit's arrest, Forsyth moved that a committee of privileges be appointed to determine the method of proceeding against Anderson, arguing that it was a recognized fact that the House was qualified to demand testimony regarding governmental activities and to punish persons for open disrespect to that body. He stated that he did not wish to extend the constitutional powers of the House beyond their proper boundaries, but maintained that an act of contempt had been committed against Chairman Williams, adding that if Anderson should be released without punishment, it would be a disgrace rather than an honor to be a member of the House. Forsyth was bitterly opposed to all suggestions and devices employed to postpone the investigation, claiming that delay would give malicious persons an opportunity to criticize the House of Representatives. The outcome of the case was a tribute to the tireless efforts of Forsyth. Colonel Anderson was brought before the House of Representatives, questioned, declared guilty, and reprimanded for contempt and violation of House privileges.[31]

Two other incidents illustrate John Forsyth's vigilance as guardian of the integrity and competence of the House. In December, 1818, the seat of an Ohio representative was contested on the ground that, at the time of his election and until shortly before he entered Congress, he had performed the duties of Attorney for the Ohio District. The contention was that according to the Constitution he was disqualified because he had held a civil office under the United States and, at the same time, had been a duly elected member of the House, even though he had not taken the oath of office. Forsyth agreed that there was a basis for the charge and offered a resolution that the Committee of Elections be instructed to investigate the rights of ten or eleven representatives whose membership might be questioned because of somewhat similar situations. He declared that he imputed no ulterior motives to the persons concerned; he merely desired a definite decision so that the issue might be clarified.[32] On February 21, 1826, John Cocke of Tennessee proposed that the House adjourn over George Washington's birthday. Forsyth replied that the members would show more respect to the memory of the first President by diligently performing their public duties, observing that there had already been too many adjournments and that even though the House had been in session for a long time it had accomplished very little. In response to Forsyth's plea, the motion to adjourn was rejected.[33]

Forsyth's devotion to national affairs did not cause him to neglect his responsibility to his constituents in matters of state importance. He was an outspoken guardian of the interests of Georgia and Georgians when the occasion demanded, during the administrations of Madison and Monroe, as well as of John Quincy Adams, when his views on state rights principles were more pronounced. Undoubtedly, sectional interests provided motivation for his actions in connection with the Indian problem in Georgia and for his ideas relative to the Tariff of 1816.

For many years Forsyth advocated that the federal government compensate the Georgia militia for services performed in 1792-1794. The claims were based on a situation which arose after the Revolutionary War when the Indians were committing depredations along the western frontier of the United States. The state of Georgia, apprehensive for the safety of its inhabitants, requested federal troops, but was informed that they were not available. In the correspondence which followed between the state executive and the national government, conflicting directions were issued by the latter. Relying upon his own interpretation of the orders, the Georgia governor called upon the state militia for police duty against the Indians. From this action, there evolved the controversial questions as to whether Georgia had been in such danger as to warrant the services of the militia, whether the governor of the state had the discretional authority to call upon the militia, and, if so, whether he had been excessive in his demands. When the federal government refused to compensate the state troops, Georgia's congressmen were instrumental in bringing the matter to the attention of the national legislature.

In March, 1818, James Tallmadge, Jr., of New York, stated that he objected to the pending bill which provided payment of the claims. He contended that the measure pertained to ancient pretensions which had been rejected repeatedly, and that the indemnification "was intended and understood by some of the Commissioners at least . . . to have been merged in the amount of $1,250,000 which the United States agreed to pay to Georgia for the territory ceded by that State to the United States."[34] Forsyth replied that a just claim should be paid, regardless of its age or its past repudiations. He asserted that Tallmadge's second contention had no force, for it was based on the impressions of General Levi Lincoln, who was only one of the commissioners, and that the other two agents had denied unequivocally that Georgia's militia claims had been liquidated by the 1802 convention.

In February, 1825, the Georgia militia claims were again discussed and rejected by the House. To the reasons previously advanced for such action was the added charge that the militia had been employed, not in defensive operations, but in offensive expeditions against the Indians. Forsyth, in rebuttal, again attempted to show that Lincoln's opinion was based on vague recollections and had been contradicted by the other two commissioners. He maintained that it was the volunteers, and not the militia, which had proceeded against the Creeks and Cherokees. Furthermore, he said, these offensive operations were in retaliation for crimes committed by the Indians. Forsyth remarked that whether the Georgia governor had or had not exceeded his authority was immaterial to the case. He insisted that the real facts to consider were:

The troops were called out by him [the governor] as the agent of the United States; the U. States are bound to pay. The U. States have paid the contractor who supplied them all the expenses incident to the service; have paid troops from Tennessee, employed under similar circumstances, and have not been absolved from their liability to the Georgia militia by the compact of 1802.[35]

Forsyth continued his support of the Georgia claims, despite the many rejections. In December, 1826, during his last term in Congress before assuming the governorship, he objected to the suggestion that consideration of the claims be transferred from the Committee on Military Affairs to a select committee. He explained that the Georgia delegation wanted only a fair and impartial report and, while select committees were usually favorable toward measures referred to them, the report of a standing committee was regarded as more important and would consequently have greater influence. Forsyth's objection was sustained by a House vote.[36]

Forsyth defended his fellow Georgian William Harris Crawford against the attacks of Ninian Edwards in an attempt to discredit Crawford and injure his chances of succeeding Monroe in the White House. In January, 1823, Edwards, a senator from Illinois, wrote a letter, under the pseudonym of "A. B.," charging that the Treasury Department had willfully omitted evidence in a report concerning the deposit of public funds in various western banks. This letter, which appeared in the Washington *Republican,* was followed by others accusing Secretary of the Treasury Crawford with intentional mismanagement of the public monies. A House committee investigated the charges and eventually reported that the conduct of the Treasury Department had been justified.

The following year, Edwards, seeking support in the Senate for nomination as Minister to Mexico, denied, in private conversations, that he was the author of the letters. But after his appointment, and while en route to his ministerial post, Edwards forwarded a communication to Speaker Henry Clay in which he reiterated his charges of misconduct by Crawford and acknowledged his identity as the author of the "A. B." papers. He maintained that the charges and specification could be easily proved if the House would order an investigation. On April 19, 1824, Clay complied with Edwards's request that the correspondence be brought to the attention of the House.[37]

Although the time for adjournment of Congress was near and the accuser was absent, Crawford's supporters were anxious to vindicate the Secretary's reputation before the approaching presidential campaign. When John Floyd of Virginia moved the appointment of an investigating committee, Forsyth approved the motion and took opportunity to remark upon the actions of Edwards. The Georgia representative denounced Edwards for the latter's failure to give complete testimony during the previous investigations and for withholding his address to Congress until after his confirmation to the diplomatic post. He also charged that the former senator had intentionally forwarded his accusations while on the verge of leaving the country, expecting his absence to prevent his being required to substantiate the charges. A select committee was then appointed, with Floyd as chairman. Forsyth was not chosen to serve on the committee.

The following day, Forsyth submitted a resolution that President Monroe be officially informed of the pending investigation in order that Edwards might be instructed to remain in the United States. On April 21, the committee voted to dispatch a messenger to bring Edwards back to Washington. Forsyth, according to John Quincy Adams, complained of the committee membership, and especially of Daniel Webster, who the Georgian said was unfriendly to Crawford. Adams said that "Forsyth knows better, but there is policy in giving this out."[38] Adams believed that Webster had been secretly promised an important position in the event of Crawford's election to the presidency, and that Forsyth wished to camouflage the cordial relations which existed between the two politicians.

The subject of adjournment was discussed in the House in May, with opposition by those wishing to postpone the action until after the arrival and questioning of Edwards. Forsyth declared that he would not vote for adjournment until after Edwards's appearance or refusal to return. He stated that the investigation was of such importance to the nation that the House should remain in session, regardless of the additional expense and personal sacrifice entailed. In his opinion, the charges had been advanced merely to damage the possibilities of Crawford's success in the coming election, and, in justice to the Secretary, the "investigation should be fully prosecuted, unless this House means to make itself a party in the projects of the individual who has addressed it."[39] When Daniel Pope Cook, representative from Illinois and Edwards's son-in-law, objected to the personal references in the Georgian's remarks, Forsyth replied that his conclusions had been formed from a simple survey of the facts.

In spite of Forsyth's impassioned plea, the House and the Senate agreed to adjourn on May 27. On May 25, the select committee reported its findings, based on all available information, and exonerated Crawford of malfeasance in office. However, since Edwards had not arrived to testify, the committee recommended that it be allowed to continue in session after the adjournment of Congress. This request was granted the following day.

Forsyth remained in Washington in order that he might take an active part in the examination of Edwards and of additional witnesses. Throughout the hearings, which closed on June 21, 1824, he was persistent and aggressive in his questions to the witnesses. In addition, he presented testimony favorable to Crawford and made an emphatic address to the committee denouncing Edwards for deceitful activities and contradictory testimony. Forsyth concluded with the statement that "nothing, affecting the Secretary, and depending upon the oath of Mr. Edwards, can be taken as proved."[40] Edwards's failure to substantiate his charges caused the committee to issue a report corroborating the previous findings. The members declared their unanimous opinion that no proof had been offered which would impugn Crawford's integrity or his proper administration of office. The day following the conclusion of the committee's sessions, Edwards, still protesting that the charges were valid, addressed a letter to President Monroe, in which he tendered his resignation as Minister to Mexico.[41]

Forsyth was an active supporter of Crawford in the presidential campaign of 1824, and was an interested participant in the election by the House of Representatives in 1825. Since the War of 1812, the Republican organization had been, to all intents and purposes, the sole party in the United States. Nominations for the presidency and vice-presidency were made through the process of the caucus, a method by which the candidate was chosen by the party members of Congress, meeting in public assemblage in Washington. As there was only one national party, nomination by the Republican caucus was tantamount to election. However, by 1824, there was widespread discontent over the caucus method, for the people considered it a procedure which made the executive dependent upon the national legislature. In addition, many voters desired a direct method of voicing their opinions on vital subjects. The system was also opposed by those candidates who saw little likelihood of their being named by the party organization. During Monroe's second term, several eminent personages emerged as eager aspirants for the succession to the presidency, the most prominent being Secretary of State Adams, Secretary of War Calhoun, Speaker Clay, General Andrew Jackson, and Secretary of the Treasury Crawford, with the latter being generally regarded as the most likely candidate to receive the caucus nomination. Calhoun later withdrew from the contest in order to concentrate on the vice-presidential position.[42]

Despite the fact that Crawford was stricken with paralysis in

September, 1823, his adherents completed their plans for a congressional caucus. John Forsyth was one of the eleven congressmen who signed the notice calling for a Republican caucus to
meet in the chamber of the House of Representatives on February
14, 1824. The meeting was attended by approximately one
thousand spectators, but by only sixty-six congressmen, a number
of whom were described by the Washington *National Intelligencer* as "the pillars of the party."[43] After some discussion as
to a postponement because of the lack of a majority, the decision
was made by the group, predominantly Crawford supporters,
to proceed with the business. Whereupon Crawford and Albert
Gallatin were chosen as the presidential and vice-presidential
nominees, respectively. Forsyth cast his ballot for his fellow
Georgian. Forsyth's participation in the meeting was defended
by the Milledgeville *Georgia Journal,* which replied to the charges
of the Washington *Republican* that Forsyth, though a man of
high principles, had allowed himself to become the willing tool
of designing persons. Declaring that the editor of the Northern
print had gained little respect from Georgians by his attack on
such a popular personage, the Milledgeville newspaper maintained that the *Republican's* statements pertaining to Forsyth
were contradictory, and hence the charges were meaningless.[44]

According to Samuel Houston, who was hostile to Crawford,
the friends of the latter seriously contemplated the possibility
of his withdrawal from the campaign because of illness, in which
case they planned to support Clay for the presidency and Forsyth
for the vice-presidency.[45] In spite of Crawford's physical condition, Forsyth continued his tireless efforts in support of his friend
and was gratified to report to Martin Van Buren, in September,
1824, that Crawford had improved to the extent that his only
difficulty was an inability to speak distinctly.[46] Forsyth traveled
to New York, New Jersey, and Connecticut, where he consulted
with influential persons, and he became unduly optimistic about
the prospects of gaining the votes of those states for Crawford.[47]

After the electoral college had failed to make a decision and
the election was before the House of Representatives, Forsyth
was less confident of victory, but insisted that Crawford's friends
would remain loyal to their principles and to their candidate.
He expressed an opinion that the House would elect no one on
the first day and that it was conceivable, in the event neither Jackson nor Adams received a majority of the votes during the early

balloting, that Crawford would eventually obtain enough ballots to insure his election. Forsyth proved to be a poor prophet. On the first ballot, during which Forsyth acted as teller for his state, Adams received the necessary thirteen state votes for election, with Jackson obtaining seven, and Crawford four. Forsyth's vote and those of the entire Georgia delegation were cast for Crawford. Forsyth was disappointed with the position which New York had taken, and especially with General Stephen Van Rensselaer, who he had expected would vote for Crawford or Jackson rather than for Adams. In a spirit of resignation, Forsyth commented that "the thing is over & I am not sorry if this was to be the result that it terminated at once."[48]

Adams's election was followed by speculation as to the composition of his cabinet. In an effort to pacify the Crawford faction of the party, the President-elect invited the Secretary of the Treasury to enter the new cabinet in the same capacity. Upon Crawford's refusal, it was generally believed that a conciliation might be effected by appointment of Forsyth to a cabinet post, possibly to head the Department of War or of the Navy. Although the Georgia representative had some expectation of being included among Adams's advisors, he was able to see a personal advantage in the situation when no offer was received. Writing to his brother-in-law, Forsyth expressed regret over the omission because of the salary which would have been involved; but, at the same time, he admitted that it allowed him to pursue an independent course in politics. He predicted that, if Adams's policies were not satisfactory, "he shall meet from me a decided opposition in Congress & out of Congress. . . ."[49] As later events were to prove, Forsyth's threat was no idle boast.

John Forsyth's position on questions involving the Negro was closely associated with his desire to protect the interests of Georgia. His views and activities on the Negro problem were those of a practical politician representing the constituents of a slave state. Being a man of limited financial means, he owned only a few slaves, and those chiefly household servants. The 1830 census for Richmond County, Georgia, lists under his name a total of seven slaves: two males between the ages of twenty-four and thirty-six, one female between ten and twenty-four, one female between twenty-four and thirty-six, one female between thirty-six and fifty-five, two females between fifty-five and one hundred.[50] The census of 1840, for the District of Columbia, credits him with two male and one female slaves whose ages were less than twenty-four years, and one female between thirty-six and fifty-five.[51]

Forsyth believed that the southern states were handling the Negro problem in a satisfactory manner and that neither the national government nor any other agency should interfere, unless its cooperation was deemed necessary by the states concerned. He was particularly opposed to any deliberate attempts made to exercise the members of Congress on the subject. When, in December, 1826, a representative from New York proposed an investigation of an alleged act of the District of Columbia authorizing the sale of a free Negro for jail dues, Forsyth stated that if such a law existed, it was unconstitutional, and therefore a matter for the judiciary. While insisting that he favored inquiries into acts of injustice, he declared that there was another reason why the proposed resolution was unnecessary. In accordance with a presidential recommendation for institution of a penitentiary system, it was probable that a House committee would soon begin an examination and revision of the laws in the District of Columbia. It was his opinion that the resolution had been introduced to create excitement and irritation among the House members, since it embodied a controversial issue. That issue, said Forsyth, was whether a free Negro of New York had the right to enjoy the same privilege in every other state. He denied such a right and succinctly pronounced the views held by the southern delegation on the subject as follows: "We hold . . . that we have the right to exclude free People of Color, to eject them, and to limit their privileges, when we admit them to reside among us."[52]

In March, 1825, Forsyth introduced a House resolution which indicated his convictions respecting the foreign slave trade. He denounced the practice as piracy, which should be vigorously prosecuted and punished under the law of nations. He advocated that the United States pursue an independent policy in its efforts to abolish the slave trade, for agreements with foreign countries would expose American vessels to the annoying process of search.[53]

Forsyth's attitude toward the American Colonization Society was expressed in the House in February, 1827, during the debates over a naval bill, which included appropriations for the transportation and maintenance of Negroes sent to Liberia from the United States. The Georgian said that he respected the motives of many members of the Society, but he charged that the organization had mismanaged its affairs. He contended that, under the auspices of the Society, the program was a failure. He claimed that, under the existing conditions, the Negroes at Mesurado were no more contented than American slaves, and that their situation in Liberia was worse than that of the free Negroes in the United States.[54]

Early in his congressional career, John Forsyth's ability was recognized. On September 21, 1814, he was given the important post of chairman of the House Committee of Foreign Relations, a position he retained until his elevation to the Senate in 1818. Upon his return to the House in 1823, he again was selected to head the committee concerned with foreign affairs. He proved conscientious and diligent in the performance of his duties, so that the Madison-Monroe administrations appeared to bestow complete trust upon him. In 1817, Secretary of State Adams recorded that President Monroe, in directing him to notify Forsyth of all important circumstances in the realm of foreign affairs, remarked that "any confidence might with perfect safety be reposed in him [Forsyth]."[55] When Forsyth was elected to the Senate, Crawford expressed the opinion that it would be difficult to find a person as competent as Forsyth to fill the position of chairman of the Committee of Foreign Relations.

Forsyth's duties as chairman of this committee were concerned with varied subjects. One of his first reports from the committee was a reply to a presidential recommendation that authority be granted to deal with the Dey of Algiers, whose pirates were preying upon American vessels engaged in Mediterranean commerce. Forsyth favored adoption of vigorous measures against the Dey, and the committee report reflected his opinions. The measure, which became an act on March 3, 1815, authorized President Madison to send fully armed vessels to war on the Algerian cruisers, to commission privateers, and to take such action as a state of war would justify.[56]

On December 29, 1815, Forsyth reported a bill from the committee designed to regulate commerce between the United States and Great Britain, in accordance with the treaty for that purpose which had been signed on July 3, 1815, and ratified on December 22. There followed an extended debate, concerning the relative powers prescribed by the Constitution to the legislative and executive branches of the government. The particular question involved was the extent of legislation necessary to execute the provisions of a treaty which had been duly signed and ratified.

In opposition to many members of the House who contended that no legislation was required, Forsyth declared that existing laws pertaining to tonnage and import duties were affected by the convention and that these measures could be changed only by an act of Congress. He maintained that, in addition to decisions on appropriations, the House had, in the past, legislated on such matters as would cause a treaty to go into effect, citing as one example the admission of Louisiana into the Union. The Georgian explained that the bill before the House was a desirable measure even though it was merely a declaration that the laws in violation of the convention were no longer applicable. Otherwise, said Forsyth, there could be no future guarantee that the President and the Senate, acting through their treaty-making powers, would not encroach upon the constitutional rights and privileges of the House.[57]

The Treaty of 1815 did not apply to the United States commerce with the British West Indies, or with the British colonies in North America. Therefore, one objective of American diplomacy was to obtain removal of the discriminations against United States trade in the British West Indies and, as a move in this direction, the Committee of Foreign Relations conducted an investigation. In February, 1818, Forsyth submitted the result of the committee's findings, complete with tables of statistics indicating the extent of the discrimination. The report recommended that, since American trade with the British West Indies was denied those advantages granted trade of other nations, the United States should resort to retaliatory measures and impose discriminating duties on all trade confined to British vessels.[58] However, Congress substituted a different method of retaliation. An act of April 18, 1818, closed United States ports to British vessels coming from the British West Indies.

A situation concerning American trade was the basis for a report made by Chairman Forsyth in 1825, entitled "Piracy and Outrage on Commerce of the United States by Spanish Privateers." The report was in response to President Monroe's recommendation that Congress consider what measures should be taken against pirates and privateers who were protected by the laxity of the laws in Spanish-owned Cuba. The committee, headed by Forsyth, denounced pirates as "the common enemies of mankind" who should be apprehended and punished by all nations, and accused Spain of being responsible for depredations committed by privateers acting under Spanish commissions. The committee recommended that the House refrain from legislative enactment for the time being, contending that the United States should once again resort to negotiations, in the hope that Spain would recognize the necessity for correcting the deficiencies. If Spain did not react favorably, the committee believed that more positive action on the part of the United States would be justified.[59]

Neutrality was a subject which engaged the attention of the chairman of the Committee of Foreign Relations. In the conflict between Spain and her South American colonies, the revolutionists violated American neutrality by using the United States as a source of ships, money, supplies, and men. President Madison found that the existing neutrality laws were not adequate for the prevention of these violations and, in a special message to Congress in December, 1816, requested additional powers for suppressing the activities of belligerents.

The subject was referred to the Committee of Foreign Relations, and the following month Forsyth reported a bill to prohibit the sale of American war vessels to the citizens of a foreign country and to prevent the arming and equipping of vessels to be employed against nations friendly to the United States. In the debates which followed, Forsyth was meticulous in explaining and defending the measure, which he considered proper and judicious.[60] The bill became a law on March 3, 1817. In the succeeding Congress, many members, reflecting the hatred of the American people toward Spain, attempted to weaken or to repeal the neutrality act. Favoring only such amendments as would strengthen the law, Forsyth again took the lead in advocating a strict impartiality on the part of the United States.

On at least one occasion, Forsyth was not in agreement with the Monroe administration. In March, 1818, he told Secretary of State Adams that the Committee of Foreign Relations was contemplating the proposal of a bill authorizing the President to seize East Florida from Spain. He inquired whether Adams had any objections to the proposal. The Secretary answered that, as a member of the administration, he was prepared to share any responsibility assumed by the government. Believing that Monroe was not in sympathy with the plan, Adams suggested that Forsyth first obtain the opinion of the President. The Georgian replied that, in spite of a previous conversation in which Monroe had expressed disapproval of the idea, he intended to proceed with the project. Hearing of Forsyth's intention, the President became agitated and, declaring that the plan would evoke a war with

Spain, warned that he would veto such a bill. Upon request of Monroe, Crawford attempted to dissuade Forsyth from the proposed motion, but he failed to convince his fellow Georgian. Crawford argued also that Forsyth's proposal would not be supported by a majority of the members of the committee.

Crawford's prediction proved accurate. Forsyth was overruled by the Committee of Foreign Relations. Cognizant of the increasing opposition of Monroe, Clay, and other administration leaders, Forsyth became convinced of his inability to reach his objective and consequently abandoned the project. According to John Quincy Adams, there was a reason for Forsyth's unusual conduct in proposing a motion so unfavorable to the Monroe administration: Clay, in the House of Representatives had taunted Forsyth with being a dependent tool of the President; in refuting the charge, the Georgian had extended his disavowals to the point of advocating measures known to be objectionable to the administration; once committed to the project, Forsyth could not, with propriety, withdraw. However, it seems more likely that Forsyth, realizing the proximity of East Florida to Georgia, visualized the benefits to be derived by his state if the United States should take possession of the poorly-governed Spanish territory. His desire to protect the interests of Georgia seems to have been the dominant reason for his unorthodox action.

On the question of sending ministers to the Panama Congress in 1826, Forsyth again differed with the majority in the Committee of Foreign Relations. In so doing, his position was in conformity with his usual opposition to the policies of the Adams administration. The committee reported a resolution stating that it was expedient to appropriate the funds necessary for the mission. In the ensuing House debates, Forsyth stated that, since the Senate had approved the mission, he favored the granting of the necessary expense money, but only on condition that the activities of the United States delegation be confined to certain limits. He proposed that the ministers attend the Congress, not as members, but merely as diplomats, who would express the interest of the United States in Latin American affairs, would explain the foreign policy of the United States if requested, and would forward any propositions which the assembled powers wished to offer for consideration by the government in Washington.

In defense of his proposal, Forsyth questioned the motives of the administration and asserted that Adams's message to the

House on the subject was ambiguous and contradictory. He vehemently opposed giving the ministers the power to negotiate treaties. He feared the danger of entangling alliances, and in support of his position referred to the Monroe Doctrine and to George Washington's Farewell Address. Concerning the former, Forsyth insisted that negotiation of an inter-American defense pact was not necessary for implementation of the non-colonization principle; with reference to the latter, he declared that Washington's admonition was as applicable to the Spanish American countries as to the European states. On April 22, 1826, the bill with the necessary appropriation for the Panama mission was passed in the House by a vote of 134 to 60. Forsyth's ballot was in opposition to the measure.[61]

At various times, Forsyth's committee was required to conduct inquiries about claims involving foreign affairs. On March 10, 1826, Forsyth submitted a committee report concerning claims of certain persons who were inhabitants of East Florida before the cession of that territory to the United States. The petitioners sought compensation for property losses allegedly sustained through American invasion and occupation of a part of East Florida in 1812. Forsyth reported that, while no supporting evidence had been appended to the memorials, the committee considered the general facts sufficient to warrant a decision. In the judgment of the committee, payment should be denied, for the Adams-Onis treaty provided the petitioners no basis for claim upon the United States. The House concurred with the recommendation made by the committee.[62]

In the same year, Forsyth's committee was instructed to investigate the claims of the heirs of Caron de Beaumarchais, with a view toward liquidating the claims as partial adjustment for those of American citizens against the French government. The original Beaumarchais claims had amounted to 2,700,000 *livres*, or approximately $500,000; they included payment for supplies furnished by the fictitious Rodrigue Hortalez and Company during the American Revolution. When settling the claim in 1805, the United States Treasury had deducted approximately 1,000,000 *livres*, or about $200,000, contending that this amount had been paid to Beaumarchais by the French government. The heirs of Beaumarchais did not deny that the French money had been received, but they maintained that it was used for other purposes; they therefore asked that the United States pay the sum which had been deducted.

Although Presidents Jefferson, Madison, and Monroe had favored payment, succeeding Congresses had questioned the legitimacy of the claims. In the report to the House on May 16, 1826, Forsyth referred to the fact that the American minister to France, in 1824, had been instructed by President Monroe to examine and adjust all claims of French citizens against the United States. Since the committee assumed that similar instructions had been issued to the present United States minister in Paris, the committee requested that it be discharged from further consideration of the matter. The request was granted by the House.

The Richard W. Meade claims also came within the purview of Forsyth's committee. Meade, a citizen of Pennsylvania, had settled in Spain as a merchant. During the Peninsular War, he had advanced large sums of money to aid the cause of the patriots against the French troops. After the war, his claims had been presented to the Spanish government, which in 1820 had awarded him a certificate of debt in the amount of 9,823,072 *reals vellon* and 11 *maravedis,* or $491,153.62 in American money.

Since the Adams-Onis treaty of 1819 provided that claims of American citizens against the Spanish government were subject to review and possible assumption by the government of the United States, Meade had submitted his claims to the latter agency. On the last day of its sessions, the Board of Commissioners appointed to survey the American claims had rejected Meade's memorial, because of the lack of important supporting documents which the Pennsylvanian had previously presented to the Spanish government and which the latter had not returned.

On April 22, 1826, Forsyth presented a report on Meade's petition which had been referred to the Committee of Foreign Relations. The committee called attention to the fact that both the petitioner and the commissioners had requested the necessary documents from the Spanish government, but they had not received the papers prior to the termination of the period designated for the investigations. Therefore, Forsyth reported a bill which would allow Meade the opportunity of establishing his claims, even though the Board of Commissioners had ceased to exist. In the House debates, Forsyth spoke in favor of reconsidering the Meade claims, declaring that they had never received a fair and adequate examination from the United States government. He explained that Meade had submitted to the commissioners a written acknowledgment from the Spanish government that the sum was due him, but that the Board had insisted upon seeing the vouchers, which were in Spain. Forsyth contended that the unsettled state of affairs in Spain had contributed to the non-receipt of the supporting documents and that Meade was being penalized for something over which he had no control.

In spite of Forsyth's appeal, the Meade claims were never paid. Forsyth's sympathy for Meade's difficulties must have been genuine, for, as United States minister, the Georgian had had an opportunity to obtain a personal view of the unfavorable conditions in Spain and to participate in disagreeable negotiations with the Spanish government.

Forsyth could look back, with some degree of satisfaction, upon an outstanding performance of duty in the national legislature. He had established a reputation as a respected and competent member of Congress, one whose debating abilities were unquestioned and whose thinking processes were more than adequate. Generally classified as a vigorous supporter of the Madison and Monroe administrations, he had on several occasions demonstrated his political independence. Nor had he neglected the interests of his Georgia constituents; his general support of broad nationalism had been tinged with the doctrine of state rights. Devoting his efforts to a variety of legislative measures, he had demonstrated a special interest in the realm of foreign affairs. His services motivated a contemporary newspaper to remark, "He said much in Congress—and much to the purpose. Congress Hall was the field where some of his greenest laurels were gathered. . . ."[63] At this stage of his career, Forsyth seemed destined for even greater honors.

III

Mission to Madrid

On FEBRUARY 25, 1819, the Washington *National Intelligencer* joyously announced that "A TREATY OF AMITY, SETTLEMENT, AND LIMITS, BETWEEN THE UNITED STATES AND SPAIN . . ." had been unanimously approved by the Senate.[1] The newspaper was referring to the convention which, after prolonged negotiations, had been signed by Secretary of State John Quincy Adams and Luis de Onis y Gonzalez, Spanish Minister to the United States, on February 22, 1819, and approved by the Senate two days later. By the treaty the boundary between the United States and Spanish territory in the West was to extend from the mouth of the Sabine River, at the Gulf of Mexico, follow that stream northward to 32° north latitude, thence due north to the Red River, follow that body of water westward to 100° west longitude, thence due north to the Arkansas River, follow the course of the southern bank of that river to its source, thence north to the 42nd parallel of north latitude, thence westward to the Pacific Ocean. South of the line established by the 42nd parallel, the United States surrendered all her territorial claims to Spain, while the latter transferred all her claims to territory north of that line to the United States.[2] Thus, the United States ceded her claims to Texas, and Spain abandoned her pretensions to the Oregon territory.

With respect to the eastern part of the continent, the King of Spain ceded the Floridas to the United States; also, the inhabitants of the ceded territory were promised religious toleration and were to receive the full status of citizenship when the area was admitted to statehood. Each nation assumed the claims of its citizens against the other, though the United States limited its responsibility to $5,000,000. The treaty was to take effect when duly ratified by the United States and Spain, such ratifications to be exchanged within six months after the signatory date.

Article VIII of the treaty was destined to cause controversy. It confirmed all land grants in the Floridas made by the Spanish King, or his legal advisers, prior to January 24, 1818, and rejected all such grants made subsequent to that date. After the treaty had been signed, Adams discovered that there was a possibility that three large grants had been made by the Spanish monarch before January 24, 1818, instead of after that date as the Secretary had previously assumed. The recipients of the grants were three court favorites: the Duke of Alagon, the Count of Punon Rostro, and Pedro de Vargas. Adams consulted Hyde de Neuville, French Minister to the United States and mediator during the treaty negotiations, who declared that it was his impression that the specified grants had been considered by Onis as being null and void. Questioned by Adams, Onis replied that he had signed the treaty with the understanding that the grants had been authorized after January 24 and hence were invalid. He promised Adams that he would notify the Spanish government that he had intended the grants to be void.[3]

So that there might be no misunderstanding about the matter, Adams drafted a declaration to be delivered to the Spanish government at the time of the exchange of ratifications. The declaration stated that the treaty had been signed with complete agreement on the part of each plenipotentiary that the grants of Alagon, Punon Rostro, and Vargas were among those considered null and void; that, in exchanging ratifications, the United States did so with the explicit understanding that the specified grants were invalid. When the draft was read to the President, he authorized exchange of ratifications even if the declaration should not be acceptable to the Spanish King. The person selected to exchange the ratifications and to deliver the declaration was the recently appointed United States Minister to Spain, John Forsyth.[4]

Forsyth's active service as chairman of the House Committee of Foreign Relations, his evident interest in and knowledge of foreign affairs, and his reputation as a firm supporter of the administration were all strong recommendations for the appointment to Spain. On several occasions, he had been prominently mentioned as a prospective appointee to a diplomatic post. As early as 1816, he had been suggested as a possible choice for Minister to Russia.[5] During the winter of 1818-1819, there were rumors that

Forsyth was to succeed George William Erving as Minister to Spain and, after being informed by Crawford that such an appointment was pending, Forsyth began a study of the Spanish language. Realizing that the commission might afford him the opportunity of negotiating for a cession of the Floridas, he wrote to Biddle that "my good fellow citizens would love me infinitely if I can procure this little slip of Territory for the U. S. especially those of them who have Speculated largely in land & negroes in the expectation of a speedy Cession of it."[6] Forsyth undoubtedly considered himself well informed and qualified for the assignment, for in addition to his legislative activities concerning Spanish affairs, he was familiar with the negotiations which were being conducted between Adams and Onis.[7]

When, by direction of President Monroe, Adams offered Forsyth the Spanish post on December 18, 1818, the Georgian accepted with alacrity. He immediately made inquiries regarding the personnel of the legation and the details of the journey to Spain. Upon being advised that Thomas L. L. Brent would remain as secretary of the legation at Madrid, he stated that he was gratified because that experienced official was doubtless thoroughly familiar with the French and Spanish languages. Informed that he would travel by frigate and was expected to arrive in Spain during the early spring season, Forsyth expressed his satisfaction, since he wished to spend some time in Georgia prior to his departure. Later, on February 17, 1819, he was notified to prepare for embarkation as soon as convenient after the adjournment of Congress; he was also told that the substance of his instructions would depend upon the result of the negotiations with Onis.[8]

John Quincy Adams did not share Forsyth's opinion that the latter had the proper qualifications for the Spanish mission. The Secretary of State had recommended Henry Middleton for the position and was disconcerted over Forsyth's selection, complaining that it was not the first time that machinations had been responsible for an appointment in his department. He claimed that Forsyth owed his appointment to the influence of Crawford, whose efforts were prompted by the fact that Forsyth's wife was the daughter of Josiah Meigs, commissioner of the General Land Office of the United States, and the niece of Return Jonathan Meigs, Postmaster General. These two officers were responsible for considerable patronage. Adams believed that an unfortunate choice had been made, for in his opinion Forsyth "had neither the experience, nor the prudence, nor the sincerity, nor the delicacy of sentiment suited for such a station."[9] However, Forsyth's appointment was confirmed by the Senate on February 15, 1819. Two days later, his letter of resignation from the Senate was read in that body, whereupon James Barbour, president *pro tempore,* advised Governor William Rabun of Georgia of the existing vacancy.[10]

Although Forsyth had not intended to leave the United States before April, the completion of the Adams-Onis negotiations in February caused him to make the offer, which was accepted, to forego his visit to Georgia so that he might be the bearer of the treaty to Spain. Forsyth was unduly optimistic concerning his venture, believing that the Spanish government would not dare to refuse ratification of the treaty, and that he would be able to bring the protracted affair to a successful conclusion before the end of May.[11] Several newspapers, not so confident, expressed forebodings as to the reactions of the Spanish authorities. One editor declared that Forsyth's mission might be rendered critical by the reported disorganized state of affairs in Spain; [12] while another remarked that "we should not be surprised if the king of Spain should tantalize and fret us a good deal before he gives them [the Floridas] up to the United States." [13]

On March 9, 1819, Forsyth called at the State Department, where his instructions and other documents were delivered to him. Included among the latter were the following: a commission, a letter of credence to the King of Spain, a cypher, the ratified copy of the Adams-Onis treaty, a letter of credit upon the London banking firm of Baring Brothers and Company, various volumes containing laws and state papers, fourteen volumes of *Niles' Register,* and a passport. The following day, Adams dispatched supplementary instructions stating that a declaration form was inclosed and giving the reason for its being drafted. In conformity with Monroe's specific directive, Forsyth was instructed to exchange ratifications even though the Spanish government refused receipt of the declaration.[14]

According to Forsyth's general instructions, he was to proceed to Boston, where the United States frigate *Hornet,* commanded by Captain George C. Read, would transport him to Cadiz. With respect to the Adams-Onis treaty, the general instructions stated that the first object of his mission was to exchange ratifications of the convention. When the ratifications were effected,

he was to receive the Spanish copy and forward it to Captain
Read at Cadiz, who would convey it immediately to the United
States.

Since the Spanish troops in the Floridas were to be transported
to Havana in ships furnished by the United States, Forsyth was to
obtain copies of the orders and transmit them with the ratified
copy of the treaty. He was to remind the Spanish government that
orders should be issued for the delivery to the United States of
all the archives and documents pertaining to the Floridas. He
was to advise the State Department when Spain appointed officials
to aid in surveying the western boundary, as specified in the
treaty. In order to provide information for the commissioners appointed to investigate the assumption of claims, Forsyth was instructed to direct his efforts toward collecting and forwarding all
pertinent documents regarding claims of United States citizens
against the Spanish government. Finally, Forsyth was ordered to
be observant and to make frequent reports of all political movements, particularly those which might be of interest to the United
States; if a change of government in Spain should affect his credentials, and thus delay the exchange of ratifications, he was to
urge the expediency of transferring the ceremony to the United
States.

The new minister received personal instructions also. Forsyth
was advised that, in the event of his contemplated return to the
United States in the autumn, the experienced Thomas L. L.
Brent should be left in charge of the legation. During any temporary absence, Brent was to receive the salary of a chargé
d'affaires, while Forsyth's annual compensation of $9,000 was to
cease from the time of his departure until his return to Spain.

The final sentence of his personal instructions was not satisfactory to Forsyth and, before leaving the United States, he wrote
to Adams objecting to the proposed deprivation of salary during
a temporary absence from Spain. By specifically asking that
Monroe rule on the matter, Forsyth probably did little to endear
himself to the Secretary. In his letter, Forsyth explained that had
he not offered to leave the United States at an earlier date than
anticipated, he would have received his salary while attending
to his private affairs in Georgia; that, if he had visited his residence
there would have been no necessity for his temporary return to
the United States and consequent loss of compensation. He declared that it had been his impression, in conversation with
Adams, that mutually satisfactory arrangements were to be made

between himself and Brent, whereby he would reimburse the
latter for any exceptional expense incurred during the period of
absence from Spain.[15]

Forsyth received an answer to his letter after his arrival in
Spain. He was informed that the President agreed that the circumstances warranted a continuance of salary during the interval
of leave from Spain; however, the absence was not to extend beyond six months and he was to be accountable to Brent for any
extraordinary expenses incurred by the latter.[16] Forsyth replied
that he was satisfied with the decision, would not abuse the privilege, and was confident that the arrangement with Brent would
be entirely agreeable to him.[17]

Forsyth, accompanied by his private secretary, F. Columbus
Fenwick, left Washington on March 10, 1819, and traveled to
Baltimore, thence to Philadelphia, where he attended a party at
the home of Nicholas Biddle, thence to New York, and on to
Boston, where he arrived on March 21. A few days' delay then ensued while the *Hornet* waited for favorable winds. Finally, on the
morning of March 26, 1819, Forsyth, together with Fenwick and
a Negro servant named Cyrus, left the Boston wharf and was received on board the *Hornet* with a salute of seventeen guns.
The sloop of war soon set sail and, on passing Fort Independence,
the Minister was complimented by a salute from the land instal-
lations and the rendition of patriotic music by the Fort band.
Forsyth's state of mind and his reaction to the music are revealed
in his journal:

I know not whether the notes were softened by our distance from
them or mellowed by passing over the water or whether the melancholy emotion of leaving the U. States for the first time, gave to them
their touching tone, but musick never before fell so sweetly upon my
ear or filled my soul with a greater variety of pleasing & painful
feelings.[18]

After passing the Boston lighthouse at the mouth of the harbor,
the commander of the *Hornet* decided that prevailing winds
were unfavorable, and therefore returned the vessel to Nantasket
Roads. Although Forsyth was inclined to return to Boston until
the weather improved, he was induced by Captain Read to remain
on board the frigate. When the Georgian awoke the following
morning, he discovered that the vessel had released the harbor
pilot and had put to sea.

The voyage to Spain proved a disagreeable one. Although there were some days of pleasant weather, the *Hornet* for the most part encountered rain, hail, snow, and strong gales. The passengers found it difficult to sleep or retain food. Maintaining that "the ship rolls about like a rocking-horse and creaks at every motion," Forsyth became dejected and consistently wished that he had never left the United States. Extracts from his journal are indicative of his feelings:

Fenwick very sick. Cyrus still worse. One in a birth [*sic*] & the other on the floor. The Ship very wet & not comfortable in any part of her. . . . The day was like most days at sea in bad weather, dull and gloomy. I wished from the bottom of my soul that I was safely stowed away in our cottage on the S. Hills with my wife & children around me, without other riches than those necessary to provide for their comfort and improvement. . . .

We passed two vessels a Ship & brig lying to bound into the U. S. Their situation was less pleasant than ours but they were bound homeward & I was silly enough to envy those on board & repine at a lot brought upon myself & which has been frequently the object of strong desire. Such is the condition of human life. We wish to strive for an object our fond imagination paints to us in colors vivid & delightful. Time & perseverance enable us to reach it, & all its beauty is fled. It is the fabled fruit of the Dead Sea, tempting to the eye, but touched in bitterness & ashes.[19]

In spite of his uncomfortable situation, Forsyth engaged in various activities during the voyage. Seeking to familiarize himself with the country to which he was going, he attempted to converse with another passenger, a Spanish patriot by the name of Radal, but found the effort ineffectual, since the Spaniard spoke only broken English, while the Georgian's use of Spanish was confined to monosyllables. He spent some time more profitably in reading Spanish history and travel accounts—while imbibing a punch made from fresh limes and peach brandy.

Forsyth became interested in the *Hornet* and her personnel. He learned of Captain Read's feats during the War of 1812 and was impressed with the vessel's distinguished naval history. He observed the discipline maintained by the crew in its drills and in the trial of offenders, who were punished by having their grog allowances discontinued for various periods of time, depending upon the magnitude of the offense. Forsyth discovered that the sailors were amused with Cyrus, who was the only African aboard the ship, and that they insulted the Negro's dignity by addressing him as "Joe." The Minister did not envy the young officers or the seamen, forced to endure the wet and cold weather of ocean voyages. He concluded that "the Ocean is the last resort I should take for the means of subsistence. . . ."[20]

The wearisome voyage to Spain came to an end on April 14, 1819, when the *Hornet* anchored in the bay before Cadiz. Since the regulations at Cadiz required all United States vessels to observe an eight-day quarantine, a restriction which Forsyth considered unnecessary, the Georgian was prevented from landing until acting United States Consul Tunis obtained pratique for the frigate. Late on April 15, the Minister went ashore and dined with Tunis. He then was escorted to the English Hotel, where rooms had been provided for him.[21]

On the following day, Forsyth's baggage was landed. When a clerk from the consulate was dispatched to bring it into the city, the Administrator of Customs sent word that regulations required examination of the baggage. The Georgian refused to give up his luggage keys. Instead, the angry Forsyth addressed a note to the Governor-General of Cadiz, Count Abisval, stating that he expected not only the delivery of his trunks, but also the exaction of a punishment upon the customs officer, whose conduct he regarded as insolent.

Count Abisval ordered the baggage released, but the customs administrator insisted that the trunks be sealed until their arrival in Madrid. In order to effect a literal compliance with the rules, Count Abisval requested that Forsyth surrender his keys, and promised that the trunks would not be opened. Forsyth refused the Governor-General's suggestion, claiming that such a compliance would be equivalent to an inspection, or at least to an acknowledgment of the right to examine. Maintaining that the Count was not familiar with the practice of regarding exemption of a minister's person and property from the laws of Spain, Forsyth directed Tunis to inform the Governor-General that the luggage must be delivered promptly or be returned to the *Hornet,* where it would remain while a remonstrance was being made to the King of Spain. On the following morning, April 17, the trunks arrived at the English Hotel.

Later, the dispute with the customs official was renewed. Forsyth, preparing to leave Cadiz for the Spanish capital, applied for passports, but was notified that the customs administrator would not sign them until the Georgian's trunks had been inspected or until a seal had been placed upon them. Forsyth went to the customs house to see the obstinate Spaniard. He listened to what the administrator had to say and then, through an interpreter, told the official "that my baggage would be passed thro' the City in the course of one hour and that whoever dared to stop it should do it at his peril."[22] Shortly thereafter, the properly attested passport was received by the Minister.

The exasperating affair of the baggage evidently had two effects on Forsyth: it caused him to have a poor opinion of Spanish procedure, and it gave him the idea that forceful language and actions were necessary to arouse the Spanish authorities from their lethargy. Unfortunately, the latter method was not the approved form for diplomats.

After his disembarkation from the *Hornet*, Forsyth remained in Cadiz for almost ten days before proceeding to Madrid. He explained to Secretary of State Adams that the delay was caused by his difficulties with the Spanish customs official and his failure to secure convenient traveling accommodations. During this period, Forsyth had an opportunity to visit the places of interest in and near the Spanish port city, and also to observe the Spanish people and their customs. He made an official call on Count Abisval, a man of Irish parentage whose family name was O'Donnel. The Governor-General was extremely courteous to the American and expressed regret over the baggage difficulties.

On his tour of the city and surrounding area, Forsyth enjoyed everything—the churches, the homes, the coffee-houses, the cockpits, the streets, the bay, the architecture, the paintings. He was not favorably impressed with the Spanish women, whom he at first mistook for mulattoes. Later, he observed "a few of them on the Alameda with the famous Mantilla or head-dress and short petticoats of black. . . . Neither are becoming, the first looks brazen & the other something worse."[23]

Accompanied by Read, Tunis, and Fenwick, the Minister visited Chiclana, the summer retreat usually reserved for persons of wealth. The party traveled in two *calesas,* heavy and awkward vehicles, each drawn by a horse and attended by a *calesero.* After arriving at their destination and partaking of a supper consisting of fish and salad, the group retired to a home, rented by Tunis for the summer, where Forsyth spent an uncomfortable night bothered by fleas. Upon his return to Cadiz, the Georgian was entertained by Gypsies dancing the *zapoteo,* the *bolera,* the *fandango,* and the *cachucha.* Concerning the performances, Forsyth wrote his wife: "I cannot describe the dances to you, but I may say that they were the most indecent exhibitions I ever saw particularly the Cachucha."[24] During his stay in Cadiz, the Minister made some purchases. As a token of appreciation to the crew of the *Hornet,* he bought and sent three hundred oranges to the vessel. He also purchased, for delivery to his home in the United States, five casks of wine and a box of mats; these items were transported by the frigate on its return voyage.[25]

Forsyth, Fenwick, Cyrus, Read, and the latter's servant left Cadiz for Madrid on April 24, 1819. To guard against the robberies common on the Spanish highways, an escort of soldiers accompanied the group along the route. Captain Read was included in the party because Forsyth considered that it would be an advantage to have the ratified Spanish copy of the treaty returned to Cadiz by a person of known fidelity; also, he reasoned that the naval officer's short stay in Madrid would entail only a slight increase of expenditures over those incurred by employing a special messenger, since the latter would have to be paid, not only for bearing the treaty to Cadiz, but also for his return trip to the Spanish capital. It turned out that the *Hornet* commander remained in Madrid longer than anticipated, not returning to Cadiz until June 26.

After a tiresome overland journey, Forsyth and his party arrived in Madrid on May 9, 1819. Within a few days, Forsyth had presented his credentials to the Marquis of Casa Yrujo, Secretary of State, and had received permission to appear before King Ferdinand VII. Since Erving had taken his leave of the Spanish court, the Georgian included the former minister's letter of recall when he presented his own letter of credence to the King on May 18, at which time he also had audiences with other members of the royal family. On the same day, he informed Yrujo that he was prepared to exchange ratifications of the treaty on as early a date as possible.[26] Anxious to learn whether a definite date for the exchange had been established, Forsyth called on the Marquis on May 25, but was informed that the Council of State had not made a decision, though Yrujo hoped for one in two or three days.

Failing to receive any information on the matter, Forsyth decided that Read's departure from Madrid might be a means of hastening action on the part of the Spanish government. Accordingly, he applied for the naval officer's passport on June 2, and received it without difficulty. On June 3 he conferred with Yrujo, who professed a desire for an early exchange of ratifications, but stated that the King had not made a formal disclosure on the subject. Forsyth replied that a prompt ratification of the treaty by Spain would insure better relations with the United States; on the other hand,

the arrival of the Hornet in the U. S. with the information that the Treaty was not ratified by Spain, would necessarily produce mistrust and suspicions of the intentions of the government, which a subsequent and later ratification could not entirely remove.[27]

The Secretary expressed the opinion that Forsyth should write a note, to bring the matter to the attention of the King. Although the Georgian complied with the suggestion, he received no immediate answer.

Forsyth wrote to Adams that he had heard indirectly that the opposition in the Council of State to the treaty was based on the fact that Alagon had considerable influence over the King, and that Alagon and Punon Rostro anticipated profitable advantages from the land grants. Forsyth understood that the grants to Alagon and Punon Rostro were dated February 6, 1818, but that the two court favorites were going to contend that the February date applied to the cedula and that the initial order of the King had been issued prior to January 24, 1818. The Georgian informed Adams that, if on the exchange of ratifications the declaration was not acceptable to the Spanish government, he intended to use the refusal as the basis of a request for authentic copies of the grants to Alagon, Punon Rostro, and Vargas. Forsyth was positive that the Spanish authorities would ratify the treaty, though he believed that they might delay until the last moment, in an effort to find some means to prevent the land grants from being declared invalid.

Forsyth called on the Spanish Secretary of State on June 12, to confirm a report which he had received from the French Ambassador, the Duke of Laval. The latter had stated that, in a previous conversation with Yrujo, the Marquis had remarked that it was reasonable to expect an exchange of ratifications within ten or twelve days. Yrujo told Forsyth that, while he could not give a positive assurance, he was "morally certain" that a final determination on the subject would be made by the cabinet at its impending session. Forsyth replied that, under the circumstances, Read would be detained in Madrid for a short time; however, he insisted that he could see no reason for the extensive consultations and the consequent delay.

The Spaniard explained that before the cession of territory could be formally approved, a cautious examination of the entire subject was necessary. Speaking unofficially, Yrujo stated that he regretted that the treaty failed to stipulate an exclusion of the disputed grants; that consequently, the King was faced with a dilemma—if he accepted the United States' interpretation of the treaty, he would be accused of acting in fear of retaliation; if he did otherwise, the United States would charge a lack of good faith. Forsyth defended the position of the United States by asserting that his government, in signing and ratifying the convention, had relied upon the correctness of Onis's statement that the grants had been issued after the date specified in the treaty. Yrujo repeated his desire to expedite the affair and asked that the American diplomat be patient. Forsyth left the Secretary's office with the conviction that the matter would be settled before the expiration of the time fixed for Read's departure from Madrid.

On June 13, the Marquis of Casa Yrujo, his family, and several other Spanish authorities were banished from the court of Ferdinand VII. Manuel Gonzales Salmon, brother-in-law of Onis, was appointed termporarily to discharge the duties of Secretary of State. Forsyth was surprised by the turn of events and feared that it meant a further delay of the exchange of ratifications. According to Forsyth, various rumors were afloat about the overthrow of the Yrujo ministry. One report stated that the change was a result of a court intrigue and was only remotely connected with the Florida question. Another interpretation was that the King, when ratifying the treaty, would represent the act as an unpleasant obligation forced upon him by the banished officials, who had, in turn, been punished for alienating Spanish territory.[28]

Forsyth lost little time in approaching the acting Secretary of State. On June 14, he talked with Salmon, and after giving him the details of his conversations with the former Secretary, declared that he considered Yrujo's pledges binding upon the present ministry. Salmon replied that since he had been absent from Madrid and had had no opportunity to obtain information from Yrujo, he was not thoroughly familiar with the subject. Nevertheless, he promised to study the matter and discuss it during his first audience with the King.

Two days later, Forsyth, accompanied by Brent as interpreter, had another conversation with the Spanish official. Salmon stated that no decision had been reached, but that he would send an official communication to the United States Minister within a few days. However, he warned that the note, instead of containing a final conclusion made by the government, might merely acknowledge the fact that the subject was still under consideration. He suggested that it might be better for all parties concerned if the *Hornet,* rather than return to the United States without the treaty, should remain in Cadiz until a definite determination had been made concerning ratification.

The acting Secretary of State also remarked that Spain should not be censured for the delay, since the treaty allowed six months for the accomplishment of the object. Forsyth disagreed with the latter interpretation, contending that the treaty stipulation was made because the distance between the United States and Spain required an extensive time for the transmission of documents. He explained that the United States, by graciously sending its ratified copy of the convention to Madrid for an exchange, had given proof of its desire to accommodate the Spanish government, and that his country had a right to expect a corresponding consideration. He pointed out that if he should return the ratified copy of the treaty to the United States for exchange there, the King would be required to make an immediate decision in order to complete the affair within the specified time. Forsyth refused to order a further detention of the *Hornet* unless he was assured that the promised message would contain a definite reply. He left Salmon's office with no idea as to when to expect a termination of the transaction.

Although Read was to leave Madrid, Forsyth instructed the naval officer to remain in Cadiz for a few days after his arrival, so that he might receive any dispatches which the American diplomat wished to transmit. Forsyth considered it wise for the *Hornet* to return to the United States and inform his government of the situation, so that it could formulate a policy to be followed in case of Spanish nonratification. While Forsyth continued to express belief that the Spanish authorities would ratify the treaty, he admitted that since the government was so erratic and corrupt, it was impossible for him to predict with any degree of certainty what Spain would do under given circumstances. On June 17, he wrote to Adams that if the treaty was not ratified by Spain, he intended to forego his contemplated visit to the United States until he received further instructions.

Two days after Forsyth addressed his communication to Adams, Salmon wrote to the American Minister that the King, realizing the importance of the convention, was determined to give it a cautious and deliberate examination before reaching a final decision.[29] The continuance of the Spanish policy of procrastination infuriated the Georgian, who replied on June 21 with a tactless note:

Perhaps you are yet to learn that the delay of the last month has given rise, at the seat of his Majesty's government, among his own subjects, to the most monstrous and absurd suppositions. Among the subjects of Spain, those who best know the integrity of the King and the purity of his Councils, it is asserted that an act, required by the policy of the government, essential to the interests of the Kingdom and demanded by the honor of the King, will not be performed. Yes Sir the King is calumniated in his very Capital by a most unjust surmise, that there will be a refusal to do that, which she dare not refuse. Your Excellency will not understand this as threatening his Majesty's government with the consequences which might ensue from the resentment of the United States, if it were possible for Spain to act in this business with bad faith. Threats are used by conscious weakness, not by conscious strength. I know too well the abundant resources, the expanding power, the youthful vigour of my country, to degrade her character by using language unworthy of it. If not by my respect for Spain, I should be prevented by the fear of the deserved resentment of my own Country; I should not be easily forgiven for condescending to say, how she would punish an act of perfidy. It is by her acts, & not by the railings of her Ministers, that she will be known to those who violate the faith pledged to her. But there is this, which a just government will more cautiously avoid than even the well founded resentment of a powerful nation,—the degradation of conscious baseness. No wise King will dare to do an act which would deprive him of the respect of all nations, sully the reputation of his Kingdom in the eyes of the civilized world and deprive his people of the strongest incentive to virtuous exertions under every dispensation of heaven, the confidence in the integrity of their government.[30]

Forsyth also informed Salmon that, while the exchange of ratifications would prove the falsity of existing impressions, the motive for delay might be misunderstood. After asserting that he hoped his apprehensions would not be verified, Forsyth advised that he would address no more notes to the Spanish government on the subject, but was prepared to exchange ratifications at any time prior to August 22, 1819.

Sailing from Cadiz on July 2, the *Hornet* crossed the ocean and anchored in New York harbor on July 20, 1819. Captain Read soon started his overland journey to Washington where, on August 2, he delivered Forsyth's June dispatches to the State Department. At a cabinet meeting on August 10, President Monroe proposed two questions for consideration: whether, in the event of Spanish nonratification, he should recommend to the December Congress that the United States seize Florida; also, whether instructions should be sent to Forsyth by special messenger and, if so, what directives should be included therein.

On the first question, there was unanimous agreement among the cabinet members present that the Executive should make such a proposal. On the second inquiry, the President and his advisers agreed that a special messenger should be dispatched to Spain, but they expressed a diversity of opinion as to the substance of the instructions. Monroe proposed that Forsyth be instructed to notify the Spanish government that the United States was agreeable to an exchange of ratifications, even though the stipulated time had expired, but that a further delay or a refusal on the part of the Spanish authorities would result in the President's recommending to Congress that Florida be occupied by the United States. Crawford suggested that Forsyth be directed to demand an immediate ratification and, if the Spanish government refused to comply, the Minister should request his passports. The Secretary of the Treasury stated that such a positive action would intimidate the Spanish authorities and force them to approve ratification of the treaty.

Calhoun and Monroe disagreed with Crawford, believing that Forsyth should remain at his post, even though it meant cancellation of his authorized visit to the United States. Adams agreed with the President, except that the Secretary of State wished to omit the reference to the threatened United States seizure of Florida, since it might antagonize Spain. He contended that the proposal might also offend Congress, whose members might resent the move as a dictatorial act on the part of the Executive. These latter views were finally approved by Monroe. At a subsequent cabinet meeting, on August 17, Adams's draft of the instructions was read and examined. The President designated Captain Read as the special messenger, and the instructions left New York, aboard the *Hornet,* on August 24, 1819.[31]

Forsyth's new instructions, dated August 18, directed that he demand an immediate ratification and at the same time notify the Spanish officials that a delay of more than one week would be interpreted as a refusal. He was instructed to accept the Spanish ratification after August 22, provided there was sufficient time to permit a transmission to the United States before the Decem-

ber meeting of Congress and provided Spain should declare the
disputed grants null and void. He was told to advise the Spanish authorities that if the ratified Spanish copy of the treaty had
not arrived in the United States by the time specified, the President would make a complete report to Congress which, in turn,
would adopt such measures as it considered expedient; that regardless of the nature of congressional action, the Spanish government would be held responsible for all damages and expenses
resulting from delay or refusal to ratify.

If the Spaniards ratified the treaty, Forsyth was, under no circumstances, to exchange ratifications without submitting the declaration concerning the grants. If the Spanish authorities failed
to ratify, he was to present a remonstrance against the grants and
against the circumstances involving their issuance. The instructions also included a lengthy discourse on the obligations of a
monarch to ratify a treaty which had been negotiated by a minister with full powers. In conclusion, Forsyth was informed that
he might use his leave of absence if the exchange was effected;
otherwise, he was to remain in Madrid pending further instructions.[32]

While his instructions were being formulated and sent to him,
Forsyth was experiencing further difficulties with the Spanish
government. On August 10, Salmon addressed a reply to
Forsyth's harsh note of June 21. The Spaniard asserted that certain phrases of Forsyth's communication, besides being superfluous, "cannot fail to appear very extraordinary, which your ardent zeal for the interests of your Nation has doubtless prompted
you to employ, but in which you have been carried further than
really could have been wished." [33] In addition, he denounced the
style as being foreign to diplomatic usage. While professing the
King's good faith, the acting Secretary informed Forsyth that
Ferdinand had decided that he could not give a final approval
to the treaty until several questions had been solved. Consequently, in an effort to remove all obstacles and to effect a successful conclusion of the affair, the monarch intended to send a new
representative to the United States for discussions with that
government.

Forsyth received Salmon's note on August 12, and made a
prompt reply. He disclaimed any intention of showing disrespect
to the Spanish government; he regretted that the contents of his
previous note had been misunderstood, but maintained that they
could not be deemed objectionable if they were interpreted

correctly. As for the criticism that certain phrases were superfluous, the Georgian stated that it was proper for his own government, and not the Spanish, to approve or censure. If his style
was considered undiplomatic, he would seek consolation in the
fact that his just opinions had been advanced in plain terms. Forsyth charged that the Spanish procedure concerning ratification
was more likely to create discord between the two nations than
any excessive zeal on the part of an agent of either country. He
remarked that their past actions seemed inconsistent with the
protestations of the Spanish authorities that they wished to establish a firm understanding with the United States.

Since the time limit for exchange was to expire in ten days,
Forsyth claimed that it was useless to send an envoy to the United
States for discussions, and that the only hope to be derived from
such a venture would be the beginning of new negotiations.
After inquiring whether the Spanish authorities were not stu-
diously avoiding the usual procedure of discussing pertinent diplomatic affairs with the American Minister, he asserted that he
was prepared to clarify any portions of the treaty which the
Spanish government desired.[34]

Salmon answered Forsyth's note on August 19. The Spaniard
stated that his government had not changed its opinion regarding Forsyth's previous assertions and that the disagreeable subject was not to be mentioned again. He declared that the
deliberations of the Spanish cabinet had been devoted ex-
clusively to the ratification problem, and it was only after careful
consideration that the members came to the conclusion that certain phases of the treaty must be clarified before they could arrive at a final decision. Saying that these elucidations could be
obtained only through discussions in Washington, Salmon reiterated that the King had resolved to send a new minister to the
United States for that purpose. The Spanish government believed that the expiration of the time limit should prove no obstacle to a successful conclusion of the affair. The acting secretary
hoped that Forsyth's dispatches to Washington would remove
all doubts as to the good intentions of the Spanish monarch.[35]

Forsyth replied that he regretted, but was not surprised, that
the Spanish government had failed to ratify the convention. He
stated that as a result of the Spanish decision the provisions of
the treaty would not be obligatory upon the United States after
August 22. While declaring that he would not comment upon the
activities of the Spanish authorities lest he be accused of disre-

spect, he remarked that the previous rumors, which he had considered calumnies upon the Spanish government, had proved to be correct. He promised to transmit the assurances concerning the King's good intentions, but described the Spanish statements as "unfruitful professions that cannot but produce all the effect they deserve and all that could be rationally expected from them."[36]

Forsyth was not advised by Salmon as to the particular obstacles which the Spanish government wished removed, but he informed Adams that he was confident that the following should be listed among the Spanish objections to ratification of the treaty: the United States should not be permitted to invalidate the disputed grants; no cession should be made without United States guarantee of Spanish-American possessions and non-recognition of the South American provinces. The Georgian also wrote to Adams that he realized he could accomplish nothing with regard to the treaty, especially since the Spanish government was determined to continue discussions in Washington. Accordingly, he asked that President Monroe renew permission for him to make a temporary visit to the United States.[37]

The new instructions from his government caused more controversy between Forsyth and the Spanish officials. He applied for authentic copies of the grants made to Alagon, Punon Rostro, and Vargas. When his request was denied, he declared that he would be forced to procure them elsewhere. Subsequently, the Georgian secured, from private sources, a copy of Punon Rostro's grant and a description of the other two.[38] On October 18, 1819, Forsyth submitted a remonstrance to the Spanish government concerning the disputed grants. He accused Spain of offering to cede territory and then attempting to make the cession worthless. From what he had been able to learn, he was convinced that no title had been vested in the grantees prior to the issuance of the cedulas. He claimed that the action of the United States, with reference to the grants, was just and proper, and that "a denial of this position would fix upon the spanish government a charge of an attempt to commit a deception for which the language of decorum has no appropriate name."[39]

Forsyth's severe remonstrance was returned by the Duke of San Fernando and Quiroga, who had been appointed Secretary of State. The Spaniard asserted that the document was too offensive for presentation to the King. Assuring the Georgian that he would transmit any future notes, provided they were couched in correct and befitting terms, San Fernando upbraided the American Minister for using expressions which were "equally unprecedented and repugnant to the delicacy and attention which are peculiar to and are invariably observed in all diplomatic communications."[40] In his reply, Forsyth answered that "from the nature of the subject but few sacrifices could be made to diplomatick courtesy."[41] The Georgian informed the Spanish official that he would retain the remonstrance if he were given some positive assurances concerning the grants; otherwise, he proposed to send a carefully translated copy of it to San Fernando for the latter's re-examination.

Forsyth wrote to Adams that he was surprised when the remonstrance was returned to him, and after due consideration had decided that if the document was not received by the Spanish government he would leave Madrid. He believed that his departure would be a source of gratification to the Spanish authorities, for he had been *persona non grata* to them since his note of June 21, 1819. If he did leave his post, it would not be until January 1, 1820, and he would remain in France for at least two months, with the expectation of learning, before the expiration of that period, what steps Congress had determined to take with regard to Spain. He also informed Adams that he had learned unofficially that Major General Francisco Dionisio Vives had reluctantly accepted the appointment as Spanish Minister to the United States.[42]

Forsyth did not leave Madrid, as he had resolved to do if the remonstrance was not accepted by the Spanish authorities. On December 16, 1819, San Fernando addressed a message to the Georgian requesting the latter to inform his government that Vives had been selected for the mission to the United States and would proceed immediately. The Spanish Secretary also advised the American Minister that, in view of the new mission, he considered any further Madrid discussions of the controversy as superfluous.[43] Not satisfied with the Duke's note, Forsyth contended that it did not mention the specific powers granted to Vives and did not definitely request a suspension of the Madrid correspondence. However, he decided to delay the return of the remonstrance until he learned the contents of the President's message to Congress or received further instructions from his government.[44]

The harsh tone adopted by Forsyth in his correspondence with the Spanish government received general condemnation in the

United States. One newspaper reported that his conduct was more disgraceful than that of any minister in recent years.[45] When Freeman Walker of Georgia considered introducing a resolution in the Senate requesting that the President submit further information on Spanish affairs, Adams told the senator that the full publication of Forsyth's dispatches would cause dissatisfaction throughout the United States and would prove embarrassing to the American Minister's friends. Agreeing to the postponement of his resolution, Walker remarked that although he was one of Forsyth's most intimate friends, he could not condone the language used in that part of the correspondence which had already been made public.

Although the general tenor was a thorough criticism of Forsyth's activities, there was some qualified censure. The editor of the Milledgeville *Southern Recorder* wished to see Forsyth's instructions before being completely satisfied that the Minister merited such absolute condemnation.[46] When Hyde de Neuville remarked on the harshness of Forsyth's language, John Quincy Adams replied that Spain's conduct had been even more offensive. Later, Adams recorded that while he could not justify the Georgian's phraseology or his determination to leave Spain without instructions to do so, "yet great allowances were to be made for the provocation under which he had acted."[47]

Forsyth's conduct failed to gain the approbation of Monroe. The President's attitude was so unfavorable that he considered issuing a reprimand, but finally decided that he would grant Forsyth permission to return to the United States, and after he had arrived would revoke the appointment. Adams agreed with the decision of the Executive. John C. Calhoun was critical of the envoy, while William H. Crawford regretted that Forsyth had not been warned when the first of his offensive notes had been received at the State Department. On February 11, 1820, Adams informed Forsyth that the President had authorized the Georgian's visit to the United States, and that Brent was to be left in charge of the legation. The Secretary also expressed the hope that the communication would find Forsyth in Madrid, since a removal from that place without proper instructions would be displeasing to Monroe.[48]

Meanwhile, the political situation in Spain was undergoing a change. In accordance with his instructions to report any occurrences which might be of interest to the United States, Forsyth had on several occasions advised Secretary Adams of intermit-

tent insurrections carried on by the Spanish liberals against the
rule of Ferdinand VII. On March 9, 1820, he transmitted the information that a military revolution had forced the monarch two
days earlier to accept the Constitution of 1812, which transferred
sovereignty from the King to the people. Consequently, the
King no longer had the power to alienate territory. Forsyth was
dubious as to whether the Cortes had such power, and was apprehensive as to the effect of the revolution upon the Adams-Onis
treaty. However, he hoped that the alteration of government
would result in an amicable settlement of affairs between the
United States and Spain.[49] In a subsequent dispatch, Forsyth informed his government that in view of the changed situation he
realized the importance of his being in Madrid at the time of the
convocation of the Cortes in July.

Forsyth's relations with the new Spanish officials were a decided improvement over those which he had had with the preceding government. In a conversation with acting Secretary of
State Juan Jabat, he was assured that the treaty affair would be
presented to the Cortes, and that the controversial subject would
undoubtedly be settled to the satisfaction of both nations.[50] At
a later interview, conducted in a friendly atmosphere, Jabat suggested that the Georgian attend the impending meeting of the
King's circle. Forsyth had absented himself from social affairs
since postponement of the treaty ratification, but he accepted the
Spaniard's proposal. When he presented himself at the next coterie
he was received as if his visits had never been interrupted.[51] The
amicable relations were continued with Secretary of State Evaristo
Perez de Castro, who exhibited evidence of the changed circumstances by dining with the American Minister on July 4.

In spite of the assurances given by the Spanish authorities, the
treaty matter was not presented to the Cortes immediately after
its convocation. On August 26, Forsyth, anxious to learn the reason for the delay, visited de Castro, who informed him that the
activities of the government had been concentrated on important
domestic matters. However, the Secretary had just notified the
Cortes that he was prepared to submit the documents pertaining
to the treaty affair.[52] On the same day, de Castro appeared before
a secret session of the national assembly where, according to Forsyth, he earnestly recommended a prompt conclusion of the transaction. The matter was then referred to a committee. On October 2, 1820, the committee made its report to the Cortes and
three days later the assembly, in secret session, authorized that

the Floridas be ceded to the United States. The Cortes also decided that the disputed land grants were null and void.[53] Forsyth
received an official notification of the decision on October 6.

Forsyth suggested to de Castro that the ratified treaty be sent
to Washington along with orders for the evacuation of Spanish
officials and troops from the Floridas, and also with instructions
for the delivery of pertinent territorial archives to the United
States. As a result, he contended, the United States could begin
preparations for the transportation of the Spaniards to Havana. De
Castro accepted the proposal and later sent copies of the orders
to the Georgian. Forsyth wrote to Adams that the treaty obstacles
had been overcome in a manner favorable to the United States.
He believed that the recent delay was caused, not from serious opposition to United States pretensions, but from the peculiar situation of the revolutionary government, and from the latter's desire
to give first attention to domestic affairs.[54]

On October 24, 1820, de Castro notified Forsyth that a special
courier carrying dispatches to Vives would leave Madrid on the
following day. He suggested that the American Minister might
wish to take advantage of the opportunity to forward communications to the latter's government.[55] Subsequently, the Georgian
informed Biddle that the special messenger was conveying the
ratified treaty to Washington. After the convention was delivered
to the United States government, without condition, the Senate
consented to its ratification on February 19, and the exchange of
ratifications between Adams and Vives took place on February 22,
1821. The protracted affair thus came to an end two years after
the signing of the treaty by Adams and Onis.

Several factors were responsible for Forsyth's unusual behav-
ior in the matter of treaty ratification. His lack of diplomatic
experience and the procrastination of the Spanish government
were contributory causes. According to one historian, "the very
firm tone of Adams' instructions of August 18, 1819 gave Forsyth
appreciable backing for his peremptory communications."[56]
Furthermore, the Georgian evidently developed the idea that
strong language was necessary if his objective was to be accomplished. Confronted with apparent failure, Forsyth's actions
and words became those of an exasperated individual.

Regardless of extenuating circumstances, Forsyth's conduct left
much to be desired. For the most part, his activities were no
credit to his country or to himself. However, in the later proceedings, he showed to better advantage than in his earlier en-

deavors. His friendly relations with Spanish officials of the revolutionary government indicated that he was not likely to repeat his mistakes. President Monroe undoubtedly gave this fact consideration when he permitted Forsyth to return to Spain after visiting in the United States.

IV

Land of the Dons

IN SPITE of the vexations which he experienced in Spain, John Forsyth found much of interest in the land of the Dons. Even the tiresome journey from Cadiz to Madrid in April-May, 1819, afforded him numerous opportunities for satisfying his curiosity concerning the Iberian country and its people. After he and his party departed from Cadiz on April 24, they crossed the bay and landed at Port Saint Mary's, a bustling fishing village. For $55 they hired a four-horse carriage and a *calesa* to convey them to Seville, a distance of approximately sixty miles. At Seville, where he found the streets narrow and the pavement of small round stones, Forsyth took a walking tour of the city, during which he visited the famous Moorish Alcazar. For the journey from Seville to Madrid, the group procured, for $175, a coach drawn by seven mules.

Leaving Seville, and passing though an area which reminded the Georgian of the sandy region near Savannah, the party arrived in Cordova. Here Forsyth visited a cathedral which had been converted from a mosque. Continuing his journey, he was impressed with the royal palace and gardens at Aranjuez, and with the productivity of the soil in the region around Madrid. In the various villages along the route, Cyrus was an object of intense curiosity to the Spaniards. With reference to the Negro, Forsyth described an amusing incident:

At Tembleque a serious application was made to him by a prudent maidservant for some of his hair, she understood it to be very good to alleviate the pains of woman in labour and altho' she was not married or likely to be so, she thought it but wise to provide for emergency that might in the order of nature occur.[1]

In Madrid, Forsyth made visits to the public parks, the art galleries, the palaces, and the theaters. He admitted that his ignorance of the Spanish language lessened his enjoyment of the theater performances. On at least one occasion he attended bull fights at the *Plaza de los Toros*. Here, amidst eight thousand to ten thousand fanatical spectators of both sexes, he witnessed a spectacle in which "twelve horses were killed, two men severely wounded & another had the horn of a Bull thro the Seat of his Breeches."[2] The national pastime of Spain did not meet with the Georgian's full approval.

While Forsyth enjoyed the Spanish scene, he was constantly aware of his difficult situation. During the months when he was conducting the disagreeable and unsuccessful correspondence with Yrujo, Salmon, and San Fernando, he displayed an increasing desire to return to the United States. In August, 1819, he wrote to Adams and stated that because of the derangement of his affairs in Georgia his wife might be in need of funds. He requested that she be advanced such sums as she required and that the amounts be charged against his salary.[3] In January, 1820, he informed the American Secretary of State that his position in Madrid was unpleasant, that he was practically useless to his government, and that his private affairs in Georgia demanded his attention. On another occasion, he declared that his continuance at Madrid was extremely irksome, that he regarded his efforts as being of little value in advancing the interests of the United States, and that he was tempted to leave Spain. Later he wrote to Biddle that "fretting at this [Spanish] government worrying myself about my return to America aided by the dryness of this atmosphere & variableness of the Temperature had reduced me to a very genteel but not comfortable thinness."[4]

After the revolutionary government came into existence, Forsyth disclosed his immediate plans in a dispatch to Adams, dated April 13, 1820. Since he could accomplish nothing until the meeting of the Cortes, he had decided to leave Madrid for twenty or thirty days. He declared his intention to visit Bordeaux and possibly Paris, where he might "purchase articles of personal comfort . . ." which were not obtainable in Spain.[5] Forsyth notified Jabat of his intended absence, and applied for a passport to France. He also gave Brent a memorandum of instructions and a letter of introduction as chargé d'affaires, which was to be presented to Jabat in case the duties of the legation rendered it necessary. According to the instructions, Brent was to correspond frequently with Forsyth, and to transmit the information contained in all official communications. He was not, however, to conduct any diplomatic affairs unless they required immediate attention, nor was he to open personal letters.[6] Having completed his preparations, Forsyth boarded a post chaise and departed from Madrid on April 15, 1820, arriving in Bordeaux after a journey of six days.

During his sojourn in Bordeaux, Forsyth found pleasure in visiting the public parks, in strolling along the beautiful avenues, and in attending the opera and the ballet. He especially enjoyed the turbot, the liqueurs, the claret, and "all the good things that flesh is heir to."[7] He visited *La Bede,* the birthplace and former residence of Charles Louis de Secondat, Baron de Montesquieu, near Bordeaux. On his return to Spain, he traveled through Bayonne, the birthplace of the bayonet; through Biarritz, renowned for its sea baths; and through Burgos, noted for its magnificent cathedral. During the journey, Forsyth had two unpleasant experiences in which attempts were made by his Spanish attendants to overcharge him for services rendered. On each occasion he refused to pay the extra amount.[8]

Two items of information caused Forsyth to curtail his French vacation. After his arrival in Bordeaux, he read in the newspapers that the Spanish King had issued a decree for the convocation of the Cortes in June instead of July. He also received the instructions, forwarded from Madrid, which gave him permission to visit the United States. According to William H. Crawford, Forsyth was irritated at the delay in authorization of his visit home and placed the entire blame for the delay on Adams.[9] As a result of the information which he had obtained, Forsyth decided not to go on to Paris, since his time was limited and he found he could shop satisfactorily in Bordeaux. He wrote to Biddle that he intended to visit the French capital en route to the United States. Forsyth left Bordeaux on May 2, 1820, and arrived in Madrid on May 8, to learn that the King had issued no such decree as reported in the French newspapers.[10]

On October 11, 1820, Forsyth notified Adams that as soon as the ratified treaty was dispatched to Washington, he planned to use the President's permission to return to the United States. Later, he wrote that he proposed to travel to Bordeaux, from which port he would embark for New York. On November 5

Forsyth informed de Castro of his intention to visit the United States, requested an audience with the King, asked for a passport and for post horses to Bayonne, and advised that Brent would be charged with American affairs during his absence from Spain.[11] The King was convalescing at the Escurial, and since he was not expected to return to Madrid for some time, Forsyth confided to Adams that there might be a dispensation of the leave-taking ceremony. He received permission to see Ferdinand VII, however, and on November 16 went to the Escurial. The following day he dined with the royal family, after which he took formal leave of the King.[12] Subsequently, the American Minister notified de Castro that he would leave Madrid on November 26.[13] Writing from Bordeaux on December 18, he informed Adams that he was preparing to sail from the French city on the vessel *Stephania*.

Forsyth arrived in New York on February 15, 1821. After a visit of a few days, he proceeded to Washington, where his family had maintained its residence.[14] He interrupted his stay of about a month in Washington to go to Philadelphia, only to learn that Biddle was absent from the city. Before departing for Georgia, he called on President Monroe, to offer the cutomary felicitations and to solicit the appointment of Obadiah Rich, consul at Valencia, as secretary of the legation in Madrid. He stated he had a high regard for Rich's abilities, and that the selection would meet with the genuine approval of the Spanish government, since many of the officials were personally acquainted with the consul.[15] Forsyth also called at the State Department where, on one occasion, he submitted his contingent expense account, complete with vouchers. On another occasion, he presented Adams with a copy of Onis's pamphlet regarding the treaty negotiations, which the Secretary declared was filled with distortions and untruths.[16]

Forsyth received a mixed reception in the United States. A friend of the family, Mrs. Samuel Harrison Smith, who saw him in Washington, observed that he was pale and emaciated and appeared to be unhappy. She remarked that "he has received none of that public approbation so supporting and gratifying to men in public life, so absolutely necessary to an ambitious one."[17] She surmised that if he had offered his resignation it would have been accepted, but since he had no other means of livelihood, he had no alternative but to return to Spain. Forsyth fared better in Georgia. The Augusta *Chronicle* praised him for accomplishing the object of his mission, and suggested that the citizens of the city compliment the Minister with a testimonial. Accordingly, he was honored with a public dinner on April 6, 1821, at the Planter's Hotel in Augusta, an affair which was attended by state and city notables.[18]

After his Georgia visit Forsyth returned to Washington. On May 16, he and his family left Washington, arriving in New York three days later, where they planned to visit the family of Henry Meigs before leaving for Spain.[19] The Minister arranged for passage for himself and family on the vessel *Fabius*, which sailed from New York on June 28, 1821. After a voyage of twenty-five days, the ship reached Cadiz and, on August 17, 1821, the Forsyths arrived in Madrid. The following day Forsyth addressed a note announcing his return, to the Spanish Secretary of State, Eusebio de Bardaxi y Azara.[20]

Though Mrs. Forsyth and the children were not happy with the prospect of living in Spain, where they expected to be in virtual retirement, their stay in the land of the Dons proved to be an interesting experience. In their Madrid home, with daughters Julia and Mary acting as interpreters, the Forsyths had numerous visitors, the favorite being the Pope's nuncio. They entertained with dances and served refreshments of cake and lemonade. Forsyth's wife enjoyed walking along the Prado, where she observed the Spanish men with their fine cloaks and the Spanish women with their costly dresses and habitual fans. She found an attraction in the stone bridges, the fountains, and the works of art. Writing to her brother, she remarked that the family intended visiting Sacedon, St. Ildefonso, and the Escurial; that they expected to see the sights of France on their return journey to the United States. She found the Spanish climate, with its lack of storms and snow, a special delight.[21] Mrs. Forsyth was presented to the King, Queen, and other members of the royal family; at the ceremony she almost committed the unpardonable mistake of turning her back on the royal dignitaries, but compensated for her error by making "a few additional curtesies [*sic*]. . . ."[22] Later, Ferdinand asked Forsyth if Clara's tall stature was characteristic of the American people.

During Forsyth's tenure of office in Spain, he suffered a number of personal inconveniences. One evening, in 1820, he rode out of Madrid and did not return until after the gates had been closed. He was refused admittance at two different entrances, and was forced to drive around a portion of the city before locating an officer who would permit him to enter. The Georgian complained to de Castro that since he had received no copy of the order requiring the gates to be closed, he believed foreign diplomats were exempt from its provisions. He stated that he was not asking for officials to be punished, but suggested that they be advised that the order was not intended to apply to members of the diplomatic corps.[23] On another occasion, a carriage was purchased for Forsyth and sent to Spain from France. It was first detained in Bayonne, and then not permitted to leave Irun, and Forsyth had to write to the Spanish Secretary of State requesting that an order be issued which would insure the delivery of the vehicle to Madrid.[24]

One morning, in 1822, Forsyth and his son were walking along a Madrid street, when a uniformed Spaniard passed them in such a hurry that the end of his musket struck the Minister's hat. Forsyth gave the gun a stroke with his cane, and suggested to the soldier that he should be more careful. The Spaniard became angry, used profane language, denied the allegation concerning the musket blow, and threatened to attack Forsyth with his gun or bayonet. Although the Minister identified himself, the soldier refused to give his name and expressed no concern over the fact that he was speaking to a foreign diplomat. Forsyth followed the Spaniard to the *Plaza de los Toros,* where he learned from the military commander that the offender's name was Manuel Rey. The Minister addressed a communication to Evaristo San Miguel, Secretary of State, complaining of the indifference shown by Rey and requesting that the soldier be punished.[25]

There followed a lengthy correspondence between the two ministers. San Miguel declared that Rey was an amiable man, had professed ignorance of the American's identity, and had denied using abusive language or instigating the incident. Instead, Rey contended that he had been insulted by Forsyth's cane thrust. If the Georgian would present the necessary witnesses, the Secretary promised to submit the case to the proper tribunal. In reply, Forsyth insisted that he was not interested in Rey's character and had not complained of the musket blow, which was considered accidental. His complaint was based on Rey's subsequent actions and language which, in his opinion, were not justified. Forsyth maintained that it was impossible for him to obtain witnesses, but that, in the future, he would be prepared to protect himself against such an attack. San Miguel answered that Forsyth's previous notes had been misunderstood and that proceedings would be instituted against Rey, who would be punished if found guilty. Forsyth expressed satisfaction with the final decision made by the Spanish Secretary.

On occasion, Forsyth's personal inconveniences were associated with matters pertaining to the legation. He became dissatisfied with Brent, and while in Washington, informed Adams that the legation Secretary was useless except as a copying clerk. After his return to Spain, Forsyth claimed that Brent seldom appeared at his office and was negligent in copying the official correspondence into the record books of the legation.[26] In May, 1822, Adams notified Forsyth that Brent was being transferred to Portugal and would be replaced by John James Appleton.[27] The new official arrived in Madrid in August.

The delayed receipt of American newspapers was a source of irritation to Forsyth. He complained that he was frequently embarrassed when forced to acknowledge ignorance of items which had appeared in American journals and which had been reprinted by the European press. While visiting in the United States, he had recommended that the State Department stop forwarding the *National Intelligencer* to the Madrid legation unless a more prompt system of delivery could be arranged. He was assured that a new method was being adopted; but after his return to Spain he discovered that the problem was not solved by sending the newspapers via Gibraltar and Valencia. Forsyth suggested that the papers be sent to Cadiz, from which point they would reach Madrid within twenty days after arrival in Spain. He explained that he himself did not expect to benefit by the change because his tenure of office was drawing to a close, but that the suggested mode of transmission should prove useful to future residents of the legation.[28]

As the accredited representative of the United States to Spain, Forsyth's duties were not confined solely to the negotiations pertaining to ratification of the Adams-Onis treaty. Other diplomatic problems arose which required his attention. When he first went to Spain, in 1819, he was instructed to seek a release for those citizens of the United States who had been captured while allegedly engaged in the service of the revolutionary provinces of South America, and who were confined in Spanish prisons or in fortresses along the coast of Africa. The United States recognized the correctness of the principle which declared that all foreigners taking part in the conflict were subject to the same treatment accorded the insurgents, provided the latter were regarded as participants in a civil war.

However, Forsyth's government maintained that there were extenuating circumstances which favored the liberation of the United States citizens. The claims were advanced that many of the prisoners had surrendered after being promised amnesty, and that the British subjects incarcerated in like manner had been freed. Some of the prisoners, though captured in the revolutionary colonies, denied that they had borne arms against the Spanish government. Finally, the United States pointed out that her imprisoned citizens constituted a financial burden upon the Spanish government, and that their discharge would strengthen the friendly relationship between the two nations.

After his arrival in Madrid, Forsyth learned that representations had been initiated by Erving and by Brent for the release of certain United States citizens imprisoned at Malaga, who had been adjudged innocent by a Spanish tribunal. On May 18, 1819, Forsyth submitted a note to the Spanish authorities requesting that the decision of the court be sustained. Receiving no reply to his message, Forsyth, during an interview, called Casa Yrujo's attention to the matter. The Spanish official's reply was an unsatisfactory statement that the case was being reviewed by the Council of War. As the weeks passed and no action was taken by the Spanish government, Forsyth again addressed a note, this time to Salmon, pertaining to the release of the Malaga prisoners. He also discussed the situation with Salmon; but on August 22, 1819, he admitted to Adams that he had received no written answer and no satisfactory verbal one.[29]

During the first few months of his residence in Madrid, Forsyth, except for his efforts in behalf of the Malaga prisoners, refrained from mentioning the subject of captive Americans to Spanish authorities. He preferred to place no obstacles in the way of an early and a successful ratification of the treaty. After his failure to secure Spanish approval of the Adams-Onis convention, Forsyth determined to press the matter of the detained persons, even though he realized that the attitude of the irritated Spanish officials augured little success.

On September 6, 1819, he informed the United States consul at Cadiz that he was endeavoring to secure a general liberation order.[30] In his note to San Fernando, dated September 21, he declared that his government had received no official explanation for the detentions. Relying upon "conjecture and doubtful report . . . ," Forsyth classified the captive Americans in several groups: those peaceful citizens whose only offense was that they had lacked passports when apprehended in the South American provinces; those who had not possessed the proper passports; those who had been forced into the service of the insurgents and who had surrendered to the Spanish when promised amnesty; and those who had allegedly borne arms against Spain. Forsyth charged that some of the American prisoners had received a more severe treatment than captured Spanish subjects; that the former had been transported, under distressing conditions, from one hemisphere to another, while the latter had been punished or pardoned.

In the interests of better relations between the two nations, Forsyth suggested that every American captive be freed. If the Spanish government considered this inexpedient, he demanded the liberation of all those whose crimes were not immediately specified. Any other action, he asserted, would "not be tolerated by the spirit of the american [sic] people."[31] San Fernando did not reply to the Minister's note.

Immediately after the Spanish revolution in March, 1820, Forsyth directed Jabat's attention to the matter of the American captives. The acting Secretary professed a desire to cooperate, and promised to bring the subject before the King, provided Forsyth would submit an official note. Forsyth complied and the communication, submitted on March 31, attained the desired result. On April 12, Jabat notified Forsyth that Ferdinand had determined to release all citizens of the United States who were imprisoned in Spain for alleged participation in the South American insurrection.[32] When Forsyth expressed his appreciation and suggested that the release orders be applicable to all Spanish-held citizens of the United States, wherever confined, Jabat promised that such action would be taken. Thereafter, Forsyth advised the United States consuls stationed along the Spanish coast, of the King's decree and authorized any necessary expenditures for transporting the captives to the United States.[33] The Spanish decree was submitted officially by Vives to the Washington government, which, a few months later, expressed its approbation to Forsyth and notified him that the discharge of the pertinent prisoners had been effected in Spain, Africa, and Havana.[34]

Forsyth's original instructions of March, 1819, stated that the Spanish government had imposed discriminatory tonnage duties

and restrictive regulations upon American shipping. He was directed to seek a discontinuance of the oppressive tariffs and rules.
After the convocation of the Cortes in July, 1820, he discussed
the matter with de Castro, submitted an informal memorandum,
and, receiving no reply, addressed a second note to the Spanish
official. De Castro then explained that no action could be taken
until the Cortes had decided upon a general commercial system.[35] Before its dissolution, the Spanish legislative body issued
decrees which satisfied Forsyth. He wrote to de Castro that the
new policy provided for a removal of the principal inconveniences to American commerce and for an imposition of tonnage
duties "in such a form as to remove the objection made to them
on the part of the United States."[36]

There was, however, concern on the part of the Washington
government that the commercial changes might not be as beneficial as Forsyth believed. He was instructed to be especially observant and to take every advantage toward promoting American
trade. The fears of the United States government were realized
and Forsyth considered it necessary to discuss commercial policy
with the Spanish Secretary of State, Eusebio de Bardaxi y Azara.
He pointed out that goods shipped into Spain in foreign vessels
were subject to a 25% higher duty than the same articles brought
in by Spanish ships. Bardaxi agreed that such an obstruction to
American commerce should be removed, and promised to present
Forsyth's views to the Cortes, provided they were submitted in
writing. Forsyth transmitted an official note on October 20, 1821,
in which he included the complaint that captains of American
vessels were not permitted to amend the manifests delivered to
the Spanish port officials, while commanders of other foreign
vessels were allowed eight days to do so. A few weeks later, in a
dispatch to Adams, Forsyth had to admit that the representation
had produced no advantageous effect.[37]

Shortly thereafter a complaint from the United States Consul
at Valencia prompted Forsyth to address another note to Bardaxi
on the subject of commercial restrictions. After calling attention
to the fact that such American imports as fish, stoves, and raw
cotton were subjected to discriminatory tariffs, he declared that
the United States commerce with Spain "could scarcely have been
in a worse situation if it had been the study of government so to
frame its regulations as to do us injury."[38] Bardaxi's reaction
to Forsyth's communication was an expressed belief that the Cortes could not make any changes in its commercial policy, but

that the succeeding legislative body, in 1822, might be persuaded
to modify the system. Nevertheless, Forsyth asked that his representations be submitted to the existing Cortes. However, the
changing fortunes of Spanish politics soon effected a revision of
the cabinet, and Forsyth was forced to admit that he saw little
likelihood of any positive action by the Spanish government.[39]

The extraordinary Cortes, which met in 1822, reduced the
duties on American fish and stoves. Forsyth informed the Spanish
Secretary of State, Francisco Martinez de la Rosa,[40] that while the
alterations were an improvement, the commerce of the United
States continued to be on an unequal basis as compared with
that of other foreign nations trading with Spain. He maintained
also that no improvement had been accomplished in regard to
the manifests or the tariff on raw cotton. However, he expressed
satisfaction that the tonnage duties had been equalized.[41]

Another problem which required Forsyth's attention was the
official establishment of United States consulates in the Spanish
dominions. The Russian consul had been received at Manila but
the United States consular officials to that port and to Tenerife
had not been accorded recognition by the colonial governors.
Forsyth was instructed to secure recognition for the two American
consuls and to obtain permission for the dispatch of similar
agents to Havana, Porto Rico, Campeche, and Vera Cruz. Forsyth
informed de Castro of the situation, impressing upon the Spaniard
the desirability and the necessity of having United States consuls
in the Spanish colonial ports. Later, he wrote an official note,
but de Castro did not favor any action until some policy had been
adopted by the Cortes. After the issuance of the legislative decrees
concerning foreign trade, Forsyth notified his government that
consuls might be sent to all the Spanish dominions where commerce was permitted.[42] He also requested de Castro to issue
orders for recognition of the United States agent who was already
in Manila.

Evidently Forsyth's endeavors produced no positive reaction on
the part of the Spanish government, for Brent, during the Minister's visit to the United States, made several unsuccessful attempts to gain admission for the American consuls. Upon his
return to Spain, in 1821, Forsyth was instructed to resubmit the
subject. The subsequent discussion with Bardaxi accomplished
nothing. The Spaniard asked for time to study the previous correspondence on the matter before committing himself to a definite answer. Forsyth agreed, since "pressing him at present would

be of no immediate service & might be injurious hereafter."[43]
On later occasions, the American envoy continued to advance
the issue concerning consular recognition, but he failed to change
the policy of the procrastinating Spanish authorities. Forsyth's
successor, Hugh Nelson of Virginia, was informed of the Georgian's extensive correspondence with the Spaniards and was directed to exert his efforts toward a successful consummation of
the affair.[44]

Problems arising out of the cession of the Floridas to the
United States required Forsyth's attention. According to Article
VIII of the treaty, Florida grants made by the Spanish King before January 24, 1818, were to be confirmed by the United States.
Realizing that many individual demands would be presented,
Forsyth asked Bardaxi for permission to examine the Spanish
records in order to distinguish the valid from the fraudulent
claims. The Spaniard was apparently agreeable, but suggested that
a formal note be transmitted to him. In compliance, Forsyth repeated his request in a communication, dated October 4, 1821,
and asked that Obadiah Rich, United States consul at Valencia,
be allowed "to examine the archives of the Indies [and to]
select and procure copies of such documents as may be important
to effect the object in view."[45]

Receiving no reply to the message, Forsyth had an interview
with the Spanish official and repeated the proposal. Bardaxi
countered with the statement that such an examination was unnecessary, for there were no more than fifty pertinent land titles
on record in Spain and all of these might be located in the Cuban
or Florida archives. Since Forsyth expected a written answer to
his note, he merely reminded Bardaxi of his apparent acceptance
of the idea during the previous interview.[46]

Bardaxi's communication of December 17 proved to be a
repetition of the evasive tactics employed by the Spanish government. Without giving a positive denial to Forsyth's request, the
Spaniard stated that an examination should be made only when
there was a doubt involving a specific grant. In addition, he maintained that a general examination of the archives would be
prejudicial to various legitimate grantees of Florida lands, for
some of the grants had originated in America and there was no
record of them in the Madrid collection.[47]

Forsyth did not agree with these contentions. He replied that
an immediate examination was preferable so that the information
might be readily available when a claim was presented in the

United States, and a prompt and just decision rendered. He denied the allegation that the United States would consider all land cessions invalid unless they were recorded in the Madrid archives. Instead, he asserted, once the Cuban archives were delivered to the United States authorities, due consideration would be given to the grants recorded therein. Forsyth requested that the subject be re-examined and that the solicited permission be granted or that it be specifically refused.[48]

The acting Secretary of State, Don Ramon Lopez Pelegrin, answered Forsyth's note on January 23, 1822. The American Minister was informed that Rich would not be allowed to make the requested examination. However, the King would order that a list of the grants be prepared for the use of the United States government. Forsyth was criticized for his persistent activities on the subject and was told that "reasons of delicacy" forbade granting permission for a stranger to examine the records of the Spanish government.[49] Forsyth replied that the action promised by the King was satisfactory, but asked that authenticated copies of all information pertaining to the grants be prepared. He was displeased with the criticism, declaring that he had not proposed an indiscriminate examination of Spanish records, but only an investigation of pertinent grants under the supervision of the Spanish archivist. Noting that it was the general practice for nations to permit public examination of similar records, Forsyth testily commented that he had "no desire to press the Govt. of H[is] M[ajesty] to do anything inconsistent with its own ideas of decorum and delicacy, however unfounded those ideas may appear to me."[50]

Almost a year passed and Forsyth had not received the promised list of grants. He became convinced that the Spanish authorities regretted their promise and he expressed doubts to Adams that the survey would ever be compiled. Nevertheless, he made repeated personal inquiries, which always occasioned vague answers, such as: there was a scarcity of pertinent records, the archives were in general confusion, individual injury might be done if a legitimate claim was not included in the list. On December 19, 1822, he addressed a formal note to the Spanish government declaring that he was ignorant of the progress of the report and asked that it be expedited.[51] There is no indication in Forsyth's later correspondence that he ever received the promised list.

Another vexatious problem which resulted from the Florida cession concerned other records besides those in Madrid. Article

II of the treaty provided that the Spanish archives and documents in the New World relating to the Florida provinces were to be transferred to the United States authorities. Colonel James Grant Forbes, with a royal order from the Spanish King, was dispatched to Havana to receive the records, but the Governor-General of Cuba delayed so long that Forbes was forced to return to the United States without the desired documents.

In a note dated September 1, 1821, Forsyth presented the situation to Bardaxi and requested that a "new and peremptory order" be delivered to the Governor-General of Cuba.[52] Bardaxi refused, and suggested that delivery of the archives had been made. Forsyth, thinking that the Spanish government had immediate information which justified such an expression, cautiously replied that compliance by the Governor-General would render further correspondence on the subject unnecessary.[53]

Within a few months, Forsyth was forced to reopen the subject. In a note dated December 25, 1821, he informed Bardaxi that according to information received from the United States the archives had not been transferred; he asked for an immediate delivery. Nothing was accomplished. Adams's instructions of May 30, 1822, advised Forsyth that the Governor-General of Cuba still retained possession of the documents.[54] In June of the same year, Forsyth notified his government that in almost every interview with de la Rosa he had urged an immediate delivery of the archives; in addition, he had submitted another formal note on the subject to the Spanish government. A reply had not been received, and disorders throughout Spain had caused the formation of a new ministry, which included Don Evaristo San Miguel as Secretary of State.

Forsyth wrote to San Miguel, called attention to his previous correspondence on the subject, and suggested that an order be sent to the Governor-General of Cuba which would "leave no room for evasion or delay."[55] He accused the Governor-General of having issued contradictory statements. In 1821 he had admitted to the American representative that twenty boxes of archives had been brought from Florida, but that it would require some time to separate the relevant documents from the irrelevant; later, in 1822, he denied that there were any records in Cuba which were to be transferred under the provisions of the treaty.

Forsyth's first note to the new Spanish Secretary was followed by another, and in two interviews he urged that an explicit order be transmitted to the Governor-General of Cuba. Finally San

Miguel informed him that a second order would be sent to the official in Havana. Although the royal decree was dispatched, Forsyth found it advisable, on December 19, 1822, to suggest that specific instructions on the matter be given to the recently appointed Governor-General of Cuba, Major General Francisco Dionisio Vives, who was preparing to sail from Spain to Havana. Forsyth further requested that he be informed if such instructions were issued, so that he might advise his government. The information would enable the United States at an early date to dispatch an authorized representative to Cuba for the purpose of receiving the archives.[56]

In spite of Forsyth's efforts, the transmission of the desired records was not completed during his tenure of office. General instructions to his successor, Hugh Nelson, stated that Thomas Randall was preparing to proceed to Havana for the purpose of demanding the documents.[57]

In May, 1822, Forsyth notified his government that he had given his Georgia friends permission to enter his name as a candidate for the next House of Representatives. If elected, he expected to resign his Spanish post before March 4 in order to qualify for the congressional position. If not elected, he was anxious to make a business trip to the United States during the summer of 1823, and he wished information concerning the disposition of the legation affairs during his absence.[58] On December 17, Adams replied that because of the critical relations between the two nations, the President had decided to appoint a new minister to Spain, who might arrive before Forsyth's departure.[59] Before receiving this information, Forsyth had learned of his victory in the Georgia elections, and had written to Adams reiterating his determination to leave Madrid before March 4, 1823.[60]

On February 8, 1823, Forsyth, accompanied by Appleton, visited San Miguel and informed the latter of the Georgian's impending resignation. The visit was followed by a formal note, dated February 25, in which Forsyth explained that, under the provisions of the Constitution of the United States, his election to the House of Representatives necessitated the relinquishment of his Spanish post before March 4. He asked for an audience with the King in order that he might take his leave of the Spanish court, and stated that Appleton would remain in charge of the legation until the arrival of a new minister. In conclusion, he requested a passport and an escort to France if the Spanish disorders should require one.[61] Permission was granted for a royal interview, to be held on March 2. In his audience with the King, Forsyth repeated his reasons for leaving Spain prior to March 4 and gave assurance that in the future he would seek to "do justice to the merits . . ." of Spain and its government.[62] Describing the event to Adams, Forsyth stated that both the King and San Miguel seemed well satisfied with the remarks expressed in his speech.

Forsyth and his family left Madrid on March 5 and arrived in Bordeaux on March 22, after experiencing frequent delays because of the lack of horses and because of the concentration of French troops along the roads. Subsequently, the Forsyths visited Paris and England[63] before taking passage on the vessel *Othello*, bound for the United States. They sailed from Bordeaux on April 28, arriving in New York on June 2. Thereafter, the family established a temporary residence in Philadelphia. Later in the year, Forsyth visited Georgia, arriving in Augusta on October 30, 1823.

Forsyth's labors in Spain did little toward enhancing his reputation or toward satisfying the expectations of his government. Cognizant of his failure and seeking to defend himself, he included in his final dispatch from Madrid the following:

In closing this last Despatch I request that you [Adams] will express to the President my regret that my labours in Spain since my return from the United States have not been more useful to the Public. The causes of my want of complete success in the Several matters submitted to my care have been beyond my controul [sic]. indeed [sic] have principally arisen from the peculiar position of our Government in its relations with Spain and the Spanish Governments. I have now the satisfaction to leave our relations with Spain on a friendly if not a cordial footing.[64]

Forsyth was diligent in obeying instructions from his government and did succeed in a few minor enterprises. However, the procrastination of the Spanish officials continually handicapped his efforts. With reference to the treaty affair, one author has commented:

Indeed, a more experienced man than Forsyth might have been forgiven if he despaired of making sense out of what was going on. No diplomat, however gifted, can divine a policy where no policy exists.[65]

The same explanation might be applied to the situation in Spain after the treaty ratification was accomplished. Forsyth's Spanish mission was the nadir of his career.

V

His Excellency, The Governor

THE POLITICAL SCENE in Georgia in 1827, the year John Forsyth became governor, shows that state parties had grown up. The story of their evolution begins immediately after the establishment of the federal government, when the Georgia Federalists, essentially democratic frontiersmen, appropriated the western lands of the state. The action resulted in a vicious counter-attack by the conservative, aristocratic element, led by General James Jackson, who succeeded in effecting a rescission of the Yazoo sale and the consequent discrediting of the Federalist party within the state. Shortly thereafter the frontiersmen abandoned their unnatural alliance with the national Federalist party and became associated with the Jeffersonian or Republican party. Since James Jackson's group was the declared Jeffersonian party in the state, the action taken by the frontiersmen meant that, for many years, Georgia was destined to have only one national party which, in turn, was composed of two antagonistic state factions.[1]

The transition was not a simple matter of the ex-Federalists in toto forming the anti-Jackson faction; actually there occurred a general re-alignment of political allegiances. The Jackson party, as it developed, was generally a union of the aristocrats of the coastal region and the equally aristocratic upcountry element, originally from Virginia, who had settled in the vicinity of Elbert County. When James Jackson died in 1806, he left a well-organized party headed by William H. Crawford and George M. Troup. After Crawford's election to the United States Senate in 1807, he became increasingly occupied with national politics, so that Troup eventually became the active leader of the state organization. The anti-Jackson faction included as its essential ele-

81

ments the small farmers of the frontier and the North Carolinians who had established settlements in the vicinity of Wilkes
County, just south of the Broad River location of the Virginians.
This opposition group was led, first by General Elijah Clarke,
and later by his son, General John Clark.

In the early years, the two factions did not include the entire
population of Georgia. After a period of relative quiet during
the War of 1812, bitter rivalry flared, and it was then that fac-
tional activities spread to all parts of the state and the two
groups emerged with distinct party characteristics, each competing
for all county and town offices as well as for the state positions.

Actually, there was little difference in the doctrines or beliefs
of the rival organizations. It was an era of acrimonious personal
politics; the vote of the electorate was based, not on national,
state, or local issues, but principally on personalities. It was an
age when ballots were cast for men rather than for measures.
There were no platforms from the parties and no stump speeches
from the candidates. In 1827 newspapers did not generally pub-
lish discussions or analyses of pertinent political issues; on the
contrary, they published editorials and articles which violently
attacked or generously praised a certain aspirant for office. In
analyzing the Georgia political scene, a newspaper of a later date
was forced to remark that "no State in the Union has perhaps
been so long distracted by political parties of nearly equal
strength as Georgia."[2]

It was only natural that young John Forsyth should become
affiliated with the Jackson-Crawford-Troup organization. Jackson
had deliberately inaugurated a policy whereby promising young
men were attracted to his party. A continuation of this policy
through the years produced leaders of similar background: most
of them were lawyers by profession, had acquired formal instruction in the academy or its equivalent, and were graduates of
such colleges as Princeton.[3] Thus, Forsyth's qualifications were
consistent with the prevailing pattern. Being a Virginian by
birth and descent, his aristocratic temperament was in harmony
with the characteristics of the party. According to one historian,
the Jackson-Crawford-Troup faction was stronger than the Clark
clique during the first decade of the nineteenth century.[4] Forsyth
undoubtedly preferred the party which would be more likely to
satisfy his personal ambition for political office. Although he was
later to forsake the faction of his early choice, by 1826 he had

attained such prominence that the party was willing to entrust him with the duties of the governorship, which was being vacated by Troup.

The possibility that Forsyth would be a candidate for governor was asserted by the *Constitutionalist* of Augusta during the summer of 1826. The newspaper referred to the Fourth of July celebrations throughout Georgia, and declared that various toasts offered on the occasions indicated strong public preference for Forsyth as the next chief executive of the state. The editor asked for an end to party strife and urged all factions to unite in elevating such an able statesman to the responsible position.[5]

The Savannah *Georgian* did not agree with the *Constitutionalist* and the two newspapers resorted to editorial warfare, in which charges and countercharges were hurled. The Savannah editor contended that the Augusta paper was being presumptuous; that the opinions voiced were those of Forsyth's friends and not those of the majority party. Also, the *Georgian* maintained that the Republican caucus should be permitted to select from several available candidates without undue pressure.[6] The *Constitutionalist* denied using dictatorial methods, reiterated that Forsyth would be a popular choice, and accused its rival of seeking to destroy party unanimity.[7]

In addition to the *Constitutionalist*, the Milledgeville *Georgia Journal* revealed a preference for Forsyth. On the other hand, both the Augusta *Chronicle* and the Savannah *Georgian* preferred to support Edward Fenwick Tattnall as the Troup faction candidate. However, Tattnall was plagued with a protracted illness which eventually caused his resignation from Congress, and his indisposition hindered any chances which he might have had to obtain the nomination. The issue was finally settled in December, 1826, when the Troup caucus, meeting in Milledgeville, chose Forsyth over Tattnall by a vote of 90 to 20.[8]

The Clarkites at a later date selected Colonel Duncan G. Campbell to be Forsyth's opponent. Soon reports were circulated that Campbell had declined the nomination; but the Macon *Telegraph* denied the allegations, asserting that the Forsyth supporters were resorting to unethical tactics in order to influence the voters. Nevertheless, the rumors became an actuality when, in July, 1827, Campbell notified a leader of the Clark faction that he was no longer a candidate for the governorship. He explained his reasons:

A necessity from which I cannot exempt myself, requires that I should spend a portion of the next winter out of the state—and what is of more consequence, the present and prospective health and interest of my family require that my attention to them, and to my own affairs, should be constant and exclusive.[9]

As a result of Campbell's withdrawal, the Clarkite candidate became Matthew Talbot, who had almost defeated Troup in 1823.

In the campaign which followed Forsyth was both excoriated and acclaimed. The opposition was persistent in reciting its interpretation of his conduct in the Washington medals affair. The incident which precipitated the charge occurred in February, 1827, when the United States House of Representatives was considering the appropriation of a sum, not exceeding $500, for the purchase of medals once owned by George Washington, and at the time being offered at auction. If the medals were obtained, they were to be placed in the Library of Congress. Forsyth objected to the purchase of the medals on the ground that the Constitution did not authorize such a purchase. Furthermore, he declared, it was improper to consider the proposal unless it was recommended by the joint committee which had jurisdiction over the library. In the course of his remarks he stated that there was nothing in Washington's service to his country to merit such a high evaluation. Obviously Forsyth was concerned with constitutional violation; but his enemies claimed that the reference was to the proposed amount of the appropriation and that consequently he had been disrespectful to Washington's reputation.

Forsyth's friends attempted to refute the charge. They denounced the opposition for having distorted his remarks and contended that the voters would show their disapproval of such tactics by redoubling their efforts in behalf of the maligned candidate. They maintained that the critics had produced no evidence to substantiate their interpretation and that Forsyth had demonstrated his veneration for Washington on numerous occasions. Forsyth wrote to several of his House colleagues and asked their recollection of his words; in reply, they assured him that he had expressed no derogatory remarks concerning the memory of Washington.[10]

Forsyth's opponents constantly accused him of apostasy to republicanism. They declared that he had been an adherent of Federalist doctrines, but had changed to the Republican party because the latter offered better means of political advancement.

They charged him with having been a follower of John Adams,
a defender of the Sedition Act, an opponent of the War of 1812,
and an advocate of the tenets of the Hartford Convention. As
proof of his former sentiments his accusers recalled that Forsyth,
in 1802, had proposed a public toast to an outstanding Federalist,
Charles Cotesworth Pinckney.[11]

In reply to the apostate charge, a pro-Forsyth newspaper admitted that its candidate, while immature, had been influenced
by prominent Augustans and had exhibited a tendency toward
Federalist dogma. However, the publication asserted, "when he
became a man he put away boyish things, detected the errors of
the heresy and embraced in heart and mind the true republican
faith."[12] Forsyth's adherents denied the other accusations, claiming that had the alleged antecedents been pertinent to Forsyth
he would never have been the frequent Georgia choice for Congress, nor President Monroe's selection for the important Spanish
mission.

The Clarkites directed numerous other accusations toward Forsyth. They claimed that he was guilty of an attempt to defraud
the Richmond Academy, that he was friendly to the presidential
aspirations of Andrew Jackson, and that his prolonged absence
from Georgia rendered him unfamiliar with the problems and
needs of the state. They attacked Forsyth's record in Congress,
contending that his many speeches had no meaning and were
delivered solely for publicity purposes, and by consuming too
much time caused an increase of expenditures. The critics also
endeavored to create dissension within the Troup party. They
reported that Tattnall and his friends were hostile to Forsyth,
and that the latter no longer approved of Troup's Indian policy.

The Forsyth supporters offered explanations and extolled the
merits of their candidate. As to the Richmond Academy fraud
charge, they declared that the entire affair had been the result
of a misunderstanding and that Forsyth had never questioned
the validity of the debt he owed to the institution. They explained
that Forsyth was transferring his support from Crawford to Jackson only because Crawford's ill health had necessitated a withdrawal from the presidential contest. While condemning the
opposition for its attempts to create discord among the Troup
leaders, Forsyth's friends emphatically denied that their candidate's Indian policy was at variance with that professed by Troup.
They pointed out that Tattnall had expressed a personal preference for Forsyth and that even had he remained quiet, party

loyalty would have guaranteed both his own support and that of
his adherents.

The Forsyth newspapers expressed confidence that their candidate, enjoying the respect of the voters, would be elected governor by an overwhelming margin. They claimed that he had not
sought the office but had been drafted by the people. Citing his
public record, they declared that he had devoted his services to
the best interests of Georgia and that his qualifications were
superior to those of Talbot. Although there was little personal
abuse directed toward the Clark candidate, there was ample
criticism regarding his practice of entertaining with barbecue
feasts. The Troup party contended that the practice constituted
political bribery, and that the gatherings were held "with intent
to charm the people by a powerful compound of hog homminy
[sic], and the essence of rye, into the support of Captain Talbot."[13]

Approximately two weeks before the election, the 1827 gubernatorial contest took an unexpected turn. On September 17,
Matthew Talbot suddenly died, a victim of fever, at his residence near Washington in Wilkes County. Thus, Forsyth was
left without a serious opponent for the office. When the election
was held, on October 1, 1827, there was a scattering vote for
local favorites, including Tattnall; but the final result was a
victory for Forsyth by a vote of 22,220 to 9,072.[14]

The Clarkites insisted that the circumstances made Forsyth's
election an accident. The contended that he was not the popular
choice: many Georgians had not cast a ballot, and others had
voted for him because he was the only avowed candidate. In
spite of these declarations, one of the most antagonistic newspapers, the Macon Telegraph, announced that Forsyth had received a fair election and that its future policy would be one of
cooperation with the governor-elect.[15] The post-election statements of the Forsyth forces were that numerous friends, realizing
the impotence of the opposition, had not voted and that Forsyth's victory was decisive because he had defeated the local favorites. In the latter instance, however, they neglected to mention
that there was no organized opposition following the death of
Talbot.

After his election as governor, John Forsyth vacated his seat in
Congress by submitting a letter of resignation to Governor
Troup.[16] His inauguration took place in Milledgeville, before
both houses of the legislature and a crowded gallery, on November 7, 1827. Attended by Governor Troup and important state

executive, judicial, and military officials, Forsyth entered the
chamber of the House of Representatives, where he took the
oath of office and made a brief address to the General Assembly.

Expressing both gratitude for the honor conferred upon him
and apprehension lest he disappoint the expectations of his constituents, he promised to cooperate with the legislators, who in
the final analysis were burdened with the principal responsibilities of government. He stated that he was not attempting to
evade his responsibility, but without the aid of the legislature the
state executive had little power. He paid tribute to his predecessor, asserting that it would be difficult for the incoming administration to make as favorable a record. He declared that, although
lacking experience and knowledge pertinent to the position, he
would execute his new duties with the best intentions and with a
deep sense of obligation to the people of Georgia.[17]

As governor, Forsyth believed in rigid adherence to the laws
of his state. His controversy with George Rockingham Gilmer
showed how literally he interpreted the laws. In 1828, Gilmer
was re-elected to the United States House of Representatives
for a term beginning March 3, 1829, but he failed to give notification of his acceptance within the time limit prescribed by
law. Consequently, Forsyth issued a proclamation declaring the
seat vacant after March, 1829, and calling for a new election
to be held the following October.[18]

The two men soon became involved in a bitter exchange of
words, the contest being waged through the medium of circulars,
each addressed to the constituents and publicized by the newspapers. Gilmer explained that he left Georgia for Washington
before the result of the election was announced; that when he
learned of his victory he submitted an acceptance of the office,
although it was impossible for the note to reach Milledgeville
within the specified time. He maintained that Forsyth was dictatorial in attempting to veto the will of the people, and that
the Georgia voters should not be subjected to the inconvenience
of another poll.[19]

Gilmer's principal argument was that certain articles of the
election law were unconstitutional. He stated that compliance
with the acceptance clause had never been considered obligatory,
but merely a formality. He asserted that the United States Constitution had established the requisite qualifications of a congressman and that they could not be augmented or modified by state
laws; yet the Georgia measure specified, in addition to notifica-

tion of acceptance, a state residence for the three years preceding
an election. Gilmer remarked that in the final analysis the United
States Congress was not required to recognize the Georgia law,
for each house of the national legislature had the constitutional
right to judge the elections and qualifications of its own members.

Referring to Forsyth's election to the House of Representatives
while minister to Spain, Gilmer said that the Georgian had not
fulfilled the residence requirement of the state act. Nevertheless,
he had been seated after the House members, in adjudicating
the matter, had advanced the opinion that official duty in a foreign
nation did not preclude habitancy in the United States. Gilmer
claimed that the House of Representatives in rendering such a
decision had disregarded the Georgia measure and thereby had
given evidence that Congress did not consider itself bound by
the state law.

Forsyth denied most of Gilmer's allegations. He maintained
that there was only one real issue in the case, the question concerning acceptance, and Gilmer had admitted his neglect in com-
plying with that provision of the election act. The Governor
remarked that his enforcement of the law was not a veto but
a compliance with the will of the people.[20]

Forsyth declared that he had never regarded the acceptance
procedure as a mere formality. As evidence, he produced his
letter of August 5, 1822, written while he was residing in Spain.
In the communication, he informed the governor of Georgia
that he was submitting his acceptance in advance of the election
so that if he won, his notification would arrive within the time
prescribed by law; if his advance acceptance was illegal, he asked
that the Georgia legislature grant him a special dispensation.

Forsyth agreed that the Georgia qualification of three years'
residence was inconsistent with the United States Constitution;
that, in case of a dispute over the seating of members, the state
regulations would be disregarded by Congress. Regardless of his
opinion, however, it was incumbent upon the governor to enforce
existing statutes. The provision requiring notification of acceptance was considered constitutional by Forsyth, since it was not a
qualification, but a precaution to insure full state representation
in Congress should an elected candidate refuse the mandate of
the people. The Governor repudiated the charge that the House
of Representatives had adjudicated his right to a seat in that
body. He explained that, in the process of examining the eligi-

bility of another member, the investigating committee had referred to his election while he was minister to Spain. He insisted that the reference had pertained to a constitutional interpretation and that there had been neither an allusion to, nor a mention of, the Georgia election law.

The newspapers became interested in the controversy. Some commented that Forsyth's action had been precipitate and would cause unpleasant feelings, possibly a division of the Troup party; that a new election was unnecessary, since Gilmer was certain to be elected. The press was practically unanimous in praising the ability and past services of Gilmer, and in expressing regret that the incident had occurred. However, the general opinion was that Forsyth's position was the correct one, and that he had acted impartially in his strict adherence to the law.

Although there were reports that Forsyth and Gilmer had been intimate friends, at least one editor claimed that they had been personal and political enemies.[21] Gilmer later denied any political feud, adding that his acquaintance with Forsyth was limited; that, while they differed on certain constitutional questions, they were members of the same party, receiving the support of common associates.[22]

Gilmer not only refused to be a candidate for re-election, but in May, 1829, resigned his seat in Congress. He stated that while he did not doubt the tenability of his position, he did not wish to oppose the will of the people as expressed in their approval of a new election. His participation in the controversy had been prompted by a desire to prevent unconstitutional restraint upon the rights of the electorate. Since his principles had been repudiated by his constituents, he did not think it expedient that he should continue to represent his state in the House of Representatives.[23]

Gilmer's action caused many of his supporters to advocate his re-election by acclamation, explaining that he would not refuse to serve if drafted for the office. By the time of the October election, however, the ex-representative was no longer available for the vacated congressional seat; following Forsyth's refusal to offer for a second term, Gilmer had announced his candidacy for the governorship.

Forsyth showed fervor in upholding the state laws on other occasions. Wilson Lumpkin, when accepting a congressional seat in 1828, failed to furnish evidence of tax payment. The Governor informed him that no commission would be issued until there was a compliance with the Georgia election act.[24] Forsyth cancelled land grants in those instances where payment for fractions was not in specie or where the amount was not paid within the time specified by law.[25] Refusing to take a partisan attitude in local politics, he ordered new county elections in cases of irregularities or indefinite decisions. According to Georgia statute, no compensation was authorized for magistrates in their capacity as election officials. Forsyth would not permit an exception.[26] The city of Savannah passed an ordinance providing for the conveyance to the state of a plot of land, upon which was to be constructed an arsenal, the transfer to be made on condition that the municipality share in the use of the building. Referring to an act of the General Assembly, the Governor advised that he could not accept the lot unless the stipulation was removed.[27]

Although admitting a sincere interest in the advancement of public education, Forsyth nevertheless was determined that the laws on education should be observed. Appropriations for the maintenance of poor or free schools and of certain academies were distributed through the Governor's office, but Forsyth frequently withheld funds because of negligence by responsible officials. He insisted that justices of inferior courts complete a census of new counties so that the counties might receive the benefits of the poor school fund. He was constantly reminding trustees of both the academic and poor school funds that they would receive no payment of dividends until they had submitted satisfactory reports concerning expenditures of previous disbursements. To aid in the accounting, the Governor publicized, through the newspapers, a legislative act on the subject. Undoubtedly the situation was a matter of concern to Forsyth, for he said that "the poor School and Academic Funds are now sources of more trouble & vexation to the Executive than all the other funds of the State . . . ."[28]

Not only did Forsyth believe in a strict adherence to the laws, but he also advocated that the laws be codified and improved. Soon after his inauguration he transmitted a message to the lower house of the General Assembly in which he referred to article III, section 8, of the Georgia Constitution of 1798: a provision requiring the codification of the civil and criminal statutes of the state within five years after the adoption of the Constitution. The Governor contended that those digests that had been published were incomplete and not in conformity with the intentions of the framers of the Constitution; he maintained that substantive common, as well as statutory, law should be included. He urged that in spite of the expiration of the time limit, the legislators fulfill a solemn obligation.[29] Although his appeal was repeated to a subsequent legislature, it was not until 1858 that provision was made for a proper codification and not until 1862 that the first such code appeared.[30]

Forsyth recognized the need for improvement in the judiciary system of the state. The superior court judges were the highest judicial officers, each having supreme authority in his circuit and not bound by decisions of his predecessors or contemporaries. Decrying lack of uniformity in judicial opinions, Forsyth suggested that the Constitution be amended to provide for establishment of a court for the correction of errors. His recommendation was disregarded by the General Assembly, so that many years elapsed before the type of tribunal contemplated by Forsyth became a reality in Georgia. In 1835, a constitutional amendment made provision for a state supreme court; however, the legislature failed to enact a law for such a court until 1845.[31]

Governor Forsyth placed particular emphasis upon reform of the penitentiary system and revision of the penal code. The penitentiary system, in operation since 1818, was a source of considerable disagreement among Georgians. There were complaints that it was a drain upon the state treasury and should be abolished; that the system was mismanaged and neither prevented crime nor rehabilitated offenders. While admitting its unpopularity, advocates of the system declared that once its defects were corrected, the state would derive a permanent benefit. They directed attention to the success attained in other states, objected to the abandonment of valuable property, and expressed concern over a wholesale release of convicted criminals.

Forsyth, so that Georgia might profit from the experience of other states, wrote to several governors requesting copies of penal codes, and any information pertinent to penitentiary systems.[32] Once received, the information was presented to the General Assembly for consideration. In his first annual message, the Governor declared that abolition of the penitentiary system would constitute a reproach upon the state. However, there were defects, one of the most prominent, in his opinion, being the inadequacy of the penitentiary buildings. He asked that the legislature devote serious deliberation to the amelioration of conditions, and also to the correction of errors in the penal code, which was too harsh and inconsistent.

Although Forsyth's appeal for betterment of the penal code was disregarded, his recommendation for improvement of the penitentiary system was referred to a committee, which returned a favorable report. Subsequently, the General Assembly passed an act giving the Governor direct supervision of the penitentiary. He was empowered to appoint, subject to the approval of the Senate, all penitentiary officials except supply contractors; to dismiss any inefficient or dishonest officer; and to receive a quarterly report of conditions from the inspectors of the institution.[33]

In the exercise of this additional authority, Forsyth required a more rigid enforcement of discipline, audits of prison records, submission of weekly progress reports, and information concerning employee efficiency. He also insisted upon inventories being made of raw materials, manufactured articles, and tools belonging to the institution. Recognizing the corruptive influence exerted upon young inmates by hardened criminals quartered in the same room, he suggested that the prison be altered so as to afford a separate cell for each convict. During his administration the penitentiary was managed with skill and economy. At the close of his administration, Forsyth was able to report that the usual institutional indebtedness was non-existent and "the appropriation of the last year for the support of the Penitentiary remains undisturbed in the Treasury."[34]

Forsyth's tenure of office occurred during an era of state participation in the banking business, made possible by purchase of stock in individual banks or by sole ownership. Georgia was a stockholder in the Bank of Darien, situated approximately seventy miles from Savannah at the mouth of the Altamaha River. This bank had suspended specie payments in 1825, thereby causing a depreciation in its currency. When Forsyth assumed his gubernatorial duties, resumption of specie payments had not been realized and the bank's financial condition had become critical.[35]

The new Governor soon identified himself as an advocate of sound financial principles and of legislative supervision of state banks. Upon notification that a meeting of the Bank of Darien's stockholders was to be held December 3, 1827, with the purpose of investigating the affairs of the bank and recommending measures for redemption of its notes, Forsyth appointed three persons to represent the state.[36] He furnished them with all available information on the subject, and instructed them to observe the unit rule in voting, so as to avert decisions of "dangerous or of fatal character."[37] He anticipated that a proposal would be made to grant the bank permission for negotiation of new loan contracts. Believing that the institution was in no condition to justify such a measure, he opposed the idea. In the event the plan should be adopted, however, he favored removal of the bank to Milledgeville and was positive that the General Assembly would approve the change of site.

Two days before the stockholders' meeting convened, Forsyth vetoed a bill which provided that the Darien bank, through payment of semi-annual installments of $75,000, would be permitted to redeem gradually its notes held by the state. The Governor's reasons for disapproving the measure were as follows: the proposal was impractical and would not insure ultimate redemption of the bank's debt, for the institution was in no condition to resume business; the bank deserved no further indulgence, for, while it had made a substantial reduction of its indebtedness to individuals, it had enjoyed the use of public funds without making any effort to reduce the debt owed to the state; the plan would be injurious to the public, for the bank's bills, if allowed to circulate, could not be sustained at par value; "and finally . . . no experiment should be permitted which will render more insecure the large amount now due to the Treasury by the institution. . . ."[38] In spite of Forsyth's objections, the General Assembly repassed the Darien bank measure over his veto.

Forsyth suggested that the state's members of the bank's stockholders provide him with all information pertinent to the management and affairs of the institution. The Senate, in December, 1827, had defeated a bill for removal of the bank to Milledgeville, but the Governor instructed the state's representatives to vote for petitioning the legislature on a change of location. He also urged a practical reduction in the current expenses of the bank. After the stockholders' report had been completed and submitted to the legislature, a committee of the lower house recommended that the Bank of Darien be permitted to resume specie payments. Forsyth voiced a vigorous dissent, declaring that there should be no restoration until the bank's debts were settled. He pointed out that the bank's vaults did not contain sufficient money to meet the next semi-annual payment due the state. Consequently, he questioned the institution's ability to establish an adequate metallic basis.[39] As demonstrated by later events, Forsyth's analysis of the situation was accurate. The Bank of Darien, after resuming specie payments in 1829, was compelled to suspend operations in 1841, and as a result forfeited its charter.

During Forsyth's administration the legislature established the state-owned Central Bank of Georgia and located it in Milledgeville. Chartered in December, 1828, the bank was not specifically made part of the Georgia government; this deficiency permitted an evasion of the federal Constitution's prohibition regarding issuance of bills of credit by a state. In reality, the institution became the state's treasury, receiving as deposits all taxes and other income due the state and honoring the treasurer's drafts for state expenditures. The bank was authorized to make loans to Georgia citizens, such funds being apportioned to the counties on the basis of population. Each loan was limited to $2,500 at six per cent per annum interest and to a five-year period, subject to renewal every six months. The bank's capital consisted of all funds, stocks, and bonds possessed by the state, and all obligations due it. The institution's three directors, appointed annually by the Governor, selected one of their number as president of the bank.[40] The Central Bank of Georgia began operations in June, 1829, at which time it faced the problem of satisfying hundreds of would-be borrowers.

The charter of the Central Bank received a reluctant approval from Governor Forsyth. Though he realized the value of the institution to the community, he was also cognizant of the charter's defects. He recommended that the provision regarding debts due on certain lands be clarified so that the property, if abandoned, might be sold by the bank, with the purchase money being added to the capital stock. He urged that the bank guard against unsound extension of its resources. The charter limited the power to issue notes, but Forsyth warned that the legislature, in seeking to popularize the bank, might attempt to make "experimental changes." He suggested that, in amending the charter, there be a requirement for a vote in excess of a simple majority. Forsyth declared that money collected from taxes should not be used in making bank loans. Taxation could be justified only on the basis of defraying cost of government; when collections exceeded this need, taxes should be reduced.

To provide an opportunity for the eventual cessation of all direct taxes on agricultural interests, he recommended that the Central Bank's profits be made available for payment of governmental expenditures. Recognizing that many Georgians were disappointed over failure to obtain loans, the Governor explained that the bank was unable to provide satisfaction to all applicants because of the limited amount of capital and the fixed county ratio. He considered the regulations necessary to insure institutional stability and asked forbearance on the part of disgruntled petitioners until the bank was in a position to accommodate them.[41] Unfortunately, Forsyth's admonitions were disregarded. The Central Bank of Georgia, because of overissue of notes, was forced to terminate operations in 1841, with final liquidation occurring in 1856.

Forsyth showed an interest in state development of waterways and transportation. In December, 1826, the General Assembly abolished the Georgia Board of Public Works. There was then reestablished the system of administering river improvements by local commissions, who used public funds. Forsyth insisted that these local boards function properly, not only to improve the transportation system, but also to prevent impractical expenditures. Keeping in close contact with the commissioners, he gave advice on problems confronting them and demanded an accounting of their use of public funds. The Governor instructed Hamilton Fulton, state engineer, to make a full examination of the Chattahoochee River channel between Coweta Falls and the Flint River, after which he was to transmit his findings and recommendation to the local agency in control of the river system. Forsyth, looking toward further improvement of waterways, also dispatched Fulton to other river locations, directing him to inspect conditions and to make reports to the executive department.[42]

Like many of his contemporaries, Forsyth favored a program of canal construction, in opposition to a report made in 1826 by the Georgia Board of Public Works suggesting that the state deviate from its elaborate plan of canal building to the more practical one of railroad construction.[43] Forsyth was not one of those few individuals who recognized the potential advantages connected with railroad transportation;[44] he preferred to support such a project as that being conducted by the Savannah, Ogeechee, and Altamaha Canal Company. This organization, chartered in 1826 and reinforced with a state loan of $50,000, had made moderate progress in building a canal from the city of Savannah to the Ogeechee and Altamaha rivers when, after two years, it was threatened with bankruptcy. In December, 1828, the General Assembly passed a relief measure authorizing the Governor, on behalf of the state, to subscribe for $44,000 more of company stock. Forsyth gave ready assent to the bill, appointed the state's representative to the board of directors, corresponded with the corporation's president relative to the business, and purchased the authorized shares of stock. Later, in explaining his activities to the Georgia legislature, the Governor declared:

Of the practicability of the proposed work and its immense utility when finished, no reasonable doubt can exist. The expense already incurred, is comparatively small, when that in prospect is considered. Calculations of cost should not obstruct the prosecution of a great work, where the benefit promised is of sufficient magnitude to repay the expenses. Unless the individuals who have commenced the work shall despair of success, and abandon the design, it is confidently believed that a full share of the charge will be cheerfully borne by the State; until the line of the canal reaches the Chattahoochee, and forms a channel of communication through the State, between the Gulf of Mexico and the Atlantic Ocean.[45]

Forsyth's evaluation proved erroneous. By 1831 the canal had been completed to the Ogeechee River, a distance of sixteen miles, but it was never extended beyond that point. Because of the insolvency of the company in 1836, the canal was advertised for sale, the state subsequently selling its interest for $10,000. With the advent of railroad transportation, the project for the grand trunk canal was abandoned.[46]

As governor, Forsyth had little occasion to express his sentiments regarding internal improvements at the expense of the federal government. He did, however, reveal his conviction that the national government had no constitutional authority to extend benefits where discrimination was involved. In 1828, a situation arose whereby the best interests of Georgia were threatened by promise of federal aid to a sister state. Georgia had charter jurisdiction over the Savannah River, located between that state and South Carolina, but insisted that improvement of the channel should be a joint responsibility. South Carolina, on the other hand, was reluctant to participate in a project favoring the city of Savannah over her own seaport of Charleston; consequently she concentrated her interest on that portion of the river north of Augusta. Each state, at various times, had taken steps toward a coordination of effort and expense, only to receive little cooperation from the other. As a result, joint action for improvement of navigation on the Savannah River had not been accomplished when Forsyth assumed the office of governor.

In March, 1828, Forsyth wrote to Georgia's congressmen in Washington and enclosed a copy of the state's 1823 ratification of an agreement for joint operations. He explained that he had no official information as to South Carolina's action; that as a member of Congress in the 1825-1826 session he had received no intimation from the South Carolina delegation of a desire to secure the necessary ratification from the federal government. He suggested that, if South Carolina would agree, the Georgia delegation would join the South Carolinians in an application for congressional consent. Forsyth's attempt at an immediate consummation of the partnership undoubtedly was prompted by distressing news which he had received from South Carolina: the incorporation of a company for the purpose of constructing a railroad between Charleston and Hamburg, the South Carolina village opposite Augusta. In his opinion, "the avowed object [of the corporation] . . . is to render the navigation of the Savannah below Augusta comparatively useless. . . ."[47] The Governor's effort came to nought, however, for the South Carolina delegation, lacking instructions, declined the proposal for making joint application to Congress.[48]

In his message to the Georgia legislature on November 14, 1828, Forsyth revealed Governor John Taylor's position that the Charleston and Hamburg Railroad project rendered South Carolina averse to further expenditures for Savannah River improvements south of Augusta. In view of the South Carolina governor's declaration, Forsyth asserted that Georgia would be unwise in making any agreement pertaining to partial improvements. As for the railroad project, the Georgia chief executive expressed confidence that it would fail since it could not compete with the natural course of commerce. He also voiced a complaint against that part of the plan which would insure South Carolina the use of federal funds and the services of the United States engineer. It was his conviction that money which had been paid into the national treasury by Georgians should not be used to advance a scheme designed to injure or destroy the trade of Savannah. He declared that such federal aid as might promote the interests of one state to the detriment of another was clearly unconstitutional.[49]

A perennial problem, to which Governor Forsyth turned his attention, was the undetermined boundary line between Georgia and Florida. Since the latter was a territory, settlement of the matter was dependent upon agreement between the United States government and the state of Georgia. At the close of the French and Indian War in 1763, the Royal Proclamation had designated Georgia's southern boundary as extending eastward from the junction of the Chattahoochee and Flint rivers to the source of the St. Mary's River and thence down the latter to the Atlantic Ocean. The St. Mary's had three western branches and the question as to which was the true source of the river involved the status of 1,500,000 acres of land within the disputed zone. Georgia contended that the Royal Proclamation referred to the southernmost branch of the river. The state reinforced its claim by citing Governor James Wright's commission of 1764 fixing his jurisdiction as extending to the most southern stream of the St. Mary's.[50]

Spain's acquisition of the Floridas in 1783 made the determination of a definite boundary a matter of vital importance. The matter remained in abeyance, however, until 1796, when, under a provision of the Treaty of San Lorenzo of the previous year, a joint commission was appointed to locate the line between the river junction and the head of the St. Mary's. Andrew Ellicott was chosen to represent the United States. Instead of actually running the line, the commissioners settled upon a point which they considered to be the river's source, on the middle branch and near the Okefenokee Swamp. For designation purposes, they erected a knoll which came to be known as Ellicott's Mound.

Georgia was not satisfied with the action taken, and in 1819 the state dispatched its own commissioners to investigate the matter. This group of three persons after some consideration confirmed the decision of the 1796 commission. The United States failed to take advantage of the concurrence by proceeding with an official determination of the boundary, but assumed that the controversy with Georgia had been concluded. Indeed the federal government, after obtaining Florida from Spain in 1819, sold tracts of land within the area between the middle and southern branches of the St. Mary's River.

Georgia, however, was not content with the situation; the state wanted the boundary surveyed and marked. In 1825, the Troup administration began a concerted effort toward realization of this goal. After repeated pleas by Georgia for cooperation, Congress finally responded, on May 4, 1826, by authorizing the President to take the necessary steps toward designation of the dividing line. The act provided for a joint commission and stated specifically that the line would be drawn to that point which the 1796 commission had declared to be the origin of the St. Mary's.

Thomas Spalding was selected as the Georgia representative on the commission and Thomas Mann Randolph was chosen to

act for the United States. Since Governor Troup was of the opinion that the southern branch constituted the St. Mary's source, he
instructed Spalding and his surveyor, John McBride, to establish the true position before running the line. These instructions conflicted with those given to Randolph, who was
bound by the congressional act.

Before the American commissioner's arrival, the two Georgians
concluded that Troup was correct in his assumption, McBride's
contention being that the greater quantity of water emanated
from the southern branch. Operations were started, but it soon
became evident that nothing could be accomplished until
the two governments had resolved their differences concerning
the point of departure. Consequently, work on the project was
postponed.[51] Such was the situation when John Forsyth became
Governor of Georgia.

Three weeks after his inauguration, Forsyth sent a message
to the Georgia legislature relative to the landed area within the
disputed zone. The communication contained a brief review of
the state's right to the property, an allusion to federal survey
and sale of the land, and two recommendations which were presented with a view to preventing further altercations. One of the
proposals was that the General Assembly prohibit state surveys
in the section until a distinct boundary line had been determined.
The second suggestion was for the passage of an act validating
United States grants of the disputed land on condition that the
central government within a designated time pay to Georgia the
amounts due or received from the grantees. Forsyth declared
that the proposed actions would constitute an assertion of Georgia's rights and would, at the same time, demonstrate the state's
desire to cooperate with the United States government.[52]

This tactful approach to the problem elicited the praise of an
Augusta editor who commented that, while he had favored
the Troup policy, the time had come for a change from vindictive-
ness to conciliation.[53] When the Georgia legislature acted on the
Governor's suggestion and passed the measure, Forsyth promptly
transmitted a copy to President John Quincy Adams with the request that it be included in a congressional consideration of the
boundary question.

Forsyth had sent to the President certain documents allegedly
substantiating Georgia's claim that the southern branch was the
source of the St. Mary's River. The correspondence included Mc-
Bride's deductions, a manuscript map, and the Governor's request

that Adams make a careful examination of the evidence before presentation to Congress.

After Congress had convened, Forsyth transmitted the same information to the Georgia delegation and advised the members how they should proceed when the matter was brought up. He cautioned that Georgia's 1819 agreement would be used against the state. He suggested to the delegation that instead of replying to this line of reasoning, they place emphasis upon a re-examination of the entire matter. He pointed out that the act of 1826 had been passed under the assumption that Ellicott's Mound was the true source of the St. Mary's. An investigation of McBride's findings would prove that Ellicott had erred in his observations. Furthermore, the Spanish had contributed to Ellicott's mistake by intriguing with the Indians and thereby preventing a determination of the boundary line. The Georgia governor stated that he relied upon the good faith of the United States to correct "the errors committed by the commissioner . . . errors into which he was led by the infidelity of Spain to its engagements. . . ."[54]

In response to a request from the Georgia legislature, Forsyth addressed a letter to President Adams in which he asked that the President make such recommendations to Congress as would insure justice to the state. Forsyth declared that it was imperative that the act of 1826 be modified or repealed, for it was based upon a false assumption. As a matter of fact, he contended, the commissioners had not complied with the provision of the San Lorenzo treaty; instead of surveying and marking the boundary, they had merely established points between which the line should be run. Therefore the designation of Ellicott's Mound had no legal significance. In conclusion, the Governor declared that "it would be the extremity of disgrace if the Federal Government should seek to take advantage of an error committed by its authority . . . when Providence had placed it in its power to correct the error by a simple exertion of its own will."[55] Some years later, Wilson Lumpkin described the letter as "the best argument in support of the views of Georgia which I have examined. . . ."[56]

A few months later, Forsyth wrote to the Georgia members of the United States House of Representatives that he was perturbed because the Judiciary Committee's report, laying stress upon Georgia's acquiescence in 1819, had been adverse to the state's claims. Maintaining that later developments had shown El-

licott's calculations to be incorrect, he insisted that no previous
state administration could compromise the rights of Georgia. In
addition, he contended that the committee opinion was based
upon the assertion that the southern branch of the St. Mary's was
known by a different name at the time of Ellicott's inspection.
Forsyth denounced this assertion as being unsound and one
which should not receive serious consideration from an impartial
tribunal. Therefore he urged the Georgia delegation to present
the facts to Congress in such a manner as to insure the defeat of
the committee report.[57]

Forsyth's first annual message to the Georgia legislature, submitted on November 4, 1828, disclosed that neither house of
Congress had reached a definite decision regarding the Georgia-
Florida boundary. As a reminder, he added that no congressional
verdict would be binding unless approved by the state of Georgia.[58] When the subsequent Congress adjourned without acting
on the matter, Forsyth asked the Georgia delegation to furnish
him with information concerning reasons for the postponement.
The ensuing correspondence together with the congressional proceedings and other pertinent data was used by Forsyth as a basis
for remarks contained in his final legislative message. He stated
that, after a careful study, he would not interpret the congressional inaction "as a refusal to make provision for running the
line, in conjunction with the authorities of Georgia."[59]

Despite Governor Forsyth's efforts to secure a satisfactory solution, Georgia's difficulty over the Florida boundary was not destined to be settled during his lifetime. The situation was prolonged until 1859 when, with agreement upon Ellicott's Mound,
the line was officially determined.

During Forsyth's final year in office, there was pronounced
speculation as to whether he would seek a second term. The Augusta *Constitutionalist,* in expectation of his announced candidacy, declared that the state had never had a more able governor
and that his re-election was assured. Similar opinion was expressed by other newspapers. The Athens *Athenian* also announced George R. Gilmer's decision not to oppose the incumbent.

President Jackson's appointment of John MacPherson Berrien
to the position of attorney general, thus vacating one of Georgia's
senatorial seats in Congress, heightened interest in Georgia politics. Forsyth hesitated in making known his intentions, and some
expressed the view that a conspiracy was in the making which was

designed to deprive the people of their right to choose his successor. It was rumored that the Governor would offer for reelection and, if successful, would resign in favor of the senatorial appointment expected from the Georgia legislature; the latter body, in turn, would be free to make its own selection for governor. In consequence of the rumors, the newspapers called upon Forsyth to make public his preference of offices.

Actually the choice was not difficult. Forsyth's private correspondence reveals that he was not satisfied with the governorship, but wished to return to some official post in Washington.[60] Forsyth made known his decision in the following letter to his constituents, dated July 30, 1829:

I ask you to excuse me for declining to be a candidate at the ensuing election, for Governor of this State. This step is taken without any intention to abandon public employment—It is my wish to continue in your service, if the next General Assembly shall think proper to bestow upon me another place, not less responsible than the one I now hold, but more congenial to the habits of my past life. I have no words of sufficient power, to express my gratitude for repeated manifestations of your kindness, and for your favorable judgement of the manner in which I have discharged the duties of your Chief Magistrate, an office entered on with reluctance, and which I shall leave with no regret, but that which arises from an apprehension that many of you would be better satisfied that I should remain for a term longer, performing its duties.[61]

Following Forsyth's renunciation, a crisis developed which split the Troup party. One faction favored Joel Crawford and another George R. Gilmer for governor. Crawford's adherents claimed that Gilmer should withdraw from the contest since their candidate was the first to announce. The rival faction responded with the accusation that Forsyth had selected Crawford as his successor and was determined to force his choice upon the people. They declared that the two men had traveled together from Sparta to Augusta and back just prior to the publication of Forsyth's letter declining re-election; that Crawford, forewarned, had been enabled to announce his candidacy in the same edition of the Milledgeville *Southern Recorder* that carried the Governor's decision.[62] A pro-Forsyth journal denied that there had been any chicanery.[63]

The quarrel between the two factions did not prove fatal to the party's success. With John Clark absent from the state and no gubernatorial candidate offered by his party, the majority of the

Clarkites chose to support Gilmer. The election resulted in a victory for the latter, who triumphed over his opponent by a vote of 24,204 to 10,718.[64] Thus Forsyth's tenure as Governor of Georgia came to a close with the inauguration of Gilmer on November 4, 1829.

In the meantime, there was considerable editorial speculation as to Berrien's successor in the United States Senate. One group, portraying Forsyth as an intriguing politician who placed self above party, predicted that any substantial opponent would defeat him for the position. Other editors, claiming that Forsyth's accomplishments entitled him to the office, prophesied his election by the General Assembly. Their prophecy was realized. On the day following Gilmer's inauguration, the Georgia legislature chose Forsyth to complete Berrien's unexpired term; there was no organized opposition. Forsyth took his seat on December 8, 1829, and performed his duties with such satisfaction that he was re-elected for a full term, beginning March 4, 1831.

A study of Forsyth's governorship reveals him as a competent administrator of local affairs who emphasized economy in government, orthodox monetary principles, and strict compliance with existing laws. He became well-informed on departmental operations and did not hesitate to exert his influence in governmental matters, although at the same time recognizing the limitations of his constitutional powers. Always anxious to promote the resources and interests of Georgia, he took a firm but co-operative position when the national government was involved.

Both friends and enemies expressed admiration for Forsyth's messages to the General Assembly. One political foe wrote:

We opposed the election of this gentleman perhaps more warmly than we ever did that of any other, and there is none whose elevation we more sincerely and honestly regretted. But this did not blind us to the reflection that it is our duty to judge him, while in his present office, by his performance of its duties alone; and with regard to the Message before us, we hesitate not to say that in our opinion, it is one of the most able, eloquent, and unexceptionable documents that has ever graced the Executive Chair of our State. Its style is chaste and eloquent, but easy and unaffected, and at the same time manly, impartial and energetic; and the sketch he has given of our State affairs, is drawn with a keenly discriminating eye and a master hand.[65]

That Forsyth's administration was popular, there is no doubt. When the question of his re-election was before the public, there was hardly a dissenting opinion. An unnamed opponent was reported to have said, ". . . no man in the state could now beat him."[66] Forsyth's letters exhibit his discontent with having to perform gubernatorial duties, but for no other phase of his career did he receive such general approval from the people.

VI

Creeks and Cherokees

ONE OF THE principal issues of the Forsyth administration concerned the removal of the Indians from Georgia and the nullification of land titles. Here was a controversy with the United States government which had existed for many years. In 1802, Georgia had ceded approximately eighty million acres of western land to the United States, and in return the latter had promised removal of all Indians from the state as soon as it could be accomplished peaceably and on reasonable terms.[1] In succeeding years, the federal government arranged treaties whereby the Indians were deprived of various tracts of land, the principal cessions being in southern Georgia (1814), one area south of the Altamaha River, and another around the headwaters of the Ocmulgee River (1818), and the region between the Ocmulgee and Flint rivers (1821).[2]

Nevertheless, when George M. Troup became governor in 1823, the Creek and Cherokee Indians still retained several million acres of land within Georgia which they declared not subject to further cession. On several past occasions, the Georgia authorities had reproached the federal government for failure to complete the Indian removal; but the national government, regarding the Indian communities as being independent, reiterated that they could not be removed by force. Since the Georgians considered the Indians as dependent tenants, subject to the will of the state, they became impatient and even bitter with the federal government. The Georgia settlers wanted to expand their cotton culture and particularly desired the fertile Creek lands.[3]

Troup, as Governor of Georgia, was outspoken in his criticism of the federal government for its failure to rid the state of the Indians. Determined that the obligation should be fulfilled without further delay, he expected and insisted upon the cooperation of the Georgia delegation in Congress. John Forsyth, a member of that delegation, had a profound interest in the problem. Being in thorough accord with Troup's policy, Forsyth soon became its most active exponent in the national legislature.

In response to a suggestion from Governor Troup,[4] the Georgia legislature drafted a "memorial and remonstrance" to the President of the United States on the subject of the apparent procrastination. On December 20, 1823, Troup approved the document, which specifically demanded an end to the existing situation, and forwarded it to President James Monroe. He also enclosed a copy of the document in a letter to the Georgia congressional members urging that they take appropriate action to attain the objective.[5] Representative Forsyth and Senator John Elliott were appointed by the Georgia delegation to visit the President for the ostensible purpose of learning whether he had received the memorial. Acknowledging receipt of the document, Monroe promised to transmit it to Congress. He added, however, that he did not intend to make any recommendations to the national legislature because he had already presented his views on the subject to that body. Forsyth and Elliott were disappointed and sought to convince Monroe of the necessity for immediate and decisive measures. Although the President appeared impressed with their arguments, he promised nothing more than his signature to any pertinent bill which Congress might pass.

At a later date, and in compliance with a note from Monroe, Forsyth and Elliott made a second visit to the President. In the presence of Secretary of War John C. Calhoun, the President read to the two Georgians a memorandum which was to serve as a basis for a conference with four Cherokee chiefs. These Indians, as spokesmen for their nation, were in Washington for the purpose of opposing further land cessions. Forsyth and Elliott declared that in general the memorandum was satisfactory; but they urged that emphasis be placed on Georgia's refusal to endure the Cherokee occupancy. In order that the Georgia delegation might be fully informed concerning the negotiations, Monroe promised to furnish copies of all correspondence between the Secretary of War and the Cherokee chiefs. The contents of the documents, which were delivered within a few days, were of such nature that the Georgia congressmen, surprised and angry, determined to address a remonstrance to the President.[6]

Forsyth wrote the protest,[7] dated March 10, 1824; it stated Georgia's case in unequivocal terms. The Georgia delegation criticized the method of negotiation employed by the War Department, maintaining that the Cherokee chiefs had been accorded recognition usually reserved for representatives of an independent state. Such recognition presented a threat to the sovereignty of Georgia, and as such would be met with determination by a state which regarded the Indians as mere tenants-at-will. The congressmen contended that blame for the Indian refusal to emigrate should be placed upon the federal government; that the administration's policy since 1819 was one which promoted the civilization of the Indians and emphasized their right to permanent occupation.

Declaring that Georgia would never permit the Indians to be numbered among her citizens, the delegates demanded that the national government resort to force if a peaceful removal could not be effected. In conclusion, they insisted "upon an immediate fulfilment of the obligations of the articles of cession . . . as the only means by which justice can be done to the State we represent, and the character of the general government be vindicated."[8]

President Monroe answered the Georgia protests on March 30, 1824. In a special message to Congress, he stated that the best efforts of his predecessors, as well as his own, had been employed to execute the provisions of the 1802 compact. Directing attention to the recent negotiations with the Cherokee chiefs, he declared that the Indians had been inflexible in their refusal of territory beyond the Mississippi River in exchange for their Georgia lands; furthermore, they had protested against any attempts at further cession. Consequently, immediate removal of the Indians from Georgia could be effected only by force. Monroe contended, however, "that the Indian title was not affected in the slightest circumstance by the compact with Georgia, and that there is no obligation on the United States to remove the Indians by force."[9] He reaffirmed his advocacy of Indian civilization and his desire for a removal on peaceable and reasonable terms, as stipulated in the compact.

The President's message, with an accompanying report from Secretary of War Calhoun, was referred to a select committee. Forsyth as chairman of the committee presented a decidedly pro-Georgia report to the House of Representatives on April 15, 1824. After reviewing the history of the controversy and reiterating the assertions contained in the March 10 remonstrance,

the committee offered its theory as to how the Indian title might
be extinguished without difficulty: a federal government order for
removal, on reasonable terms, would be recognized by the Indians. The committee recommended that the national government honor the compact with Georgia by arranging for complete
removal, to be effected with the least possible inconvenience to
the Indians.

Upon a motion from Forsyth, the report and recommendations
were referred to a Committee of the Whole on the State of the
Union.[10] Congress gave due consideration to the report, and on
May 26, 1824, appropriated $50,000 for the extinguishment of
Creek titles to lands in Georgia.[11] Thereafter, Forsyth's activities
(prior to his term as governor) concerning the Indians were directed primarily toward Creek affairs rather than those of the
Cherokees, although he was careful to include the latter when
there was opportunity.

The intention manifested by the federal government to deprive
them of their lands met positive opposition from the Creek Indians, particularly the Upper Creeks. In his efforts to settle
the problem, President Monroe appointed two Georgians, Duncan
G. Campbell and James Meriwether, to represent the United
States government in negotiations with the Creeks on the subject
of land cessions. At first the commissioners met with no success,
for the Creeks reaffirmed their determination in councils held at
Pole Cat Springs and Broken Arrow, Alabama.[12] Subsequently,
however, an agreement was reached with those Lower Creeks
who were under the influence of Chief William McIntosh.

On February 12, 1825, chiefs of the latter group signed the
Treaty of Indian Springs, whereby they ceded all the Creek lands
in Georgia (4,700,000 acres) for an equal amount of territory
west of the Mississippi River; removal was to be completed prior
to September 1, 1826. In addition, the federal government agreed
to pay the Creeks the sum of $400,000 to defray the expenses in-
volved in the emigration and to compensate them for losses incurred in land improvements. The treaty was denounced as illegal by the non-signatory Georgia Creeks, by the Upper Creeks,
and by John Crowell, Indian agent.[13] Although Monroe had stated
that the United States government would recognize no cession unless approved by all the Creeks, he transmitted the Indian Springs
treaty to the Senate on February 28, where it was approved on
March 3, 1825. President John Quincy Adams, who had been in
office only a few days, proclaimed the treaty on March 7. There-

after, Governor Troup began preparations for a survey of the Creek lands in Georgia.

The various aspects of the Creek negotiations were followed with interest by John Forsyth, who was vigilant in his efforts to prevent a collapse or a delay in what he considered a just settlement of the issue. When Monroe, in a message to Congress on January 27, 1825, referred to the pending negotiations and suggested that such a practical solution should be extended to similar Indian problems within the United States, Forsyth was emphatic in his protests. He stated that the plan might be expedient and humane, but he objected to any combination of Indian adjustments which might cause "an indefinite postponement of justice to Georgia."[14]

When the negotiations at Broken Arrow failed, Forsyth became disturbed, and with other members of the Georgia delegation sought to discover the reasons for the breakdown. After conversations with Duncan G. Campbell, the Georgia delegates transmitted their conclusions to the chairman of the Committee on Indian Affairs. Convinced that the commissioners were sincere in their attempts to secure extinguishment of land titles, the congressmen cited two causes for the failure at Broken Arrow: the influence of the Cherokees over the Creeks and the indifferent attitude exhibited by Creek agent John Crowell toward the negotiations. Although Crowell had been reprimanded for neglect of duty, the Georgians expressed doubt that the commissioners would receive his earnest cooperation.[15]

While the Indian Springs negotiations were in progress, Forsyth determined to avert any misapprehensions concerning the reaction of Congress toward a possible treaty. Accordingly, he advised Governor Troup that a treaty concluded with only the Georgia Creeks would receive the sanction of Congress. This information was in turn forwarded to Campbell and Meriwether for the evident purpose of reassuring them in their transactions with the Lower Creeks.[16]

Forsyth's efforts in behalf of Georgia did not cease when Adams affixed his signature to the Indian Springs treaty on March 7. Two days later he visited the President for the purpose of discussing the obligations due his state as stipulated in the compact of 1802. Adams suggested that the matter be referred to the Secretary of War, whose department had supervision over Indian Affairs. Forsyth complied by addressing a letter to Secretary James Barbour, in which he urged that there be no delay in effecting a humane removal of the Creeks from Georgia. Expressing apprehension that Crowell would resort to obstructive tactics regarding the emigration, he requested that the Indian agent's activities be scrutinized and that no confidence be placed in him.

Forsyth stated that the time was appropriate to conclude a treaty with the Cherokees, who, knowing the treatment accorded the Creeks, must realize that the United States would eventually demand the surrender of their lands also. He added that the purchase could be accomplished by the federal government without injustice to the Indians and without violation of legal principle or usage. Barbour replied that the government had already taken measures to insure the execution of the Creek treaty. The Secretary of War also stated that a letter embodying Forsyth's suggestion for a treaty had been sent to the Cherokee chiefs, who had answered with an adamant refusal. Forsyth was assured, however, that the President, anxious for a fulfillment of the obligation to Georgia, would persist in his efforts toward a solution of the Cherokee problem.[17]

Although President Adams had approved the Indian Springs treaty, he soon became engaged in a bitter controversy with Governor Troup concerning the validity of the agreement. Charges of fraud directed toward the treaty caused Adams to order investigations and to urge that Troup discontinue the land survey for the present. Troup agreed to the postponement until the Georgia legislature could take action; that body acted on December 23, 1825, when it adopted a resolution for a continuation of the survey after September 1, 1826.

Meanwhile, the correspondence between Troup and the federal government was becoming more acrimonious. The President, finally convinced that the Indian Springs treaty had been obtained by illegal methods, invited certain Upper and Lower Creek chiefs to Washington where a new agreement was signed on January 24, 1826. After declaring the previous Creek treaty null and void, the Treaty of Washington provided that the Georgia Creeks cede all their lands except one small area west of the Chattahoochee River. The Indians were to yield possession of the territory prior to January 1, 1827, and were to be compensated for all improvements on the ceded lands. Transmitted to the Senate on January 31, 1826, the treaty received its approval and was publicly proclaimed on April 22, 1826.

After a controversy with Georgia concerning the State's right to **survey the strip of** land excluded by the Washington treaty, the federal government deserted the cause of the Creeks. Congress recommended that the Indian lands in Georgia be procured and the Creeks, realizing the futility of opposition, agreed to a cession of the disputed strip on November 15, 1827.[18]

Approximately two weeks before the Treaty of Washington was negotiated, Forsyth and others of the Georgia delegation presented their views on the existing situation to Secretary of War Barbour. They upheld the validity of the Indian Springs treaty, claiming that the adverse testimony in possession of the federal government had been obtained by fraudulent means. For participation in such unethical practices, the delegation asked for the recall of Creek agent John Crowell. The congressmen added that the residents of Georgia, under the pressure of circumstances, had come to regard "the complete extinguishment of the Indian title to all the lands within the limits of Georgia . . . as vitally connected with their safety, and with the preservation of the rights of the State as a member of this Union."[19]

After the annulment of the Indian Springs treaty, Forsyth expressed his opposition in a caustic speech to the House of Representatives. He stated that Georgia, although not a signatory party to the agreement, was affected by the provisions; therefore the treaty could not be declared null and void without the consent of the state. He denounced the investigating authorities for their undue partiality for the Indians, and President Adams for his threat of the use of military force to prevent the survey. In conclusion, Forsyth asserted that the administration had misrepresented facts to such an extent that the general public had come to regard Georgia as the transgressor. His intention, the Georgian declared, was to vindicate the honor of his state.

The following day, Forsyth read a remonstrance which had been signed by the Georgia delegation in the House of Representatives. The members reiterated the contention that without the consent of Georgia the federal government lacked constitutional power to invalidate the Creek treaty of 1825. They explained that the Washington treaty was unsatisfactory as compared with the Indian Springs agreement because it extended the time of Indian removal and it did not provide for a cession of all Creek lands in Georgia. Under the circumstances, the Georgia representatives declared, it was their duty to protest against the Washington treaty as a violation of the rights of their state.[20]

A few days after the presentation of the protest, Forsyth continued his attack upon the Treaty of Washington. The opportunity came with the discovery of fraud by the Creek delegation which had agreed to the treaty. These Creek chiefs, together with certain Cherokee friends who had assisted in the negotiations, had received for their personal use approximately three-fourths of the first payment made for the Georgia lands. The War Department was cognizant of the corrupt transaction, and to Forsyth this was a clear indication that the Adams administration had resorted to chicanery in obtaining the treaty. He demanded that the honor of the United States government be vindicated by a congressional guarantee of proper distribution of funds to the Creek nation.[21]

The action of the Georgia authorities in sending surveyors into the controversial strip of Creek land prompted President Adams to transmit a message to Congress on February 5, 1827, in which he condemned the conduct of the Georgia governor and legislature as a direct violation of treaty provisions. Explaining that he had decided to meet the exigency with a recourse to civil process, he issued a warning that if legal expedients failed he was prepared to use military force.[22]

Forsyth made an immediate reply to the President's communication. Speaking before the House of Representatives, he denied that the Georgia officials had violated the United States Constitution and insisted that Governor Troup, in ordering the surveys completed, had acted under the sovereign power of his state. He maintained that the responsibility for the Creek controversy rested upon the federal government, whose agents had incited the Indians to resist the authority of Georgia; that if the administration had not intervened, the problem would have been settled without difficulty. Under the existing circumstances, Forsyth declared, the President had no constitutional authority to employ military force against Georgia.

Daniel Webster rebuked Forsyth for his remarks. Instead of being influenced by the Georgian's dictatorial tactics, Webster declared that he intended to be impartial in his investigation and consideration of the matter. Forsyth replied with a denial of any attempt to dictate to the House members. However, he continued to defend the Georgia cause and to assert that a fair and unbiased examination was all that his constituents desired. He expressed hope that the Indians would receive justice, but contended that their just claims could be satisfied without encroachment upon the rights of Georgia.[23]

After Forsyth became governor, his double objective of justice to his state and to the Indians continued to constitute the basis of his Indian policy. Although anxious for a complete removal of the Indians from Georgia, he was less impetuous than his predecessor, being content to pursue a moderate and cooperative course as long as there was a possibility of success. Once convinced that a different approach was necessary, he was not hesitant in resorting to more stringent action.

The Creek emigration question was on the verge of settlement when Forsyth was elected; consequently the issues between his administration and the Creek nation were confined primarily to border incidents and Indian depredations. However, the Cherokees, occupying the northwestern part of the state, remained a problem.

After having refused to agree to any additional cessions, the Cherokees, in July, 1827, embarked upon a plan which they hoped would insure the retention of their Georgia lands. They adopted a constitution and established a well-organized government, thereby declaring themselves to be a free and independent people.[24] Troup, in his farewell message to the Georgia legislature, made hints at a prompt and summary removal, which met with the approval of Georgia citizens, who insisted that there could never be an extensive development of their state until the Indian lands therein were inhabited by an industrious white population. In addition, the Georgians considered the erection of a state within a state as inconsistent with the rights of Georgia, and they were determined that the Cherokee government should be suppressed.[25]

Governor Forsyth did not mention the Indian controversy in his brief inaugural address, but he left no doubt as to his position in the matter when he approved a joint resolution of the Georgia General Assembly, dated December 19, 1827, and forwarded it to the President of the United States. Following a harsh indictment of the federal government for failure to honor its obligations, the measure presented an affirmation of Georgia's right to extend her authority and laws over an area within her borders. Should the Cherokees continue in their rejection of emigration proposals, the Georgia government was prepared to exercise this right. The state authorities requested that the President redouble his efforts to secure a treaty with the Cherokees and inform the Indians of the probable consequences should such attempts fail.

In conclusion, the Georgians stated their refusal to recognize the Cherokee government and recommended that the national government do the same.[26]

Convinced that the Cherokee Constitution was a violation of Georgia's sovereignty, Forsyth was anxious for the federal government to lose no time in reaching a similar conclusion. He learned that the Tennessee authorities possessed a copy of the Indian constitution and immediately wrote to the governor of that state requesting a duplicate. Having obtained it, he transmitted it to President Adams with a letter citing that portion of the United States Constitution which expressly forbade the establishment of a state within the jurisdiction of another state. He asked to be informed as to what action the administration intended to take.[27]

Adams, being of the opinion that the cited article did not apply to the Indians, referred the matter to his cabinet. After several meetings, in which the members failed to reach an agreement on the constitutionality of the question, the President decided upon a course of action. The Georgia communications would be submitted to Congress without comment, and the Cherokee agent, Hugh Montgomery, would be instructed to notify the Indians that their constitution would not be permitted to alter the relations existing between them and the United States government. Congress then appropriated $50,000 for the purpose of extinguishing the Cherokee titles in Georgia, and Montgomery received instructions from the War Department to ascertain the feelings of the Indians and the Georgians with reference to the existing situation.

Adams's ineffectual mode of procedure did not satisfy Forsyth. Seeking information for his own use, the Governor corresponded with Montgomery, and in a letter to the Cherokee agent stated his position:

The Indians within the limits of the U. States are not dependent upon us in consequence of treaties made with them containing stipulations to that effect. They are dependent upon us because they are a conquered people residing within our Sovereignty. It is true that the General and State Governments have heretofore refrained from considerations of policy to subject the Indians as individuals to the operation of the laws governing our own citizens. I think it however extremely important that the Indians should be made sensible that the right and the power thus to subject them is not doubted and will be before long exercised unless they should remove beyond the Mississippi. The Cherokees in Georgia will be inevitably subjected to the

State laws if the compact made in 1802 is not speedily executed by the U. States.[28]

In correspondence with other persons, Forsyth reiterated his determination to take the initiative, adding that Georgia could expect no aid from Washington unless there was a change in the federal administration.

The Georgia General Assembly convened in November, 1828, with the knowledge that the Cherokees still retained their constitution, their government, and their lands within the state. Forsyth, in his annual message to the legislature, devoted considerable space to the problem. He declared that, although the federal administration had given repeated assurances of its desire to remove the Cherokees, the policy being pursued was not conducive to success. He stated that the attitude of the federal government toward the Cherokee constitution was so inconclusive that the Indians were not only continuing their independent government, but were strengthening it by conferring citizenship upon white persons who wished to settle within their territory. Such a situation was intolerable to Georgians, and if the federal administration was unable to provide a remedy it was the duty of the state authorities to take the necessary action.

Forsyth insisted that there was nothing in either the state or federal constitutions which impaired Georgia's sovereign right to exercise authority over all inhabitants within the state; that in no previous instance had there been a dispute over, or a disregard of, a state's control over an Indian tribe residing within its borders. He did not wish to be unfair to the Indians, who should be protected by Georgia; but they, in turn, owed obedience to the state. Forsyth recommended that the General Assembly, to promote the best interests of both, enact legislation extending the state laws over the Georgia region occupied by the Cherokees. He suggested also that the proposed act not become operative until the President of the United States had an opportunity to determine whether the Indians preferred to emigrate or to submit to the authority of the Georgia laws.[29]

In making the latter suggestion, Forsyth could have had several advantages in mind. The federal government would be given a final opportunity to settle the question without Georgia's intervention; suspension of the act would be a means of exerting pressure on both the Cherokees and the national government, and thereby of increasing the possibilities of an early removal; the delayed operation of the measure would be indication that Georgia was prepared to act if necessary, and evidence that the state was willing to resort to arbitrary methods only after all other means had failed; the Adams administration might, within a few months, be replaced by one more favorable to the pretensions of Georgia.

The Georgia General Assembly acted favorably upon the recommendations, and on December 20, 1828, the measure was signed by Forsyth. The act extended the state laws over the Cherokee region in all matters relating to white persons; it provided that beginning June 1, 1830, all Indian residents would be subject to the jurisdiction of Georgia; and it decreed that all laws of the Cherokee nation would be null and void after the latter date.

Determined to contest the issue, the Cherokees sent a delegation of chiefs to Washington, who on several occasions presented memorials to the federal government protesting the action of the Georgia authorities. Their efforts were destined to be futile, however, for Andrew Jackson, who became President of the United States in March, 1829, had little sympathy for the Indians. Soon after his inauguration, Jackson's official position on the Georgia question was revealed to the Cherokees through his Secretary of War, John Henry Eaton. The Indians were urged to consent to a removal beyond the Mississippi River, where there would be no conflicting interests and where they would receive full protection of the federal government. In unequivocal words, they were informed that

the right of permitting to you the enjoyment of a separate government, within the limits of a State; and denying the existence of sovereignty to that State within her own limits, cannot be admitted; It is not within the range of powers granted by the States to the General Government, and therefore not within its competency to be exercised.[30]

Subsequently, Jackson reaffirmed his opinions in various messages to Congress.

The change in the federal administration was a source of satisfaction to Forsyth, for he was optimistic in the belief that Jackson's efforts would be beneficial to Georgia. He corresponded with Eaton, making certain that the President received all pertinent documents and information which would reinforce Georgia's claims. Writing to the Secretary of War that he was willing to leave the matter to the discretion of the President, Forsyth nevertheless reserved the right to express opinions in the interest of the public good. When he learned of the message to the Cherokee delegation, he was convinced that "a rigid adherence to the principles developed . . . will . . . enable the President to execute the Compact of 1802."[31]

Toward the end of Forsyth's administration, Georgians were cheered by the news that the national administration had appointed commissioners to visit the Cherokees for purposes of emphasizing the just claims of Georgia and of urging the necessity for an early removal. If the Indians could be persuaded, the commissioners were instructed to enter into treaty negotiations with them. However, the objective was not accomplished.

In his final message to the Georgia legislature, Forsyth stated that since the state's claims were recognized by Jackson, there was little likelihood of further controversy with the federal government on the subject. The Governor hoped that the Cherokees would emigrate before June, 1830; but if they did not the General Assembly should have a prepared program for the exercise of its jurisdiction over the region.

He recommended legislation which would guarantee to the Indians protection of life and property, would arrange for the establishment and operation of courts within the region, and would provide for the selection and duties of the officials to be placed over the Cherokees. He also suggested that plans be made for the imposition of a small tax upon the Indians, so that they might be counted in the next census and thereby cause an increase in Georgia's representation in the United States Congress.[32] In June, 1830, Forsyth's successor, acting in accordance with the previous state legislation, proclaimed the extension of Georgia laws over the Cherokee area.

Although the complete extension of Georgia authority was delayed until after the termination of his administration, Forsyth, soon after assuming his gubernatorial duties, proclaimed the state's criminal jurisdiction over the Cherokee lands. This meant that in the Indian region the state had jurisdiction in all criminal matters where the offense was committed by or upon a white person; it did not apply to criminal acts between Indians. Since the counties contiguous to the Cherokee area were to exercise the authority, Forsyth corresponded with judges of the superior courts, suggesting that each grand jury be informed of its additional duty.

Under the new arrangement Governor Forsyth's policy toward

the Indians was fair and impartial. On numerous occasions he advised interested constituents that the procedure for arresting, trying, and punishing an Indian offender should be the same as that employed against a white criminal. On hearing a rumor that Hugh Montgomery had declared Georgia had no right to enforce criminal jurisdiction over the Indians, Forsyth wrote to the Cherokee agent demanding either a confirmation or a denial of the allegation.[33]

Receiving a reply that the rumor was false, Governor Forsyth assured Montgomery that, in the latter's capacity as Indian agent, it was entirely correct for him to attend the court sessions and to assist the Cherokees in obtaining a fair trial.[34] In 1828, a Cherokee was found guilty of assault with intent to murder and was sentenced to four years' confinement in the state penitentiary. Forsyth pardoned the Indian upon petition by a group of Georgia citizens. At a later date, he commended a Georgia sheriff for his apprehension of several white criminals who had robbed and murdered some Indians.

Inseparably associated with the question of Cherokee removal was the problem concerning the Creek-Cherokee boundary line. Georgia claimed that the true boundary between the two tribes had been changed by an agreement between the Creeks and the Cherokees in December, 1821; that the contract was void because neither the United States nor Georgia had been a party to it. The Cherokees maintained that the line agreed to in 1821 was nothing more than a recognition of what had always been considered the boundary between the two Indian nations. Involved in the dispute were 1,167,360 acres of land, inhabited by the Cherokees, which Georgia contended belonged to her because it was included in the Creek cession.

In compliance with a joint resolution from the Georgia General Assembly, Governor Forsyth turned his attention to the procurement of evidence to substantiate Georgia's claim. He appointed Samuel A. Wales as a state commissioner in December, 1828, and instructed him to obtain testimony from all persons who might have knowledge of the boundary line prior to 1821, being particularly careful that statements were made under oath, and were detailed and explicit. An investigation having been conducted, the commissioner submitted a report, accompanied by various depositions, in which he gave his unqualified support to the Georgia contention.

Forsyth studied the report, and, convinced as to the legitimacy

of the state's claim, appointed Wales to supervise the tracing and
re-marking of the boundary. He informed the commissioner that
the object of the survey was to establish a distinct line, thereby
facilitating the work of the federal officials in their removal of
the Indians residing in the disputed region. Later, Governor Forsyth wrote to the Secretary of War stating that when the survey in
progress was completed, he intended to make application to
the President for federal expulsion of the Indians from the lands
south of the designated line. He explained that such action on
the part of the national government would serve an additional
purpose; it would be effective in influencing the Cherokees to
abandon all territory within the limits of Georgia.[35]

While the survey was being made, white settlers began moving
into the controversial area; Wales and Montgomery became concerned. The latter wrote to Eaton asking whether the survey had
the approval of the federal government and inquiring what measures he should take to protect the Indians from the intruders.[36]
The Indian agent also presented Wales a protest of the survey, in
which he contended that the state was encroaching upon a power
of the United States government and asserted that the information upon which Georgia based her action was biased and incomplete. He asked that consideration be given those Cherokees
who faced disaster if the Georgians were permitted to settle in
the disputed region. In reply, Wales denied the allegations and
refused to discontinue the survey; he made no reference to the
probable Indian distress.[37]

The War Department, already cognizant of the transgression
upon the Cherokee lands, assured the Indians that the agent would
have the white persons removed. This statement brought a reply
from Forsyth, expressing regret over the intrusion. He claimed
that the state had neither authorized its citizens to occupy the
region nor expected such a movement, until after the Indians had
been removed by the federal government. Yet the Governor
sought to rationalize the situation. He explained that his constituents were firm in the belief that the Cherokees had no right
to the land. He accused the Indians of practising discrimination
by permitting other whites to settle in the area while excluding
Georgians. Forsyth contended that, since he expected the Cherokees to be removed from the region upon his application to the
President "it will be incurring a useless expense & creating unnecessary excitement to have the white persons now on it driven
off by military force."[38]

Forsyth's communication did not deter the national administration in its announced policy. Montgomery was advised that a federal commissioner would proceed to the Cherokee territory for the purpose of ascertaining the true boundary between the two tribes. In the meantime the agent was to issue a notice that all intruders found in the disputed area after December 1, 1829, would be removed by force and their cabins destroyed.[39]

After the survey of the Georgians had been completed, but previous to the issuance of instructions to Montgomery, Forsyth forwarded to the President a map of the boundary and an application for Indian removal. Jackson's answer was delayed, because the letter miscarried, and the Governor had to send a second communication. However, in September, 1829, Forsyth was informed that the President was not prepared to offer an opinion regarding the issue. While expressing confidence that the problem would be solved by the administration, Jackson cautioned that Georgia should do nothing to antagonize the Cherokees and thereby handicap the federal government in carrying out its intentions.[40] The following month, Forsyth was told that since the President had been unable to make a decision regarding the controversy, he had determined to refer the matter to "a different tribunal." In order that the administration might render an impartial verdict, Jackson stated that he had appointed John Coffee of Alabama to collect evidence and to present the facts for his consideration. He asked that Governor Forsyth cooperate with Coffee.[41]

Forsyth gave his official reaction in his final message to the Georgia General Assembly. He declared that there was no objection to any investigation which would justify the removal of the Cherokees, but he saw no necessity for the one which was intended. He warned that the integrity of the state would be compromised if, in the investigation conducted by the federal commissioner, Georgia was represented as an enemy of the Cherokees. Admitting that his application to the President was inconsistent with Georgia's alleged right to determine such matters without intervention, Forsyth explained that he had been prompted by precedent and by a sincere desire for cooperation. He recommended that in anticipation of the verdict the General Assembly should prepare legislation for the survey and disposition of the land. Forsyth also made a statement relative to the proposed expulsion of white settlers from the disputed territory. He expressed the hope that in the interest of good relations between Georgia and the national government the Secretary of War would revoke the order before the execution date.[42]

In addition to the various Cherokee issues, Governor Forsyth was forced to contend with the problem of Creek depredations. There were continual complaints from inhabitants of the frontier counties that small bands of armed Creeks were crossing the Chattahoochee River into Georgia, where they were committing robberies and in some cases murder. Forsyth was convinced that the Indian intrusions were not part of an organized effort, but were caused by wandering individuals or groups seeking subsistence. Nevertheless, he was determined that the outrages should cease, that the perpetrators should be punished, and that the Georgians should be adequately compensated for their losses.

He instructed the county officials to obtain pertinent testimony and to apprehend the offenders if they had not fled from the state. Since there was a scarcity of white settlers in the frontier counties, he advised the militia officers of nearby areas to restrain the Indians if necessary. He was responsible for the organization of a volunteer corps in Columbia, furnishing that group with arms and ammunition from the state arsenal.

In 1828, Forsyth asked the General Assembly to enact legislation which would permit Georgia officers to disarm, arrest, and expel non-resident Indians found wandering within the limits of the state. The ensuing act decreed that no Creek could cross the Chattahoochee River into the state without a permit from the Creek agent; the pass was to specify the nature of the Indian's business and was to be valid for no longer than ten days. Georgia officials were given the authority to arrest not only the violators of the act, but also those Creeks with permits who were disturbing the peace.[43]

Forsyth, actuated by several objectives, was in almost constant correspondence with the federal government concerning the Creek depredations. In the first place, he desired the cooperation of the national government in apprehending those Indians who, after committing crimes in Georgia, had escaped to the Creek nation. Second, he wanted the administration to take precautionary measures for the protection of the frontier settlers. Finally, he wished to insure indemnification for those Georgians who had suffered from the Indian raids. In many of his endeavors, Forsyth came into acrimonious conflict with John Crowell, the Creek agent.

A few days after his inauguration, Governor Forsyth asked

Crowell for the return of an alleged offender and for the federal official's cooperation in preventing further transgressions. The Creek agent replied that he had referred the first subject to the Indian chiefs, with directions for the arrest of the Indian if he could be located. Declaring that he had no power to prohibit the Indians from going into Georgia, Crowell expressed the opinion that many of the disturbances occurred at frontier whisky shops, where it was almost impossible to ascertain whether the Creeks or the Georgians were to blame. The reply angered Forsyth, who, while censuring the Adams administration for continuing Crowell in office, asserted that "any outrages committed will be imputed to his [Crowell's] machinations or considered the result of his criminal negligence."[44]

After several months had passed, Forsyth recorded that the Indian offender whose case had been submitted to the Creek chiefs had not been delivered to the Georgia authorities. In the meantime, Crowell applied to Georgia for the arrest and punishment of a white person who had killed an Indian. Although Forsyth contended that the Creek was shot while in the act of plundering, he advised that Crowell furnish an affidavit of all the facts, together with a list of the witnesses. He promised that when the documents were received the state officials would "do their duty."[45]

The Adams administration did not agree with Forsyth's charges against Crowell; in fact, Crowell was considered one of the government's most faithful agents.[46] Influenced by Crowell's opinion, the federal administration sought to minimize the issue by declaring that many of the violent acts resulted from drunken brawls between white and Indian participants; that such occurrences, though deplorable, were inevitable. The usual reply to Forsyth's complaints contained these sentiments, plus a promise that the President, desiring to preserve peace and security on the border, would resort to powers granted him by the Intercourse Act of 1802, that the agent would attempt to restrain the Indians from trespassing into Georgia, and that any violators would be subject to the penalties provided in the measure. However, the Georgia governor was warned that Congress in passing the specified act had limited the presidential authority in matters of trespass between the two races.

The correspondence from the federal government did not satisfy Forsyth. He maintained that the Creek depredations were criminal acts and not concerned entirely with matters of trespass; therefore the administration should exercise more power than was provided by the act of intercourse. He insisted that preventing a crime was more desirable than apprehending and punishing a criminal. On numerous occasions, Governor Forsyth appealed to the national government for decisive action in restraining the Creeks from entering Georgia. Failure to act, he declared, might force the state to adopt severe measures against the Indians. He suggested that federal troops be stationed along the border; if that was impracticable, he was willing to furnish a militia force which would act under the orders of the United States government.

In July, 1828, Forsyth was gratified to learn that a small contingent of federal troops had been ordered to proceed to the Creek nation. According to instructions issued by the War Department, the stationing of soldiers near the border was to serve a two-fold purpose: to aid Crowell in preventing Indian intrusions into Georgia and to intimidate those Creeks who actively opposed emigration.

After Jackson became President, Forsyth received more active cooperation from the federal government. He asked that the Creek agent be instructed to issue permits for entrance into Georgia, the passes to be confined to those Indians who were travelling on legitimate business. The administration agreed, and even advised the troop commander to enforce the order. Following another request from Forsyth, both Crowell and the army commander were directed to cooperate with Georgia authorities and to demand of the Indian chiefs the immediate surrender of certain alleged murderers. Jackson also transmitted a message to the Alabama Creeks in which he advised the Indians to remove beyond the Mississippi River and so avoid the inevitable conflicts with the frontier Georgians. In further gestures of friendship for the state, federal reinforcements were sent to the garrison in the Creek nation and Governor Forsyth was encouraged to submit facts and opinions regarding the Indian situation.

Forsyth was energetic in his attempts to secure indemnities for the Georgians who had suffered from the Creek depredations. He commissioned Mansfield Torrance to visit the frontier for the purpose of obtaining evidence to substantiate the claims of the Georgia citizens. Once collected, the information was sent to Crowell, with a request that the claims be presented to the Creek council for payment; in addition, duplicates were furnished the War Department. In both communications Forsyth called attention to the Intercourse Act of 1802 and stated that if the Indians failed to provide compensation he expected the amount to be deducted from the next annuity due the Creeks.

He also complained to Secretary of War Peter B. Porter that in the past Crowell had refused to submit certain individual claims to the Indian chiefs unless the culprit's town was identified. Governor Forsyth, contending that such a condition was not required by the specified act, asked that the agent be so informed.[47] Forsyth's complaint was referred to Crowell, who sent his explanation to the War Department prior to receiving Forsyth's indemnity application. The agent declared that the Governor's assumption was incorrect; that the only petitions not presented to the Creeks were those withdrawn from his possession by claimants who wished them included in the Torrance investigation. He stated that, while he had suggested more positive identification of alleged offenders, he had submitted all claims other than those mentioned.

Several months later, the Creek council refused payment on the Forsyth application, whereupon the claims were referred to the War Department. The administration, after an examination of the documents, rejected the claims because of insufficient evidence. Forsyth, irritated by the decision, denied that there was a lack of authentic details. Furthermore, he declared that if the national authorities repudiated just claims, then "the promised guaranty of the United States under the law of intercourse is but a lure thrown out to the Indians to plunder and a notice to the frontier settlers to submit without the hope of redress or to take vengeance into their own hands."[48] In reply, the federal government expressed sympathy with the claimants, but refused to reconsider the verdict without more conclusive evidence. The matter was not adjusted during Forsyth's administration.

After his return, in 1829, to the United States Senate, Forsyth's interest in Indian affairs continued, particularly in those involving Georgia. He, together with Representative Richard Henry Wilde, requested that the Georgia General Assembly furnish all data pertinent to the Indian situation.[49] He supported the state's remonstrances against previous treaties between the United States and the Indian residents of Georgia. He also advocated that certain claims submitted by the Creeks be authenticated before receiving senatorial recognition and consideration. Familiar with the efforts being employed by various missionary societies and other agencies within the United States to ameliorate Indian conditions, Forsyth voiced objections to the petitions which those groups presented to Congress. He declared that the memorials, which asked that the federal government protect the Indians from oppression, were obnoxious because they "impeached the character and conduct of the Southern States."[50]

President Jackson's Indian policy incorporated the belief that the red men would improve their condition by voluntary emigration to land west of the Mississippi River where they would not be in close association with the white population or in conflict with state rights and laws. John Forsyth, in thorough accord with the idea, was active in resisting the opposition, who sought to emphasize the progress being made by the Indians in the prevailing situation.

When Theodore Frelinghuysen of New Jersey proposed that the Senate be furnished with information concerning the advancement of civilization among the southeastern Indians, Forsyth was responsible for the amendment to the resolution that included all the Indian nations within the United States. Declaring that he wished to see justice done to all Indians, the Georgia senator stated that he was agreeable to a full discussion, but was determined that the deliberations should not be limited to Indian conditions in any one section of the country. On another occasion, Frelinghuysen spoke with reference to the pending extension of Georgia laws over the Cherokees. He considered such legislation unjust to the Indians and proposed that the relevant laws be presented for the information of the United States Senate. Forsyth, in order that there might be a comparison with similar legislation, intervened and was responsible for including in the resolution the acts of all states extending jurisdiction over Indian tribes.

In April, 1830, the Senate considered a bill which proposed that the Indians be given trans-Mississippi lands and that they be removed to the western grants. Forsyth, in a speech for which he received many compliments, urged a compliance with existing treaties and an immediate removal of the Indians. He also took the opportunity to defend Georgia's decision to extend the state's authority over the Cherokees. He asserted that Georgia had conducted a full examination of the problem and intended to pursue her announced policy; that Georgia, in the exercise of her sovereign power, was not accountable to the United States Senate for the justice, wisdom, or equity of the state's laws. In 1833, the persistent Forsyth introduced a bill which was designed to procure a fulfilment of the 1802 campact.

The following year, Forsyth became involved in senatorial debate regarding a Cherokee memorial which censured President Jackson for discrimination in behalf of Georgia and which asked Congress for a redress of grievances. Not only did the Georgian object to having his state arraigned before Congress by an "insolent" Indian, but he was opposed to a petition which appealed to one branch of the government for interference in the activities of another branch. On the issue of annuity payments, Forsyth advocated that the funds be paid to the individual Cherokees rather than to the Indian council. He contended that while the tribal members became destitute the chiefs used the money for travel to Washington where they presented petitions in opposition to the President of the United States.[51]

To the end of his congressional career, Forsyth labored for a settlement of the Indian problem. While the objective was not achieved until after he had entered Jackson's cabinet, there is no doubt that his early efforts contributed to the final result. On December 29, 1835, the United States concluded a treaty with several Cherokee chiefs at New Echota, Georgia, whereby the Indians agreed to remove to lands west of the Mississippi River. Three years later, the last group of Cherokees departed from Georgia.

Over a long period of time, there was no issue to which Forsyth gave more attention than Georgia's relations with the Indians; nor did he deviate from his avowed purpose of promoting the removal of the Creeks and Cherokees from the state. On many occasions, while in Congress and in the governor's mansion, he exhibited evidence of his desire to secure justice for the Indians. But where there was a conflict with the interests of his state, justice for Georgia obliterated any concern which Forsyth had for the Indians. Forsyth's enemies criticized his aggressive tactics and declared that his objective was to gain popularity with his constituents; there is reason to believe, however, that the Georgian was sincere in his convictions. Forsyth, like Andrew Jackson, was familiar with frontier problems, and honestly believed that there could be no peace so long as the Indians and the white population resided in proximity to each other.

To Forsyth, there was no question as to the righteousness of Georgia's cause; the land belonged to the state and the Indians were only tenants. By solemn agreement, the United States had promised to remove the Indians but, while emigration had been completed in various states, Georgia had not been relieved of her Indians. In spite of his efforts to cooperate, Forsyth met with severe handicaps in his relations with the Adams administration. He fared better with the Jackson administration, although there was disagreement over the payment of claims. Of his many services in regard to Indian affairs, perhaps the most notable was his decisive leadership in the extension of Georgia's jurisdiction over the Cherokees.

During his final term in the United States Senate, Forsyth continued to speak in vindication of his state's Indian policy. He sought a delay in congressional action on Georgia's extension of authority over the Cherokees, which would permit the state, after June 1, 1830, to present an accomplished fact. He was also successful in expanding the subject of Indian affairs, so that instead of Georgia alone contending for her rights, the matter became one of general policy, involving the interests of many states and territories. Since Forsyth was the consistent champion of Georgia in the Indian controversy, it was appropriate that the state legislature should decide to give his name to one of the counties which were fashioned out of the Cherokee region.[52]

VII

Staunch Defender of Jackson

JOHN FORSYTH'S return to the United States Senate in 1829 came only a few months after the inauguration of President Andrew Jackson. In the election of the preceding year, Georgia had unanimously cast her nine electoral votes for Jackson while giving just two ballots to the successful vice-presidential candidate, John C. Calhoun. The reasons in each case are discernible. With William H. Crawford, Georgia's favorite son, no longer a presidential possibility, the majority of his adherents had favored Jackson, whose views they believed consistent with their own. On the other hand, most Georgians had refused to support Calhoun because of his past opposition to Crawford and because of his lack of consideration for what they thought were the best interests of Georgia.

Georgia's preference for Jackson and dislike for Calhoun coincided with the sentiments of the majority of Crawford supporters elsewhere in the United States. Among Jackson supporters none was more conspicuous than Martin Van Buren, the person generally credited with having managed the alliance of the Jackson-Crawford groups. This shrewd New York politician, in addition to professing principles similar to those of Jackson, recognized the expediency of being associated with the popular but aged Tennesseean. Van Buren has been described as a social favorite with both sexes because of his charming manner and intelligent, entertaining conversation.[1] Thus, both politically and socially, John Forsyth had much in common with the New Yorker. Indeed the words and tone of their correspondence give evidence that the two men were on intimate terms.[2] It would be difficult to determine how much influence, if any, Van Buren exerted over Forsyth in the Georgian's estimation of Jackson. It is a certainty, however, that Forsyth's cautious attitude became more favorable after returning to Washington in 1829. Perhaps the change was due to observation and sincere conversion; perhaps personal contact with Van Buren had its effect; perhaps there was the desire to advance Van Buren's claim to the succession; or possibly there was a combination of these reasons. But whatever the cause, Forsyth's career thereafter was characterized by a staunch support and defense of the Jackson administration and its policies.

Support of Jackson was a distinct contrast to Forsyth's views and activities during his senatorial tenure of 1818-1819. He had been a leader in efforts to censure the General for his conduct in Florida during the Seminole War.[3] Jackson's expedition into Florida, supposedly to punish the Indians for depredations along the frontier, actually developed into an attempt to wrest the territory from the Spaniards. In the course of his attack upon the Seminoles, he captured and executed two British subjects, Alexander Arbuthnot and Robert C. Ambrister. Naturally repercussions followed. While Jackson's accomplishments had made him popular with the American people, his dictatorial methods had placed the government of the United States in an awkward position with Spain and Great Britain. Had he, or had he not exceeded his authority? Upon this question there was disagreement, and Congress was determined to inquire into the matter.[4]

According to a Jackson biographer, the congressional investigations were prompted by the Clay and Crawford groups, both of which feared the General as a rival of their respective favorites for the presidency. In addition, Crawford and the Tennessean were long-time enemies.[5] Forsyth, loyal to his fellow Georgian, had shared the feeling of hostility toward Jackson. Indicative of his critical attitude was his comment that Ambrister "was executed in direct violation of the Sentence of the Court by which he was tried."[6] When Jackson was reported on his way to Washington, presumably to present his case, Forsyth anticipated that "we shall probably have some trouble with the Old Blade unless he has wisdom enough to suit his manners to his Situation."[7]

Abner Lacock of Pennsylvania proposed that the Senate investigate Jackson's conduct in Florida, but Forsyth pointed out that the upper house had no power to impeach. Nevertheless, Forsyth favored an inquiry which would result in a resolution exonerating the Senate "from a participation in the crimes that have been committed."[8] A special committee, headed by Lacock, was established for the investigation. Forsyth as a member was relentless in his efforts to discredit Jackson. John Quincy Adams declared that Forsyth's bitterness extended to such length that the committee was persuaded to charge Jackson with ulterior motives in the seizure of Pensacola, the allegation being that the General had been interested in nearby land speculation.[9] Another member of the select committee declared that of all persons he had observed, the Georgian was "the most inveterate and malignant against Jackson. . . ."[10] Forsyth's intensity of purpose was influential in the adverse report of the committee.

Over a period of years, Forsyth ceased to display intense hostility toward the military hero. His judgment became more restrained, with only a tendency toward occasional mild criticism.

In the election of 1828, Forsyth's preference for Jackson over Adams was to be expected, since the latter's participation in the Indian controversy rendered him *persona non grata*. Forsyth was confident that a change of administration would result in settlement of the Indian problem in a way satisfactory to Georgia. As to other public matters, he was less optimistic. He expressed hope for general improvement, but admitted that he was reluctant to make any further commitments until convinced of the ability of the Jackson government.[11]

Van Buren's was the only appointment to President Jackson's first cabinet that pleased Forsyth. And he disapproved of the diplomatic selections, maintaining that the ministers lacked the knowledge and skill required in handling foreign affairs. He also deplored a system which would permit choice by solicitation rather than by merit. There is strong evidence that Forsyth, despite his denial, had some expectation of being an appointee. He confided to a relative "that the publick would not have suffered if I had been called to W.[ashington] or sent to England or France."[12]

Although Forsyth was destined to change his estimation of Jackson, his attitude toward Calhoun continued to be antagonistic. Nothing gave him greater pleasure than the break which occurred between Jackson and the Vice President. Not only did the controversy serve to eliminate the South Carolinian from the succession, but it enhanced the possibility of advancement for Forsyth's friend Van Buren. One of the incidents precipitating the quarrel was the introduction of what came to be known as the

"Crawford letter." Quite by accident, Forsyth was involved in the procurement of the document.

The episode was an outgrowth of Jackson's conduct during the Seminole War. In 1828, Colonel James Alexander Hamilton, friend of Van Buren, and Major William Berkeley Lewis devised a scheme to cause a rift between Jackson and Calhoun. Hamilton was to talk with William H. Crawford concerning the proceedings of a cabinet meeting held during the Monroe administration at which there had been deliberations on condemnation of Jackson for his Florida exploits; after obtaining Crawford's views regarding whether any members had advocated punishment, Hamilton was to forward the information to Lewis.[13] In this way would the fact be revealed that Calhoun had favored a censure of Jackson.

Upon Hamilton's arrival in Georgia, he learned that Crawford was absent from home. On January 29, 1828, the New Yorker wrote to Forsyth explaining that time had not permitted him to see Crawford and requesting that the Governor secure the desired information from the absentee. Forsyth replied to Hamilton on February 8. He wrote that Crawford had authorized him to make the following disclosure: during the deliberations of the specified cabinet meeting, it was Calhoun and not Crawford who had urged the arrest and trial of Jackson.

In the spring of 1828 Hamilton revealed to Lewis the contents of the Governor's letter, but Lewis declined to mention the subject to Jackson for fear of an explosion which would endanger the General's election to the presidency. Waiting for an appropriate time, one in which Crawford's revelation might be used to injure Calhoun, Lewis did not inform Jackson of Forsyth's letter until November of the following year. In conformity with the President's request to see the letter, Lewis made a trip to Hamilton's home in New York. Hamilton refused to release the document without Forsyth's consent.

Early in December Colonel Hamilton visited Washington, where he asked Forsyth to give the President the facts concerning the Crawford conversation. The Senator at first suggested that a copy of his letter should suffice. The New Yorker refused to forward the document, explaining that propriety demanded that he (Hamilton) not be identified in the affair. His reasoning was based on his contacts with Calhoun, whose version of the cabinet meeting had differed from Crawford's. Forsyth then de-

cided that he would supply no information until Crawford had
been notified of Calhoun's contradiction and had been given an
opportunity to correct any misinterpretations found in the letter
to Hamilton. After an unexplained delay of several months Forsyth enclosed a copy of his message to Hamilton in a dispatch
which he eventually sent to Crawford.

Forsyth's letter to Crawford, dated April 16, 1830, outlined the
situation and asked if Crawford objected to his giving the information to the President. Crawford replied on April 30; with
some amplification and one correction, he confirmed the statement attributed to him by Forsyth. He denied saying that Calhoun had proposed the arrest of Jackson; instead, the South
Carolinian had recommended a reprimand. Without specific reference to the request for transmission of data to Jackson, Crawford authorized his reply to be shown to Calhoun if Forsyth so
desired.[14] Upon receipt of Crawford's letter, Forsyth forwarded a
copy to the President, to be followed a few days later by a duplicate of the 1828 letter to Hamilton. In these communications,
Forsyth carefully omitted Hamilton's name. Jackson, in turn, sent
a copy of the Crawford reply to Calhoun with a request for clarification. An extensive correspondence followed, not only between
the two executive officials, but with Forsyth and others interpos-
ing to explain their activities in the affair.

Forsyth incurred Calhoun's anger on at least two counts: first,
that he voluntarily had withheld vital information and second,
that he was an instigator in the plot to ruin Calhoun. Of the initial charge, Forsyth's transmission of Crawford's 1830 letter to
Jackson rather than to Calhoun was cited as placing the South
Carolinian at a disadvantage in the ensuing controversy. The
omission of Hamilton's name from the Crawford document was
criticized for the same reason. When Forsyth explained that the
deletion was "from respect to the personal delicacy of Major Hamilton. . . ,"[15] Calhoun replied that regardless of motive the omission was unjust and operated to prevent a fair presentation of
his case.[16] Forsyth also was criticized for neglecting to include
the Forsyth-Hamilton correspondence with the Crawford letter.
Calhoun claimed that, because of the exclusion, he was being "deprived of evidence material to my defence, and which is in the
hands of my accusers. . . ."[17]

With respect to the second charge, Calhoun realized that the
affair was a political maneuver designed to injure his relations

with the President. In the beginning, however, he was inclined to place the blame on persons other than Jackson. Forsyth's alleged suppression of information and his close association with Crawford made him a prime suspect.[18] Calhoun's insinuations drew this reply from Forsyth:

With this presumption [of a plot] I have no concern, but the circumstances under which my name is introduced by you, renders it proper that I should be distinctly informed if this charge of conspiracy against you is intended to apply to me.[19]

In his reply Calhoun expressed surprise that Forsyth should so construe his remarks as to include him in the indictment.[20]

There was a reason for Calhoun's change of tactics. A statement in Forsyth's letter, that the transmission of the Crawford message was in answer to Jackson's request for information, was interpreted by Calhoun as implicating the President, while at the same time making Forsyth only an agent. Both Forsyth and Jackson denied the accusation concerning the President's guilt, but in equivocal statements which failed to convince Calhoun.

From the available evidence it appears that Forsyth was nothing more than an instrument used by the conspirators to launch the attack on Calhoun. Although a pro-Calhoun newspaper suggested a more sinister role for the Georgian,[21] it presented no definite proof. Forsyth stated that, after writing to Hamilton, he heard nothing and thought little of the matter until approached by the New Yorker in Washington almost two years later.[22] Since Crawford's letter to Forsyth obviously was written for Jackson's perusal, the addressee was under no obligation to show it to Calhoun; the delivery of the message to the President merely constituted a compliance with Jackson's request for information. While Forsyth was apparently not an author of the conspiracy and did not wish close identification with the controversy, he made no attempt to hinder the progress of the plot against Calhoun. Once involved, however unintentionally, he recognized the partisan advantages and determined to make the most of the situation.

As a result of the break between Calhoun and Jackson, the cabinet was dissolved; when it was reconstructed, the Calhoun followers had been eliminated. In the interests of harmony, the President also had accepted the resignations of his friends Secretary of State Martin Van Buren and Secretary of War John Henry Eaton. Van Buren was particularly obnoxious to Calhoun and his adherents. Although Van Buren denied any complicity in the plot the Calhoun group rejected his protests on the ground that they came from a rival presidential aspirant.[23]

Van Buren's resignation was followed by his appointment some months later as Minister to Great Britain. Jackson nominated him after the adjournment of Congress; consequently, when the New Yorker left for London in August, 1831, his appointment had not received confirmation from the Senate. In the subsequent deliberations of the upper house, Forsyth had the opportunity of defending both Van Buren and the Jackson administration.

President Jackson submitted his nomination of Van Buren soon after Congress convened in early December. By the time it was reported out of the Senate Committee on Foreign Relations on January 10, 1832, the Calhoun-Clay-Webster faction had decided to defeat Van Buren's chances for the succession by doing what Jackson had predicted they would not dare to undertake —forcing a rejection of the appointment.[24] Their opposition, as presented to the Senate, was based on four charges against the appointee:

(1)   The instructions drawn up and signed by Mr. Van Buren as Secretary of State, under the direction of the President, and furnished to Mr. McLane, for his guidance in endeavoring to reopen the negotiation for the West Indian trade.

(2)   Making a breach of friendship between the first and second officers of the government—President Jackson and Vice-President Calhoun—for the purpose of thwarting the latter, and helping himself to the Presidency.

(3)   Breaking up the cabinet for the same purpose.

(4)   Introducing the system of "proscription" (removal from office for opinion's sake), for the same purpose.[25]

The first charge was advanced and supported by Clay, Webster, and their adherents, while the other three accusations received the attention of the Calhoun forces. Twelve hostile speakers combined to attack Van Buren's conduct as Secretary of State on the grounds that it was cowardly, corrupt, and demoralizing. Professing their distaste for having to impugn the character of so prominent and genteel a citizen, they insisted that devotion to public interests demanded that it be done.

Only four senators spoke in defense of Van Buren's nomination; of these, Forsyth presented the most able arguments. Touching with sarcasm upon the pious assertions regarding public duty, he proceeded to answer, with skill and determination, each accusation listed by the opposition. He declared that Van Buren's instructions to Louis McLane were in agreement with a subsequent act passed by Congress in 1830. The policy adopted by the Jackson administration, instead of being humiliating to the United States, had so impressed the British government as to assure reopening of the West Indian trade. With reference to the second charge, Forsyth maintained that Van Buren's public denial had never been impeached by a reputable person. As for the final two charges, Forsyth pointed out that they were based on distorted reports and that Van Buren had actually aided in keeping the cabinet together long after its usefulness had vanished.

To illustrate the untenable argument of the opposition, Forsyth stated that certain political groups attributed to Van Buren total responsibility for any misfortunes suffered by the United States during the Jackson administration. The Georgian declared that he was not asking for magnanimous and courteous treatment such as Van Buren had accorded his rivals—he was demanding nothing more than simple justice. During the course of his remarks, Forsyth defended the Union party of South Carolina and denounced those persons who would establish or patronize a partisan press for the purpose of disseminating scandal and deception.[26] In spite of his deft presentation of facts, Forsyth's speech was of no avail. Van Buren's appointment was rejected by a count of 24 to 23, with Vice-President Calhoun casting the deciding vote.

Reaction to Forsyth's speech corresponded to party affiliation. The *United States' Telegraph* showed its rancor by stating that "respect for the body of which that gentleman is a member inhibits our speaking of him as his conduct merits."[27] The friendly newspapers applauded Forsyth generously. Proclaiming his address as the most outstanding of the occasion, they emphasized that he had exposed the intrigue as one based on personal revenge and political hatred. Forsyth, informing Van Buren of the result, expressed his opinion of several opposition speakers: Robert Young Hayne had damaged his reputation, while George Poindexter, Gabriel Moore, and Stephen Decatur Miller had "no character to lose."[28]

There were two repercussions to Forsyth's speech. The Georgian's address contained a statement that one of Jackson's former cabinet members voluntarily had repeated a confidential conversation which he had had with the President. The assertion precipitated an exchange of several letters between Forsyth and Representative John Branch of North Carolina, ex-Secretary of the Navy and a Calhoun advocate. When Forsyth was asked if his offensive remark applied to Branch, he replied that he did not know the guilty person's identity. Branch then admitted that he was the official referred to and demanded that the Georgian repudiate his charge. After consulting with his friends, Forsyth agreed with them that he had placed an unwarranted interpretation upon the nature of the presidential discussion, and he withdrew his accusation. Yet, in so doing, by underscoring the word "confidential"[29] he indicated disapproval of a person who would disclose official information however classified.

The second encounter was a direct exchange between Forsyth and Calhoun on the floor of the Senate. In his denunciation of individuals who would establish and support a party newspaper for evil purposes, the Georgian was interrupted by Calhoun. The Vice-President asked if the speaker alluded to him. When Forsyth indignantly questioned Calhoun's authority to intervene, the latter replied that so direct an inference gave him the right to make inquiry. Forsyth denied the right and protested that, if necessary, he would appeal to the Senate for a ruling on a point of order. The Vice-President declined the challenge, merely remarking that if intended for him there was no foundation for the allusion. In describing the affair, a contemporary reported that Forsyth "hated Calhoun, and at times was at no pains to conceal it in debate."[30]

Van Buren's rejection as Minister to Great Britain assured his nomination for the vice-presidency in 1832. The mortification inflicted upon him not only aroused public sympathy, but brought additional support from Jackson. When the Senate's verdict was announced, Thomas Hart Benton of Missouri predicted the New Yorker's election to the nation's second highest office. Previously, the President had prophesied the same. Jackson regarded the Senate action in rejecting Van Buren as a personal insult, which would be avenged at the polls through the election of Van Buren as successor to Calhoun.[31] Van Buren, in England, received various suggestions from his friends as to when he should return. After careful consideration, he determined that it was to his best interests to remain out of the United States until the Democratic party convention had made nominations. Consequently, he planned a tour of Europe, which would delay his arrival in New York until July 5, 1832.[32]

Forsyth was one of the friends who advised Van Buren on the best course to follow. He suggested immediate return and election to the Senate, so that Van Buren would have the opportunity of facing his accusers. Forsyth thought that Van Buren should be offered the vice-presidential nomination and that he should reflect seriously as to advantages and disadvantages. The possibility of the aged President's death rendered it desirable that Van Buren be in a position to succeed to the vacancy. On the other hand, Van Buren's candidacy would increase the virulence of the campaign and raise the hopes of the opposition, who considered Van Buren's association a means of defeating the Jackson ticket.[33]

The Democratic party held its convention in Baltimore, May 21-23, 1832. Jackson received a unanimous endorsement for re-election, while Van Buren defeated two candidates for the vice-presidential nomination. John Forsyth attended the convention as a member of the Georgia delegation, which also included the United States representatives Augustin Smith Clayton, Thomas Flournoy Foster, Wiley Thompson, and James Moore Wayne. In the absence of Georgia's four remaining congressional members, these five individuals cast the state's eleven votes for the eventual nominees. Their choice of Van Buren was criticized by some Georgia newspapers because he had favored the tariff of 1828. One of the journals concentrated the attack on Forsyth, evidently considering his influence among the Georgia delegation predominant.[34]

During 1832, congressional attention was directed to the question of re-chartering the Second Bank of the United States. Forsyth participated in the deliberations and in subsequent debate on related issues, generally defending Jackson's policies. Forsyth had advocated a national bank in 1814, as the best method of obtaining funds for the prosecution of the war. He had favored the establishment of the Bank in 1816, not as a necessity, but as a measure of convenience in the restoration of a sound currency. With the passage of time, however, Forsyth came to the conclusion that the Bank, although beneficial in some respects, had become a serious menace to the welfare of the nation. Consequently, he was prepared to oppose a renewal of the institution's existing charter. He would vote for the authorization of a national bank, properly controlled.[35]

The President feared the dangers of the Bank's power. Controlled by eastern and foreign capitalists, the institution exerted a practical monopoly over the currency and credit of the United States; furthermore, it gave political influence to the wealthy classes. Convinced that depriving the Bank of its objectionable features would not be a satisfactory solution, Jackson decided against re-incorporation. At the same time, he realized the importance of a tactful approach; otherwise, there was the likelihood of a party division. Van Buren's objection to renewal was to be found in the rivalry between New York City and Philadelphia. Each wanted to be the financial capital of the nation. Elimination of the Bank, with its headquarters in Philadelphia, would promote the banking and business operations in New York.[36]

On January 9, 1832, George Mifflin Dallas of Pennsylvania presented a memorial to the Senate in which the Bank's president, Nicholas Biddle, requested a renewal of the charter. Despite the fact that the Bank's charter did not expire until 1836, Biddle had taken the advice of the Clay supporters to precipitate action. Their reasoning was based on the mistaken idea that a presidential veto would be unpopular with the electorate: the best interests of the Bank would be served by a request for renewal prior to the 1832 election; a congressional approval, coupled with executive rejection, would diminish Jackson's chances for re-election; regardless of the outcome in the contest for the presidency, the election would produce a majority in Congress sufficient to override a veto. Following Dallas's presentation, the matter was referred to a select committee, with the Pennsylvanian being appointed chairman. A bill for re-charter was reported out of committee on March 13, and submitted to the Senate for debate on May 22, 1832.

In the meantime, Thomas Hart Benton had devised a plan in support of the administration. Realizing that the Bank advocates had an adequate majority in each house for passage of the bill, he decided upon the employment of obstructionist tactics: an attack upon the evils of the institution would not only postpone congressional approval, but also would convince the voters that the veto should be sustained. A proposal for the appointment of an investigating committee in the House[37] met with approval, the Bank's friends having no desire to arouse suspicion through denial of a charter provision. The methods used in the Senate were slightly different. According to Benton,

A great many amendments and inquiries were prepared to be offered in the Senate, all of them proper, or plausible, recommendable in themselves, and supported by acceptable reasons; which the friends of the bank must either answer, or reject without answer; and so incur odium.[38]

The Missourian led the assault, aided by various administration adherents.

Although Forsyth did not speak as often as others during this phase of the debate, his efforts were employed in the diverting procedure. Showing less animosity toward the Bank than Benton, he appeared intent on alleviating the tension between the party factions. While he might seem conciliatory at times, there was no question as to his position on the matter. Even before the memorial was written, Biddle was advised that he could not expect Forsyth's support.[39] During the Senate deliberations, Forsyth made inquiries, proposed changes, and voted in favor of amendments. In June, when the original bill for renewal passed the Senate by a vote of 28 to 20, his ballot was cast with the minority. Following approval by the House of Representatives, the measure was vetoed by Jackson and returned to the Senate. Again Forsyth's status was clear; he voted with those who managed to sustain the veto.

Jackson was not content with a partial victory over the Bank and after his re-election prepared to curb the institution's power for the remaining period of its existence. Otherwise, he believed that the Bank, through loans, might bribe congressmen into voting for a charter despite his veto; also, through subsidies, the press might be employed to condition public opinion in favor of a re-charter.[40] In pursuance of his plan, the President decided that during adjournment of Congress the Bank should be deprived of its custody of government deposits. On September 18, 1833, there was read to the cabinet a paper in which Jackson gave his reasons for transfer of the public funds to certain state banks. He cited malpractices of the Bank of the United States and the necessity of establishing a new system prior to the Bank's dissolution.

Two days later, the Washington *Globe* announced the change, to begin October 1. After that date, the newspaper explained, no further government deposits would be made with the Bank of the United States; however, federal funds already in possession of the institution would remain, to be disbursed at regular intervals until exhausted.

On December 3, 1833, Jackson submitted his annual message to the new session of Congress. Discussing the withdrawal of deposits, Jackson accused the Bank of being a permanent political machine attempting to dominate public opinion through fear and distress. He indicted the institution for efforts to create a panic through curtailment of loans, the objective of the Bank being to insure a public demand for re-charter. Admittedly disagreeing with a resolution from the preceding House of Representatives, the President questioned the financial condition of the Bank and contended that the government funds were not safe in its custody. Secretary of the Treasury Roger Brooke Taney, in a subsequent report, presented his reasons for withholding deposits from the Bank of the United States. Justification for the action was based on expediency more than on alleged insolvency. Taney defended his right to order the removal by citing the Bank charter. It gave the secretary of the treasury full authority provided he inform Congress of his reasons; it made no mention of the explanations being subject to legislative confirmation.[41]

Senate opposition to removal of the deposits was led by Henry Clay, who used Taney's report to inaugurate the attack. Disagreeing with the Secretary's interpretation of authority, the Kentucky Senator asserted that the provisions requiring submission of reasons carried with them the intention of congressional investigation and decision. Upon his suggestion, the Senate consented to a special consideration of Taney's report so that the members might determine whether cessation of deposits was justified. Clay then proposed a resolution relating to Jackson's report to the cabinet of September 18, which had been publicized in the newspapers. The resolution demanded that the President inform the Senate if such a document was genuine and, if so, that he transmit a copy of it.

John Forsyth, who was to bear the brunt of the defense, challenged Clay's proposal. Declaring that there could be no doubt concerning the authenticity of the document, Forsyth asked the purpose of such an unusual requisition. When Clay resorted to an ambiguous reply, Forsyth declared that cabinet conferences, being of a confidential nature, did not come within the official purview of the Senate. Since publication of Jackson's report did not alter the situation, Forsyth inquired what legitimate use could be made of the document once it was acquired by the Senate. If it was to be made the subject of debate, the paper already was accessible.

Revealing the strategy planned by the Jacksonians, Forsyth conceded that the House of Representatives had the power to obtain the document for use as evidence in impeachment proceedings. He remarked that, if impeachment of the President was intended, it should have originated in the lower house rather than in the Senate. Forsyth declared that the resolution was designed to force the House of Representatives to institute impeachment charges, with the knowledge that the President had been prejudged by the Senate.

Forsyth, "with his suave courtesy, which was not always as innocent as it seemed . . . ,"[42] argued a good case for the administration forces. However, the opposition possessed a majority in the Senate and the resolution was adopted by a vote of 23 to 18.[43] Jackson's reply was read the following day, December 12, 1833. In dignified language, the President stated that the Senate had no authority to make such a demand on a coordinate and independent governmental agency. He was willing to cooperate with the legislature in the proper performance of its duties; he intended, however, to maintain the constitutional guarantees of the executive department. In view of his sense of self-respect and because of the constitutional rights bestowed upon the executive branch of the government, he had no choice but to refuse compliance with the resolution. There the matter rested until after Christmas.

On December 26, 1833, Clay introduced two resolutions, which were to hold the Senate's attention for three months. Although they were amended during the course of the deliberations, the substance of the proposals remained essentially the same. The first resolution, a censure of the President for his activities in the deposit affair, stated that Jackson had assumed unconstitutional and dangerous powers. The second, a denunciation of the Secretary of the Treasury, declared that his transmitted reasons for removal of funds were neither sufficient nor satisfactory. Clay's speech in support of the resolutions extended over a period of three days. Scrutinizing Jackson's entire presidential record, the Senator from Kentucky delivered an arraignment against despotism. With a warning that concentration of power was passing into the hands of one person, he appealed for Congress to apply an immediate and effective check.

Calhoun and Webster joined Clay in the attack on the administration. Forsyth responded on January 27-28, 1834,[44] in an address which caused one newspaper to comment on his "intimate . . . knowledge of facts which would only be the result of laborious research."[45] Forsyth denounced the form and substance of Clay's resolutions. He insisted that, instead of being corrective and legislative, they were censorial and vindictive. He defended the actions of Jackson and Taney, and condemned those of the Bank of the United States. Although the latter had professed abstention from politics, it had financed newspapers and publication of speeches in efforts to prevent the re-election of the President. Nevertheless, the people had not only returned Jackson to office, but also had elected a pro-Jackson majority to the House of Representatives. Having become identified with the opposition, the Bank could expect no preferential treatment from the victors. The removal of the deposits was not a retaliatory measure, said Forsyth. The President, who took full responsibility, directed the move because of the impending charter expiration.

Forsyth denied that Taney had deliberately misinterpreted information contained in his report or had willfully neglected to supply the Senate with available clarification. Taney's statement that the deposits could be removed regardless of the Bank's stability was not a new opinion. Forsyth produced a document written in 1830 by George McDuffie, a Calhoun adherent, in which the author had expressed a similar view. The charge that Taney had usurped the powers rightfully belonging to the treasurer of the United States also was claimed to be without foundation. According to precedent, the order designating state banks as depositories was within the jurisdiction of the secretary of the treasury. Taney, in issuing the directive, had exercised the same power as had Albert Gallatin, James Madison's Secretary of the Treasury, following the dissolution of the First Bank of the United States in 1811. With reference to Gallatin's action, Forsyth reminded the opposition, not without a touch of sarcasm, that

no one seems to have considered that there was any dangerous encroachment upon the duties of the Treasurer, or on usurpation, any exertion of undelegated powers; it was reserved for the acuteness of the present day to make these important discoveries.[46]

In refuting the various charges of executive usurpation, Forsyth maintained that presidential intervention was duly warranted; in fact, Jackson would have been derelict in his duty if he had not acted. He ridiculed the idea that the Bank charter made no provision for executive control over the matter of government deposits. The secretary of the treasury, though required to make a report to Congress, was not independent of the presi-

dent, who possessed the power to remove the official. Congress
had been aware of this and had intended that the President
exercise ultimate authority.

Forsyth placed emphasis upon what he considered sufficient
justification for the President's entire procedure against the Bank:
the policy had the approbation of a majority of the American people. At the same time, Forsyth showed courage in admitting that
his personal views had not coincided completely with those of
Jackson. While in accord with the President in opposition to
charter renewal, Forsyth stated his preference for a national bank
with proper restrictions upon its power. He predicted the
re-establishment of a national bank at some future date, and considered the present more auspicious than a time of dire necessity. He would have advised a delay in removal of deposits until the new House of Representatives had had an opportunity to
make known its position on the Bank charter. Then the removal
order would have been issued with the knowledge of congressional inability to pass a recharter bill over a presidential veto.
Forsyth, despite the difference of opinion, declared that he was
willing to abide by the wishes of the electorate and suggested
that the opposition do the same.

There was varied newspaper reaction to Forsyth's address.
The *United States' Telegraph* asked why Forsyth was not denounced by the administration press because of his views. It
praised Forsyth's candor and suggested that he was speaking the
sentiments of many Jackson advocates who preferred to remain
noncommittal. Another newspaper expressed the hope that Forsyth's views might serve to influence the administration. Still another criticized Forsyth's views but admitted that he was among
the administration's most able speakers, being second only to
William Cabell Rives of Virginia.[47] Still another declared that
the Senate and crowded gallery were so absorbed in the address that on occasion "you might have heard a pin drop."[48]

In a later speech, Forsyth rebuked the opposition for its alleged duplicity. He asserted that the quarrel over disposition
of the Bank was incidental, and that the real purpose of the
Clay forces was to gain political power. If the Bank was sustained,
then the President's conduct would be judged tyrannical and arbitrary. As a consequence, the opponents of the administration
expected to win possession of the government at the end of Jackson's term. This analysis of the situation was made for public
consumption. While true, it scarcely was designed to win votes

from the anti-administration bloc. As Benton commented, with reference to the first of Clay's resolutions, "it was passed by the same majority that would have voted for it on the first day of its introduction."[49] Both resolutions of censure received Senate approval on March 28, 1834. In each case, Forsyth voted with the minority.

Jackson did not tranquilly accept the condemnation of the Senate. Neither the President nor the House of Representatives was formally advised of the resolutions. Nevertheless, Jackson submitted a protest, read before the Senate on April 17, the principal thesis of which was the same as that advanced earlier by Forsyth. The censure was analogous to impeachment charges, which only the House of Representatives had authority to institute. Furthermore, the Senate action placed the President at a disadvantage in that he was given no opportunity to present a formal defense. Jackson concluded with a request that his message be recorded in the journal of the Senate. On April 21, the Senate received a supplementary message from Jackson, which was intended to clarify the protest. After the reading of each of the presidential communications, Poindexter recommended that the Senate refuse official receipt. During the debates which followed, he offered other resolutions to the effect that the protest was a violation of the Senate's prerogative.

Forsyth spoke frequently in an attempt either to prevent or to discredit the project. He chided his opponents for their inconsistency, asking to be informed how the Senate could condemn a message which it refused to recognize. He denied that the Constitution gave either house the right to pass such a censorial resolution. Since the Senate had recorded its censure, justice demanded that the President's defense be entered in the journal; only by such action would a fair presentation be made to the people and to posterity. As for the Senate's past conduct, Forsyth "was of opinion that the Senate had travelled beyond the bounds of propriety, and deserved—what he believed would, in due time, be meted to them—a sentence of condemnation by the people."[50]

Realizing that the anti-administration group possessed the necessary votes to pass the Poindexter resolutions, Forsyth resorted to a subtle move in an effort to guarantee the recording of Jackson's protest. He suggested a change in the wording of the resolutions so as to include the content of the President's messages. The opposition was on the alert, however, and Poindexter

replied that such an amendment would make the resolutions ineffectual. To counteract Forsyth's initiative, members of the anti-
administration bloc insisted that his recommendation was out of
order. Van Buren, the presiding officer, disagreed; whereupon,
Poindexter appealed from the decision. The Senate, giving further indication of its anti-Jackson feeling, reversed the Vice-
President's ruling.[51]

Forsyth's next move was equally ingenious. He presented two
amendments which differed somewhat from his initial proposal.
The first was a simple recommendation that the President's protest be entered in the Senate's journal. The second declared that
since each senator was responsible only to the people of this state,
the latter should have an opportunity to judge the Senate's competency in passing the censure resolution. As an aid in this direction, the amendment prescribed that the following documents be
sent to each governor for transmission to his respective legislature:
an authenticated copy of the censure, the roll call on the measure,
the President's protest, and Forsyth's present resolutions.[52]

These proposals constituted good tactics. If his resolutions
passed, which was not likely, the people would sustain the administration senators. If the recommendations were defeated, the
impression would prevail that the opposition senators were apprehensive of subjecting their actions to the scrutiny of their constituents. The anti-administration forces chose the latter
alternative. On May 6, 1834, Forsyth's amendments were disapproved by the Senate, the vote being 25 to 17. The following
day, Poindexter's resolutions were adopted by a vote of 27 to 16.
In both cases, the ballots were cast according to faction.

During the months of debate on the various aspects of the
Bank question, Congress was the recipient of countless memorials
and petitions concerning economic conditions. Many of the documents, inspired by Bank sympathizers, urged renewal of the
charter and restoration of the deposits as the only means of alleviating a crisis caused by the administration. Forsyth spent considerable time in rebuttal when these denunciatory papers were
read and endorsed by his Senate opponents. He admitted that
adverse conditions existed in many sections of the nation, but expressed belief that the distress was both temporary and exagger-
ated. Denying that removal of deposits was responsible for the
situation, he placed the blame upon the Bank because of its
propaganda and its policy of credit contraction. In his words,
"there was a considerable embarrassment in the country, in conse-

quence of the bank refusing to do what it had been in the habit of doing."[53]

Forsyth stated that he was not impressed by the numerous names affixed to the distress documents, for many of the same signatures appeared in both memorials and counter-memorials. Another fact to be considered was the natural disposition of human beings to offer complaints. Furthermore, he maintained that the memorials against the administration were not indicative of the opinion held by most people in the United States. Those who were satisfied with the state of affairs were not as likely to make their sentiments known to Congress as was the opposite group.

An incident which occurred during discussions of public distress will illustrate Forsyth's intensity of purpose in defense of the Jackson administration. Angered by Poindexter's inference of administration duplicity, Forsyth stated that certain of his statements were not true. Poindexter, choosing to disregard the implication that he might have been misinformed, declared that if his veracity was being questioned, he would demand satisfaction. When Forsyth refused to retract his assertion, Clay intervened with the request that both senators reconsider the matter and adjust their difficulty. His attempt at reconciliation was unsuccessful, and the Senate met in secret session following the close of the day's business.[54] The *Senate Journal* recorded the result of the meeting by saying ". . . at the instance of several members, mutual, satisfactory, and honorable explanations took place."[55]

Forsyth became involved also in the investigation of the Post Office Department. The opposition accused Postmaster General William Taylor Barry of borrowing money without the authority of Congress, of partiality in assigning and paying mail contracts, and of general ineptitude in office. The Senate Committee on the Post Office and Post Roads recommended the printing of fifteen thousand extra copies of its report containing these accusations.

Realizing that the first session of the Twenty-third Congress was drawing to a close, Forsyth resorted to delaying tactics. He immediately objected to the increase of publication as unnecessary and expensive. Newspaper accounts, said he, would furnish sufficient circulation and thereby prevent an excessive spending of the public money. Besides, he argued, the Senate's contingent fund was not intended for such use, the publications being, in effect, electioneering documents. Forsyth conceded that Barry had negotiated loans for the department in anticipation of congressional approval. While such action was a violation of the law, he pointed out the possibility that the Postmaster General was prompted by necessity, in which case Barry was following customary procedure.[56]

On several occasions, the opposition attempted to place partial or full blame upon Jackson for Barry's action by intimating that the President was familiar with the deplorable conditions in the Post Office Department and yet had retained Barry. Forsyth made the cryptic reply that the President knew his responsibility and would act accordingly. He expressed amazement that Jackson should be criticized for inactivity in the affairs of the Post Office Department after the Senate had condemned him for interference with Treasury Department matters.

Forsyth was merely laying the foundation for a proposal which he offered, to replace a resolution submitted by the opposition. The latter's resolution provided for continuation of the investigation by an interim committee, the avowed purpose being to expedite business by having information available immediately upon the re-convening of Congress. Forsyth suggested that the proper course would be to refer the subject to the President, thereby making him responsible for conducting the examination. The anti-administration clique refused to be diverted, and its resolution was adopted by the Senate.

Forsyth and other administration spokesmen were more successful with respect to postponement of resolutions based on evidence already compiled. The Senate voted on only the first of several recommendations, the one in which the existing loan contracts were declared illegal and void. The charge was so evident that even Forsyth joined in the unanimous approval of the resolution.[57]

John Forsyth's views on federal aid to internal improvements changed from support in his early years to opposition in the 1830's. In 1816, he considered internal improvements by the national government necessary in order to improve the military defense of the United States. As a member of Congress, he voted in favor of the Bonus Bill,[58] the General Survey Bill,[59] the measure authorizing federal subscription to stock in the Chesapeake and Delaware Canal Company, and the bill appropriating $150,000 for extension of the Cumberland Road.

Following his return to Washington in 1829, Forsyth's record indicates that his views on internal improvements were more limited as to what constituted national welfare. He opposed the authorization of the following federal expenditures: subscription to stock in the Louisville and Portland Canal Company; $10,400 for a canal from the Atlantic Ocean to the Gulf of Mexico; $40,000 for navigation improvement on Back Creek; subscription to stock in the Maysville, Washington, Paris, and Lexington Turnpike Company; subscription to stock in the Baltimore and Ohio Railroad Company; and $30,000 for navigation improvement on the Cumberland River. Seldom offering explanation for his vote on internal improvement bills, Forsyth stated that his disapproval of the Florida canal project was based on a conviction "that the hope of obtaining water by filtration was futile in the extreme."[60]

On two occasions, Forsyth favored federal subsidy measures: $4,500 for river and harbor improvements at St. Marks, Florida, and subscription to stock in the Washington and Rockville Turnpike Company. The first he regarded as advantageous to both section and nation; the other, he regarded as being in the interest of national security. The second measure received Jackson's veto, which the Senate was unable to overrule.

Forsyth's absence prevented a recording of his vote. Neither did the Georgian participate in the decision which sustained the President's veto of the Maysville Bill; the verdict rendered by the House of Representatives precluded Senate action. However, he had already signified his opposition to the bill. He agreed with Jackson's contention that the measure was solely of a local nature. Forsyth believed the bill offered no contribution to the nation's welfare.

A seat in the Senate of the early 1830's was not comfortable for members who spoke in favor of the administration. Yet, John Forsyth acquitted himself well. A person of less talent would have been unequal to the task of combatting the onslaughts of a powerful opposition. In tribute to his prowess, one newspaper expressed "regret that no Reporters to the Senate, have been found competent to convey to the public the galling irony and satire—the vehement and eloquent denunciation, by which he has kept at bay the whole pack of Bank orators. . . ."[61] A keen analyst, he frequently placed the anti-administration forces at a disadvantage by exposing their ulterior motives. A master of parliamentary technique, he often used finesse in his attempt to offset the numerical strength of his opponents.

In spite of his obvious loyalty to Jackson, Forsyth made no effort at evasion when he disagreed with the President. While some of the administration adherents chose to remain silent, Forsyth exposed himself to attack by proclaiming his divergent opinion. His candid remarks concerning dissent were stated not only in the Senate, but also in his correspondence. Replying to a presidential commendation of his services, Forsyth assured Jackson that "I will support you to the best of my power when I think you right and oppose you without asperity when I shall be unfortunate enough to think that you have mistaken the true path."[62]

During debate on various phases of the Bank question, Forsyth showed sincerity of purpose, exhaustive preparation, and tremendous tenacity. Possessing confidence in Taney, expressed when Taney first entered Jackson's cabinet as Attorney General, he considered the attack on the administration entirely unwarranted, and the actions of the Bank advocates detrimental to the best interests of the United States. Consequently, Forsyth's defense of the administration might be termed a crusade. On the Bank issue alone, he spoke to the Senate more than seventy times. Amos Kendall, confidant of the President, declared that Forsyth's exertions in this contest were responsible for the latter's appointment to the office of Secretary of State.[63]

VIII

~~~~~~~~~~~~~~~~~~~

Tariff and Nullification

~~~~~~~~~~~~~~~~~~~

WHEN JOHN FORSYTH relinquished the governorship in 1829, political parties in Georgia were on the threshold of re-alignment. By this time, it was apparent that in the minds of Georgians national affairs affecting the state were beginning to overshadow personalities. The voters, on occasion, began to concentrate on measures rather than on men. Among the national problems exciting interest, none was more agitating than the tariff, which was to be responsible for the elimination of old party designations and for the development of new political groups within the state.

During the War of 1812, Georgia considered domestic manufacture both expedient and patriotic. With the end of the conflict and the revival of foreign trade, Georgians, somewhat passively, accepted the prevalent nationalistic sentiment of protection to infant industries, most of which were located in the northeastern section of the United States. The tariff act of 1816 aroused little state interest, and only a small amount of protest was heard in 1820 when Congress was discussing tariff revision. By 1824, how-ever, Georgians had come to the conclusion that the protective system was harmful to the best interests of the South. In their opinion a high tariff benefited northern industries at the expense of the southern people, who were compelled to pay increased prices for manufactured articles while the sale of their own agri-cultural products suffered in comparison. The measure of 1824 found no favor with Georgia's congressional delegation; mass meetings, resolutions and memorials from the state legislature, and declarations from various congressmen left no doubt as to Georgia's opposition to the successive tariff acts.

Georgia's political parties differed regarding a remedy for the situation. The dominant faction among the Troupers, with their strong state rights principles, opposed Jackson for his nationalistic tendencies and sought to capitalize on the tariff agitation through organization of an anti-administration party. A minority of this group either accepted or came dangerously close to sanctioning nullification. Without advocating secession as a solution for the current problem, the majority declared that a sovereign state had the right to secede. They asked for joint action through a general convention of the southern states. None of these views proved acceptable to the conservative wing, of which Forsyth was a member. In the meantime, the Clarkites, for the most part, became supporters of Jackson; opposed to any movement which might jeopardize the Union, they believed that it was only a matter of time before the tariff issue would be adjusted through normal legislative procedure. By gradual transition, the conservative Troup element associated with the Clark majority, while the anti-Jackson Clarkites joined the Troupers.[1]

With party lines shattered, new political coalitions emerged which were destined to become identified with two distinct national parties. The first step in the evolution came with the realignment on the state level. There were many exceptions in both factions, but in general the Troupers formed the nucleus for the State Rights party, while the Clarkites did the same for the Union party. Soon a second modification took place and again there was lack of consistency. Generally speaking, however, the State Rights members became Whigs and the Unionists became Democrats.[2]

As a member of the House of Representatives, John Forsyth was prompted by sectional interest to comment on two aspects of the tariff of 1816. During consideration of the duty on sugar, he recommended that a tax of five cents per pound be established for importation of the product. He explained that enactment of the high impost would serve as inducement for an extensive sugar cultivation in Georgia. Despite his appeal, the proposal was defeated. Forsyth also called attention to the avowed primary purpose of the measure: to "give the necessary and proper protection and support to the agriculture, manufactures, and commerce of the country."[3] Claiming that manufacturing in his section was being denied federal protection, he protested against the injustice of taxing Southerners for the benefit of eastern industrialists.[4] His assertion indicated an early realization of the ill effect of the protective policy upon the South. Forsyth voted against the 1816 tariff measure and also the 1824 measure.

Forsyth left no doubt as to his views concerning the tariff act of 1828. His gubernatorial message to the Georgia legislature on November 4, 1828, contained a sharp denunciation of the so-called "tariff of abominations." Classifying the measure as an embodiment of discrimination and perversion of power, he pledged every legitimate effort to insure its repeal. In his estimation, the answer to the problem was not to be found in retaliation through discriminatory state excises; such procedure was neither judicious nor constitutional. Declaring that public opinion was the force which would guarantee repeal, he recommended that the General Assembly submit a solemn protest to the United States Senate and a strong memorial to the states which favored the protective system. To afford relief while the iniquity was being rectified, he suggested to the legislators and to the people certain expedients, such as reduction of state taxes, strict economy, boycott of eastern manufactured articles except necessities, substitution of domestic manufactures, and diversification and increase of agricultural pursuits.[5]

Forsyth's tariff pronouncement received considerable newspaper commendation. By outlining an explicit and prudent course, he had placed an effective check upon radical tendencies within his state. If his plan failed to bring repeal or modification, it would then be time to consider more extreme measures. However, confidence was expressed that the latter expedient would not be necessary. Forsyth's opposition to a Georgia excise was regarded as more satisfactory to the Clarkites than to the Troupers; hence he was praised for his independence of party affiliation.[6] A South Carolina journal, however, disagreed with the general impression. Declaring that Forsyth showed a lack of familiarity with both parties and also with human nature, the Columbia *Telescope* complained that such a conservative program would have no persuasive effect upon tariff exponents, who represented a majority of the nation's population. Forsyth was portrayed as advocating a policy which would lead to the ruin of southern interests; his advice was described as "insipid mawkish trash. . . ."[7]

Forsyth's recommendations met with such approval by the legislature that, within a few weeks, he was able to transmit Georgia's protest to the presiding officer of the United States Senate. At the same time, he sent a copy to the two senators, explaining that he wished them to be well-informed on a subject of probable discussion in the upper house. He also ordered Georgia's remonstrance printed in pamphlet form and distributed to both tariff and anti-tariff states. In his second annual message to the state legislature, delivered on November 3, 1829, Forsyth reported transmission of the protest but noted that the Senate had made no attempt to repeal or modify the act of 1828. He expected favorable action at the approaching session of Congress, however, for the law was displeasing to the tariff advocates. "Although deeply injurious to us of the South," said he, "it has as yet poured no golden showers into the lap of those for whose benefit it was especially intended."[8] When Forsyth returned to the Senate, he presented a resolution from the Georgia legislature instructing the state's congressional delegation to exert maximum effort and close co-operation in effecting a complete revocation of the 1828 act.

Serious congressional deliberation on the tariff began in 1832, but strange as it may seem, the first debates did not occur in the House of Representatives, which has the constitutional authority to originate revenue bills. On January 9, 1832, Henry Clay initiated the discussion in the Senate by introducing a proposal, which he placed in the category of "resolution," to instruct the Committee on Finance to report a bill which would abolish the tariff on non-competitive articles with the exception of duties on wines and silks, which would be reduced. A few days later, Robert Y. Hayne of South Carolina voiced his opposition, declaring that the proposal would afford no actual relief to the South, and indeed was unconstitutional. Hayne suggested an amendment providing for a tariff based on revenue only, to be established after liquidation of the public debt and following a gradual reduction of duties on competitive foreign manufactures.[9]

When the debate developed into a general discussion of the protective system, Forsyth suggested that both proposals be submitted for committee consideration. If this was inadvisable, the Senate should delay proceedings on the subject until receipt of a proper bill from the other house. Premature discussion of the protective principle would merely aggravate the feelings of members of the upper house. Expressing hope for a satisfactory settlement of the controversy during the current session, he declared that attainment of success would require maximum justice and moderation, two attributes which should be characteristic of the United States Senate. He wanted no misunderstanding as to the

South's determination, asserting that the opponents of protection "will fight from post to post, and die in the last ditch."[10] The latter remark drew a retort from Clay to the effect that any threat against the system would find the protectionists prepared to meet the attack. Equal to the occasion, Forsyth responded, "The gentleman from Kentucky . . . has assumed the amiable character of a defender. But, in fact, he is himself the assailant. . . ."[11]

As the weeks passed, the debate continued. During the final days of February, Forsyth spoke for more than two hours in opposition to Clay's proposal. On March 22, 1832, he stated that he was prepared to vote to refer the resolutions to committee. He explained, however, that his purpose was to obtain a committee report, which would afford a better opportunity to argue the demerits of protection. While he did not expect the report to be favorable to the South, he assumed that the Senate would not pass a bill which retained the worst features of the protective system. Forsyth's position drew extreme criticism from Hayne. He censured Forsyth for alleged inconsistency, for supporting the amendment at the beginning of the discussion and later showing preference for the original resolution, for injuring the amended proposal by predicting its defeat, and for denouncing the amendment as an extreme measure.

Forsyth conceded that Hayne's proposal contained merit, but he repeated the assertion that there was no likelihood of its receiving senatorial approval. Forsyth vindicated his conduct, as follows:

In declaring, at the commencement of the discussion, that he would "die in the last ditch," he did not mean to make a declaration of war against the Government. He would, indeed, oppose the protective system by all fair, legal, and constitutional means. He would go that far, but not one step farther. Should the majority overrule us—should the system be continued—he would not, on that account, sanction any course of opposition that would endanger the Union, or be contrary to the spirit of the constitution. God forbid that, on account of any erroneous legislation, he should be betrayed into measures that would tend to the destruction of the constitution. He would continue to urge upon Congress, in every proper and constitutional form, the necessity and propriety of an abandonment of a policy which, to a portion of the Union, is odious and oppressive; and he would rely upon the intelligence of the people, and upon their sense of justice, for an ultimate adjustment of the tariff, upon fair, equal, and constitutional principles. [He] . . . admitted that he did not, at present, expect full justice from the majority; but did the Senator from South Carolina himself expect it? It was for that reason he was willing to vote for the reference, as the best course to be adopted, under the circumstances in the case.[12]

Hayne asked Forsyth if he was accusing him or his friends of disloyalty to the United States and its Constitution. Forsyth replied that he intended no reflection upon the Hayne group; instead,

he had reference merely to a certain doctrine which had been propagated at the South, which he believed to be unconstitutional, and the tendency of which he considered as unfavorable to the permanency of the Union.[13]

On June 29, 1832, the Senate received a tariff bill from the House of Representatives, and within a few days it was reported out of committee. Forsyth suggested an amendment which would provide for revocation of the act of 1828; this, in effect, would have destroyed the pending measure, thereby leaving the tariff on the basis of the 1824 law. Realizing that his scheme would continue the protective principle, Forsyth explained that his purpose was to entrust settlement of the basic issue to the next session of Congress, whose new members would be more representative of the people. The Senate, in no mood for such tactics, refused approval of the amendment.

The tariff act of July 14, 1832, eliminated the majority of objectionable features in the previous law; however, it retained protection. Scheduled to become effective on March 4, 1833, the measure provided for a reduction of customs, principally on non-competitive articles. The average rate for all duties would amount to 33 per cent, in contrast to the current 41 per cent. Casting his vote for the bill in its final form, Forsyth asserted that his action should not be construed as a commitment in favor of the protective principle. He was influenced by two factors: first, defeat of the pending measure would result in retention of the 1828 law; second, the new bill was a modification of the "tariff of abominations." Therefore, ". . . it was not a question of protection, but of reduction of the burdens of the people; and he would continue the uncompromising, incessant enemy of the system, till it was totally abrogated by Congress."[14]

Enactment of the 1832 tariff act caused intense excitement in Georgia. Forsyth and Representative James Moore Wayne were censured and praised for having voted in favor of the measure. Oglethorpe County citizens called a meeting to consider means of tariff redress and invited all Georgia congressmen with the exception of Forsyth and Wayne to attend. Similar action was taken by Bibb County residents when they gave a dinner in honor of Representative Augustin S. Clayton.[15] On the other hand, the Milledgeville *Federal Union* insisted that the two men should be admired for doing their duty; although hostile to the system, they had voted for a protective measure because it embodied a $6,000,000 to $10,000,000 tax reduction. This paper placed the responsibility for the insults to Forsyth and Wayne on nullification advocates who desired disorganization of the Union.[16]

Anti-tariff meetings took place throughout the state. Forsyth accepted an invitation to speak in his defense at Sparta, where, at the end of his speech, the assemblage voted a grateful approbation of his and Wayne's actions. He spoke to the Richmond County residents when they met in Augusta; this meeting also adopted a resolution in support of Forsyth and Wayne. Forsyth's address, however, was subjected to harsh criticism by a local newspaper. Accusing Forsyth of misrepresentation of facts and of failure to sustain his position, the editor exclaimed that "a more milk and cider apologistical speech we hardly ever heard."[17] Most of the anti-tariff meetings were dominated by radical personnel; nevertheless, many of them expressed confidence in Forsyth and Wayne and regret for the unjust attacks being made upon them.[18]

On August 1, 1832, a meeting was held in the chapel at the University of Georgia for the purpose of discussing the tariff problem. Moderate members of the Troup faction favored the appointment of a committee to draft resolutions expressing the opinion of the assemblage. This plan met with disapproval from the more radical element of the party. Led by Augustin S. Clayton and John M. Berrien, the radical group gained control of the meeting and secured the adoption of resolutions already prepared by their leaders. After a denunciation of Congress and the tariff, the resolutions called for elections of county representatives to a state convention. The delegates were to assemble in Milledgeville the following November, invested with full power to act in preserving and defending the rights of Georgians. The declarations also provided for a committee to correspond with citizens of other states on matters of common interest.[19]

Condemning the arbitrary methods employed at Athens, the anti-nullification journals declared that a probable majority of the assemblage left in disgust before passage of the resolutions.

Members of the Clark party were advised to avoid the proposed convention. They declared the various branches of the state government were competent to deal with the tariff issue; the legislators, elected in October, would be as responsive to the desires of the people as would convention delegates selected at the same time. They accused the proponents of the convention of being nullifiers who, if given the power, would resort to rash measures culminating in disruption of the Union.[20]

At the appointed time, November 12, 1832, the convention began deliberations which continued through November 17. Forsyth, who had not been present at the Athens meeting, attended the convention as a delegate from Richmond County. He was determined to prevent action which would be injurious to the Union. Following the selection of George R. Gilmer as presiding officer, it was moved to appoint a committee, composed of twenty-one members, to draft resolutions expressing the views of the assemblage relative to the protective system and the most effective means of obtaining relief.[21] Forsyth moved to postpone action until the following day. An extensive debate ensued. Forsyth and William Cumming were opposed by Berrien, Clayton, William H. Torrance, Roger L. Gamble, and Thomas Spalding. Forsyth's motion was defeated by a count of 67 to 52,[22] and a committee was chosen. As a member of the committee Forsyth recommended calling a convention of all the southern states. His proposal was rejected by the committee.

On the second day of the convention, Forsyth offered the following proposals:

Resolved, That a Committee of five be appointed by the President to examine and report to this body at its next meeting, the authority of the persons assembled as Delegates from the different counties of the State to represent the people of their respective counties; the Resolutions, if any, under which the election in each county was held; the notice given of the time of the election; the manner of holding it; the number of votes given at the election and the number of votes in the county.

Resolved, That the individuals who have been elected as a committee of what is known as the Athens meeting, be and they are hereby requested to present to this body the correspondence which they have held connected with the object of their appointment.[23]

Forsyth's resolutions were designed to discredit the work of the convention. In his opinion, the assemblage was not representative of the sentiments held by most Georgians. There was no

doubt that many of the delegates would experience difficulty
in procuring the evidence demanded by his first recommendation;
hence confusion and delay would result, with a possibility of suppression of any anti-Union action. His second resolution was
introduced for the purpose of ascertaining whether the Berrien-
Clayton group, through the committee of correspondence, was
acting in concert with the South Carolina nullifiers.[24]

The opposition proposed, as a substitute for the initial recommendation, that a committee be appointed to which would be
referred contested elections only. Following a spirited discussion,
Berrien offered an amendment to the pertinent resolution, his objective being to prevent further delay of action on the tariff problem. He suggested that the approved report of a credentials committee be submitted, with the convention record, to the people
for a decision. Debate on the resolution and amendment con-
sumed the afternoon sessions of November 13, 14, and 16,
with Forsyth and Berrien the principals.

In support of his resolution, Forsyth questioned whether any
action taken by the convention would be binding upon the people. He desired to ascertain if the delegates actually had received
a mandate. If so, they should conform to the wishes of the electorate; they should be cautious in assuming such a high trust unless
they possessed positive proof of their power. He maintained that
the delegates were selected by a minority of the citizens; until
convinced otherwise, he refused to deliberate on so grave an
issue, no matter how respectable the members might be.

Berrien and his adherents claimed that the elections were
well advertised; that, though informally expressed, the will of a
large part of the population was vested in the delegates; that a
refusal to vote in the county meetings implied assent; and that
public officials frequently were elected by a minority of the electorate. Declaring that such a detailed investigation as proposed
by Forsyth was impractical, they denounced Forsyth for his
attempt to disrupt the convention. They also condemned his dis-
courtesy toward the delegates who had been duly elected but
whose authority he questioned. The Berrien-Clayton spokesmen
insisted that the convention had the authority to make recommendations, a privilege conceded to any group of citizens.[25]

A spectator at the Milledgeville convention recorded his impressions of the momentous and acrid debate between Forsyth
and Berrien, a contest in which the former showed to better
advantage. Berrien preferred to meditate on a question and to

organize his thoughts before expressing them; on this occasion, he was denied the opportunity by a versatile impromptu debater. Surprised by Forsyth's eloquent attack, Berrien's arguments lacked their usual cogency and vitality. According to the observer, able speakers addressed the meeting who, "in a register of debates . . . would appear equal to Mr. Forsyth; but on the floor his superiority was conceded by all, friend or foe."[26] Nevertheless, as one newspaper commented, Berrien was the convention's dictator; as evidence, the journal stated that every motion receiving his support was approved by the assembly, while those to which he was opposed were rejected.[27]

On November 16, the convention approved Berrien's amendment by a vote of 63 to 56; the action, in effect, was a rejection of Forsyth's first resolution. Forsyth withdrew his second proposal. He then displayed a paper which, said he, contained an expression of his views and those of his supporters. The convention might dispose of it as they saw fit. Depositing the document on the clerk's desk, he retired from the chamber followed by fifty-two others. The withdrawing delegates were both applauded and hissed by the gallery. [28]

The document left by the seceders was not read before the convention because of Berrien's objection that to do so would be imprudent. No mention of the protest was made in either the journal or the minutes of the meeting. Nor was it included in the published proceedings, twenty thousand copies of which were circulated among the people of the state. Nevertheless, the document appeared in various newspapers and in circular form. The protest listed three reasons for the withdrawal. First, more than twenty counties were not represented, and hence any action taken by the convention would constitute a decision by a minority of the people; second, many counties elected delegates with the understanding that they would endeavor to avert the evils anticipated from the meeting; third, the refusal by the convention of a full examination of credentials was inconsistent with individual rights and a usurpation of power. In conclusion, the fifty-three signers deemed it their duty to secede and to protest that the convention's decisions were entitled to neither authority nor influence.[29]

The seventy remaining members adopted seventeen resolutions prepared by the committee of twenty-one, and adjourned with the avowed intention of re-convening on the first Monday in July, 1833. Apparently, the assemblage realized that the people of the state were not in sympathy with extreme measures, for the resolutions were more conservative than generally expected. They asserted Georgia's sincere attachment to the Union and a desire for peaceful settlement of the tariff problem. Although opposed to protection, they would accept a gradual reduction of the tariff to begin after the payment of the public debt. They expressed a determination to resist the protective system in every way possible, either through separate or joint state action. They would postpone resistance, however, and give Congress and the manufacturing states another opportunity to act in the interest of justice and patriotism. They called for a convention of the southern states, with Georgia's delegates to be chosen in county elections to be held in March, 1833. Finally, they called for a popular referendum on the convention's action.[30]

Advocates of the anti-tariff convention denounced the seceders in general and Forsyth in particular. They accused Forsyth of being a temporizer; having accepted innumerable honors from his state, he was prepared to desert the people in order to further his own selfish ambition for high office in the federal government. In causing a division among Georgians, he had done more to rivet the tariff upon them than had all the speeches of Clay, Webster, and other protectionists. They warned him that his constituents would remember his attempt to suppress popular feeling. They charged that the seceders had held secret meetings at McComb's tavern in Milledgeville. With Forsyth as leader, these caucuses had drafted the protest and the circular.[31]

Forsyth and his friends were convinced that the real purpose of the anti-tariff assemblage was to advance the political ambitions of Berrien and his followers.[32] And if Berrien succeeded, they feared that Georgia might become involved in some nullification project. Hence, Forsyth sponsored the publication of the circular and the protest, both of which emphasized these views. The pamphlet asserted that the proceedings of the Convention were designed "to bring Georgia into the toils of South Carolina, and deliver her people en masse to the demon of nullification."[33] Forsyth voiced similar sentiments in a letter to Martin Van Buren. He stated that Chancellor Harper had promised postponement of final nullification action by South Carolina if the delegates to the Georgia convention would ask for a joint convention of the southern states. Forsyth's "impressions were that S. C. wanted an excuse to suspend or was playing a deep game to entangle Georgia in their Nullification Scheme."[34]

On November 24, 1832, South Carolina passed an Ordinance of Nullification which declared the tariff acts of 1828 and 1832 null and void. The annulment was to become effective on February, 1, 1833. In reply, President Jackson issued a proclamation to the people of South Carolina which left no doubt of his intention to compel obedience to the federal laws. Subsequently, the President requested of Congress additional authority to use military force for proper execution of the laws. He also asked for power to remove pertinent cases from state to federal courts and to transfer or close those ports of entry where officials would be prevented from collection of customs. Jackson's recommendations were incorporated into a Senate bill which was reported out of committee on January 21, 1833. The measure, generally known as the Force Bill, was called the "Bloody Bill" by many Southerners.

In conformity with his hostile views toward nullification, and as administration floor leader, Forsyth favored passage of the measure, with one major change. The bill provided that the grant of power embodied in the military provisions was to expire at the end of one year. Forsyth wanted the same limitation placed on the authority contained in the judicial provision. He declared that the entire bill should be designed to take care of a temporary situation. In his opinion, any consideration of making the judicial sections a part of the permanent legal system of the United States should be postponed until the senators were in a more placid frame of mind.

Forsyth's principal speech on the measure was delivered, without preparation, on February 18, 1833. According to the official record, he denounced nullification by declaring that

No individual State possessed the right of nullification from any sovereignty residing in her. Sovereignty . . . did not exist in the States, separately or individually, since the Union. Since that period, it resided in the United States as a whole; and by them alone could it be exercised, and in the mode defined by the constitution. Much ingenuity had been called forth in support of nullification; but mystify it as much as they pleased, it could not stand the test of argument. The doctrine was preposterous; it was a mere web of sophism and casuistry. And the arguments in its favor, if analyzed, and put through the alembic, would result in the double distilled essence of nonsense.[35]

Forsyth admitted that South Carolina's action had served one useful purpose: it had caused the nation to become more conscious of the injustice imposed upon the South by the tariff.

Nevertheless, the state's method of procedure could be neither defended nor tolerated if the Union was to survive. According to Forsyth, the time was not too distant when protection and nullification would be buried in the same grave.

Forsyth sought to disprove charges that certain actions taken by Georgia were analogous to those taken by South Carolina. He insisted that Georgia had not resorted to annulment of federal law in either the imprisonment of missionaries or in depriving the Cherokees of control over land within the state. In the first instance, Georgia was suppressing a hypocritical priesthood which was mixing politics with religion.[36] In the second case, the state, after waiting thirty years for Indian removal, was merely exercising her rights as identified in the contract with the federal government. Forsyth could detect no similarity between South Carolina's procedure and that of the American colonies toward Great Britain. In the latter case, the colonists did not complain of oppressive taxation, but of taxation imposed by a legislature in which they had no representation. South Carolina's grievance, on the other hand, was that the state did not have sufficient influence in Congress to cause a change of policy. Forsyth was critical of South Carolina's expressions of devoted attachment to the Union, and compared them with those made by the Hartford convention of 1814-1815. In each case, he declared, "they loved the Union, were devoted to the Union so much, that nobody must govern it but themselves."[37]

Two days after Forsyth's address, the Force Bill passed the Senate, with Forsyth and William C. Rives of Virginia being the only Southerners voting aye. Subsequent approval by the House of Representatives found James M. Wayne the sole member of the Georgia delegation voting with the majority. With Jackson's signature, the measure became law on March 2, 1833. The act aroused antagonism in Georgia, where there was definite opposition to federal coercion of a sovereign state. Many Georgians gave vent to their feelings by condemning Forsyth and Wayne. Forsyth was hanged and burned in effigy at Macon and at Hillsboro. He was presented by the grand juries of several counties and called upon to resign his seat in the Senate. The citizens of Butts County passed a resolution deploring and disapproving his conduct. Various Georgia and South Carolina newspapers, emphasizing his unpopularity, referred to him as an apostate and a traitor. Vicious toasts were offered at dinners and other celebrations. At Centreville, Forsyth was denounced as "an apple fair to the eye, but rotten at the core."[38] In Waynesboro, he and Wayne were cited as "the undivided supporters of the *bloody* alias *force* bill—May it be the means of forcing them into political damnation."[39]

Adherents of Forsyth and Wayne contended that public opinion was being misrepresented by the nullifiers. They denounced the effigy incidents as constituting not only a vile insult, but also disgrace and injury to the reputation of the communities concerned. One supporter called attention to the fact that nine of the twenty-two members of one jury that condemned Forsyth declared his "greatest crime, perhaps, has been his opposition to Nullification and zeal for the promotion of our present happy Union, and firm support of the administration. . . ."[40] In Milledgeville, a meeting of Union party members from throughout the state expressed similar sentiments regarding Forsyth's conduct. Forsyth was invited to several public dinners in his honor, but refused to attend any of them. He declared that he did not wish to appear triumphant over his former associates or to be instrumental in prolonging harsh feelings. He desired a calm and accurate appraisal of Union party doctrine, for he was "firmly convinced that nineteen-twentieths of the people if they do not now, will, when they are properly understood, approve the principles upon which we act. . . ."[41]

At the same time it debated the Force Bill, Congress was considering a reduction of the tariff, an action which Jackson had recommended in his annual message. The Verplanck bill, reported in the House of Representatives on December 27, 1832, proposed an immediate reduction of specified duties, to be followed by further reduction a year later. The protectionists, opposed to such radical change, added amendments until the bill became impracticable. Meanwhile, Henry Clay introduced a tariff measure in the State which was destined to receive the support of the Calhoun group as well as that of the protection advocates. This compromise bill provided that the tariff of 1832 be reduced gradually, over a period of ten years, until the duties were stabilized at twenty per cent.

Forsyth, like Jackson, favored the Verplanck bill; consequently, he objected when Clay requested permission to introduce his measure. Since the session lacked only fourteen days of adjournment, he claimed that time was insufficient for passage of the Clay bill. He urged the Senate to delay action until receipt of the bill from the House; otherwise, the latter might cease de-

liberation in deference to the upper chamber. Forsyth also reminded his colleagues that they had no constitutional authority to
initiate revenue bills, such power being reserved to the House of
Representatives. He said that he was in sympathy with what the
measure sought to accomplish and, if the Senate insisted on consideration, he would offer no objection provided there was deletion of a portion which he considered unconstitutional. Forsyth
hoped that his suggestion, if adopted, would make the Clay
proposal less acceptable than the Verplanck measure. Clay, however, refused to make the change, maintaining that the pertinent section was an essential part of the bill.[42]

More than a week elapsed before the Senate began debate on
the Clay measure. By that time, Forsyth was convinced that
distortion of the Verplanck bill had rendered it unacceptable.
He, therefore, determined to vote for Clay's measure. He explained that his acceptance was motivated by a desire to avert
armed conflict. A secondary consideration was the fact that the
measure was an improvement upon the tariff act of 1832. He
noted that there were numerous absurdities and contradictions
in the bill, all of which were to be expected since it was the
product of two diverse groups, each attempting justification before
respective constituencies. Forsyth contended that Congress had no
power to limit the actions of its successors, whether those before
or after 1842. Furthermore, he did not consider assent to the bill
as a pledge against modification or repeal; the law should be
obeyed while in existence, but there was no guarantee for its
continuance once public opinion decreed otherwise. Forsyth
could not refrain from directing a barb toward those southern
senators who had been censorious of his vote on the tariff measure
of 1832. Emphasizing the protective features of the pending bill,
Forsyth remarked that his critics were about to follow his example
of the previous year. With grim humor, he observed that "they
make the most of the circumstances of the hour; are willing to
admit some evil, that greater evil may not fall upon us."[43]

On February 26, 1833, the House of Representatives passed the
Clay bill, which had been substituted for the Verplanck measure.
The Senate, in order to remove constitutional objection concerning the origin of the measure, immediately replaced its pending
bill with the identical one approved by the House, and passed the
compromise tariff act on March 1, 1833. Forsyth's ballot was included with the majority. The following day, President Jackson
appended his signature. Forsyth's motive for opposing introduc-

tion of the Clay bill was misunderstood by some Southerners, who denounced him for seeking to obstruct reconciliatory efforts. Forsyth, however, acted in what he considered the best interests of his constituents. In 1834, he explained that Clay's proposal was more favorable toward protection, consequently less beneficial to the South, than was the measure which had the original support of the administration party.

The public land policy of the United States was an issue which, in at least one respect, was associated closely with the tariff problem. The protectionists favored a distribution among the states of the proceeds from the sale of public lands. They reasoned that if this revenue was diverted from the national treasury, the government would be forced to adopt protection as a permanent policy in order to meet necessary operating expenses. Although Forsyth seldom spoke on the public land policy, he made his position on the issue clear. In 1833, the Senate approved a distributive measure which was to be applicable for a limited period. The bill received a pocket veto from Jackson. Forsyth not only voted against the measure, but also defended the President when the latter's action was debated in the subsequent session of Congress.[44]

John Forsyth's conduct on the tariff issue was consistent. An analysis of the maze of events reveals that the Georgian's activities were based on his opposition to the protective system, his practical evaluation of the existing situation, and his devotion to the Union. As early as 1816, Forsyth foresaw the evils inherent in protection; when his apprehensions were realized, he searched for some legitimate method whereby the burden upon the South might be removed. After the tariff states refused to cooperate, he came to the conclusion that a decrease in duties was preferable to no change at all. This policy was in the nature of a temporary expedient, since he reiterated the opinion that the protective system was destined to be repealed.

Surpassing Forsyth's hostility to protection was his desire for preservation of the Union. He disliked the compromise tariff measure of 1833, yet cast a favorable ballot. He explained later that he had been forced to sacrifice the interests of his constituents in order to dissipate the imminent menace of civil war. An inveterate enemy of nullification, he told the Senate that he considered nullification more dangerous than any doctrine ever formulated in the United States. The Milledgeville anti-tariff convention gave Forsyth opportunity to strike a blow for his cause.

There was a possibility that a vigorous minority might impose its nullification views upon the state. Forsyth's endeavors made certain that such a catastrophe would not befall Georgia. Union sympathizers were in desperate need of leadership by a prominent and able person. Forsyth supplied that leadership.

IX

Affairs of State

M EMBERS OF THE United States Senate who render meritorious service in behalf of an administration frequently are given opportunity to continue their support in an executive capacity. As John Forsyth's affiliation with the administration became more pronounced, there were recurrent reports that he would be rewarded with a diplomatic assignment or a cabinet position. When the Senate refused to confirm Van Buren as Minister to Great Britain, there was speculation that Forsyth would be his replacement. Rumors of 1832-1833 differed as to which of the following departments he would head: State, Treasury, War, or Navy. On one occasion, Van Buren suggested to the President that Forsyth be appointed Attorney General. When the various vacancies were filled with other aspirants, Van Buren was consistent in his efforts to alleviate any disappointment experienced by his Georgia friend. He advised that Jackson explain to Forsyth the reasons for the respective appointments and assure him that his claims had received careful consideration.[1]

Forsyth refused to be pacified over his failure to obtain an appointment. In a bitter mood, he exposed his feelings to Van Buren in a letter dated December 30, 1832. Emphasizing his valuable services to the administration, he declared that he had received no promises from the President for the future and he expected none. His self-respect would not permit personal solicitation for office; anyone who resorted to such practice or who induced friends to advance pretensions was not worthy of the desired position. Forsyth stated that furthermore it was not within the power of the President to grant what was needed most—money. In debt and with dependent children, Forsyth threatened to quit public office once he was assured an opportunity to secure a better income for his family. He wanted Van Buren and Jackson to be under no false impressions concerning his acceptance of a presidential appointment. He would not resign from the Senate unless the proffered position was commensurate with his ability and would reflect credit upon his name. In a positive manner, he declared,

I shall not without an obligation of publick duty . . . suffer my fair pretensions to be undervalued, to gratify any man's caprice or ambition. I know the honor and the power and the respect of my present 'post and I shall take care not to drop from the Van to the rear.[2]

On another occasion, in 1833, Forsyth furnished Van Buren with further evidence of his disappointment. He complained that he had been overlooked in a second reorganization among the President's advisers; that it was improper to have a cabinet with no Southern representative. As to the rumored appointment of Edward Livingston to the French mission, Forsyth objected to sending foreign ministers during a recess of the Senate; he would not sustain the President on this subject, as he had done on previous occasions. The administration's neglect in providing for his talents would detract from his strength in Georgia, since he was thought to have influence in Washington. Feeling useless as a member of the Senate and humiliated before his constituents, Forsyth was prepared to consider an appointment as Minister to Russia, where he might "be able to satisfy our European friends that it is possible for an American minister to have the manner & look of a Gentleman. . . ."[3]

Van Buren communicated the contents of Forsyth's letter to Jackson, who remarked that the Georgian's objection to the recess appointment was not based upon a comprehensive view of the situation. As for the Russian mission, the President made the laconic comment, "I am happy to hear that our mutual friend Forsythe [sic] is contented with the prospect in view."[4] Within a few months, Forsyth reconsidered his position regarding the proposed ministerial appointment. He asked that Van Buren inform Jackson of his determination to defend himself against his political opponents in Georgia; if unsuccessful in retaining public confidence, he would retire to his home and supervise the cultivation of nankeen cotton. However, he wanted an option on the Russian assignment should it become vacant at a later date. The New Yorker transmitted Forsyth's sentiments to Jackson, who responded that he had no objections to rescission of all promises and conversations; until Minister James Buchanan returned from his St. Petersburg post, there was no necessity for choosing his successor; when a decision was to be made, Forsyth would be considered for the position. The following year, the Georgian declined the proffered appointment on the ground that it would entail a financial sacrifice which he could not afford.[5]

On June 19, 1834, the Washington *National Intelligencer* reported a rumor in the capital city that Louis McLane had resigned as Secretary of State. The Washington *Globe,* same date, commented that President Jackson, though differing with McLane on some important measures, had accepted the resignation with regret and with expressions of his high regard for the departing cabinet member. The latter statement caused the *National Intelligencer* to reply: "More fortunate than the majority of his predecessors in the Cabinet, he has, it appears, parted from the President on friendly terms."[6] A contemporary, however, thought that "the *old chief* made the place too hot for him"[7] and that McLane resigned because of his opposition to the removal of government deposits from the Bank of the United States.

There was immediate speculation as to who would be McLane's successor in the cabinet, and among those prominently mentioned for the position was Forsyth. Rumors of his appointment were confirmed when Jackson consented to the suggestion of Van Buren[8] and nominated Forsyth to be Secretary of State. The Senate approved Forsyth for the post by unanimous vote on June 27, 1834. The Georgian entered upon his new duties on July 1, at which time he resigned his seat in the Senate. A few days later, he received congratulations on his promotion to the cabinet from an old friend, Nicholas Biddle.[9] In general, the reaction to the President's choice seems to have been favorable. Even an opposition newspaper commented that

As for Mr. Forsyth, we give him credit for intellectual ability, eloquence, and adroitness, to an extent rarely found combined in a single individual . . . he has well earned the station which he occupies; a station for which he is, in some respects, remarkably qualified. . . .[10]

An English writer, visiting the United States in 1835, observed that "persons who love to watch the game of politics, and those who make a study of strong minds under strong excitements, like a season at Washington . . . ."[11] Certainly, those persons referred to must have been more than satisfied with the furore created by

France's refusal to pay the spoliation claims. This was an old diplomatic problem and among the first of major importance to be handled by the new Secretary of State.

The history of the claims may be outlined briefly. Beginning in 1806, Napoleon I had issued several decrees whereby ships and cargoes of American citizens had been confiscated. Even though the United States government has repeatedly protested the wholesale spoliations, which were estimated at approximately $7,000,000, it had been unable to secure from the Emperor anything more than indefinite assurances of redress. After the downfall of Napoleon I, United States efforts continuel, culminating in the treaty of July 4, 1831. According to the provisions of the treaty, France agreed to pay to the United States twenty-five million francs in six annual installments.

A draft was presented for the first payment, which became due in March, 1833. The French Finance Minister was unable to pay because no appropriations for the purpose had been made by the Chamber of Deputies. Subsequently, the Bank of the United States demanded fifteen per cent protest charges on the unhonored draft. Matters became worse when, in April, 1834, the Chamber of Deputies defeated a measure to provide funds for the treaty payments. Thereafter, the cabinet of the Louis Philippe government was reorganized, with promises being made to the United States that the ministry would present a bill to the new Chamber of Deputies at the latter's first meeting.

Jackson was not satisfied with events. He decided, however, to delay action until the December meeting of Congress, with the expectation that during the interval the French would have honored their obligations.[12] This was the situation which confronted Forsyth when he took office in July, 1834.

Forsyth made no effort to conceal his disapproval of the French inaction when, in October, he was visited by Louis Barbé C. Serurier, France's Minister to the United States. Although polite, the Secretary's manner was cold and reserved. He informed the French envoy that Jackson was disturbed because the treaty had not been executed and that the President intended to present his views to the next session of Congress, as he had promised to do if the matter was not cleared up by that time. According to Forsyth, Jackson was at a loss to understand why convocation of the Chamber of Deputies had been delayed until the latter part of December unless it was to prevent Congress from taking any action before adjournment on March 4.

When Serurier asked if Forsyth believed that the French government would resort to such an evasion, the Georgian replied in the negative, but emphasized the fact that it was the President's duty to inform Congress and to propose appropriate measures. When Serurier bluntly inquired whether the United States wanted the treaty executed or a war with France, the Secretary answered in favor of the former.[13] It is to be inferred that the two men were not on the best of terms when they parted.

On November 19, the French Minister made another visit to the State Department, his object being to learn the nature of Jackson's forthcoming message to Congress. Forsyth stated his belief that the President would present a complete statement of facts and leave the matter to Congress for a decision. It was his opinion that Jackson would advise Congress to take no action until the French Chamber of Deputies had made a final decision. Serurier was apprehensive as to what steps might be taken by the opposition in Congress. To this, Forsyth made the laconic reply, "Sufficient for the day is the evil thereof; but it is probable the President will stand his ground."[14]

Forsyth, despite his calm assurances, had considerable trepidation as to the contents of the presidential communication.[15] Later, when Jackson's views on the subject were revealed to the cabinet, Forsyth attempted to make them more acceptable to the French government. A contemporary has given a graphic description of the preparation of the President's message:

On that subject he [Jackson] had himself dictated the very language he would employ in uttering a threat direct to Louis Philippe. The Cabinet consulted to change the phraseology. Mr. Forsyth, the Secretary of State, was adroit in language, and wisely, he thought, changed the paragraph which the President had dictated. The change in words was but a shade different in meaning; but he sought to make the message more diplomatic in terms and more conformable, of course, to peaceful and courteous national intercourse. It was in vain. When Mr. Andrew J. Donelson, the President's private secretary, brought to him the proofsheets of the message, Mr. John C. Rives, of the Globe was present.

Mr. Donelson read, whilst the general walked the room, pipe in his mouth, smoking, and the printer the only attendant. All was quietly listened to until the reader came to the passage relating to the five millions debt due by France. Mr. Donelson was evidently desirous so to read the paragraph on that subject as to avoid notice of the change in words which had been made. General Jackson at once paused in his walk, stopped, and said, "Read that again, sir." Mr. Donelson then read the passage distinctly, and General Jackson was instantly roused, saying "That, sir, is not my language; it has been changed, and I will have no other expression of my own meaning than my own words."

He immediately and vehemently had the change erased, and his own language, even more strongly importing a threat, inserted. . . .[16]

In his annual message to Congress, on December 1, 1834, the President reviewed the controversy with France and condemned the French government for its failure to provide the indemnity. In vigorous language, he recommended that if the payments were not assured by the next session of the French Chamber, Congress should pass a law authorizing confiscation of French property in the United States. Jackson's message created great excitement. The Washington *National Intelligencer* reminded its reading public that Jackson's recommendation was his act only and probably would not be supported by Congress or the American people. The Whig journal later voiced the hope that the French Chamber would vote the appropriation before news of the President's message reached Paris.[17] The Washington *Globe* upheld Jackson and accused the opposition press of attempting to create the false impression among the French that the administration would be unable to obtain the necessary support on any redress measure.[18]

As a result of Jackson's message, the Louis Philippe government decided to recall its minister in Washington. On February 23, 1835, Serurier prepared a message to be transmitted to the State Department, in which, pursuant to orders just received from his government, he requested an immediate audience. Forsyth's cold, formal reply was that the Secretary of State was "ready to receive in writing any communication the Government of France desires to have made to the Government of the United States."[19] Serurier answered that the purpose of the suggested interview was to present personally the chargé d'affaires, Alphonse J. Y. Pageot, as the accredited representative of France in the absence of a minister; that, in compliance with Forsyth's wishes, he was taking the opportunity to make the presentation in written form.[20]

Pageot, the new French representative, was the son-in-law of Major William B. Lewis, close friend of Jackson.[21] A few days after his presentation, Pageot called upon Forsyth in order to enter a verbal protest against the recent publication of Edward Livingston's letters to the Department of State. These dispatches from the United States Minister to France had been made public when Jackson transmitted them to Congress. The Secretary of State was told that the letters were private and that their publication violated the respect due the French government. Pageot admitted that he had had no instructions on the matter, but was protesting because he felt it was his duty to do so. Forsyth informed the Frenchman that a foreign government had no right to complain of a communication which had been submitted from one branch of the American government to another.[22]

In April, 1835, after much discussion, the French Chamber of Deputies passed the indemnity bill. It included an amendment which provided that the payments were not to be made until the French government received satisfactory explanations concerning Jackson's obnoxious message. The President's attitude on the action was expressed in a letter to the Postmaster General: "I am of the opinion that France will pay the money without apology or explanation; from *me she will get neither. . . .*"[23] Since the qualified appropriation measure was regarded by the United States as being a rejection of the payments, Livingston departed from France. Upon his arrival in Washington, he tendered his resignation to the President.

On June 17, 1835, the French Minister of Foreign Affairs, Duke Achille Leonce V. C. de Broglie, addressed a note to Pageot in Washington. The communication stated that the indemnity law had received the royal sanction and that the United States could remove the remaining obstacle for payment by explaining certain passages of the President's annual message of 1834. The action of the French legislature in passing the conditional amendment was upheld. The dispatch maintained that Livingston's personal explanations could not be accepted in place of Jackson's. De Broglie stated that the French government objected to the presidential message on two points: it impeached the good faith of France and it contained the threat of reprisals if the treaty was not executed. He admitted that "it will possibly be found that passing successively from phrase to phrase, none will be met with that cannot bear an interpretation more or less plausible . . ."; but, taking the message as a whole, he felt that France had a just cause for complaint. He declared that

if it is true that the President . . . had no intention to cast any doubt on the good faith of the French Government . . . [or] to assume, with regard to France, a menacing attitude, we cannot see how he could find any difficulty in declaring it.[24]

In conclusion, de Broglie authorized Pageot to read the note to Forsyth and to furnish a copy if the Secretary of State desired it.

Pageot applied to Acting Secretary of State Asbury Dickins for permission to read the communication from Paris. Forsyth, who was cognizant of the application, wrote to Jackson while en route to Washington. He suggested that the chargé be informed that the note could not be accepted without mature reflection and without consultation with the President. Jackson, however, could see no reason for postponing the issue. He declared that no foreign government had the right to dictate the phraseology or manner in which the President corresponded with Congress. Therefore, he instructed Forsyth to take no notice of the document unless it was submitted officially; if it was made an official communication, then Forsyth should advise Pageot, in writing, "that we cannot discuss this subject nor will never permit it to be discussed by any foreign nation."[25]

When the French chargé d'affaires conferred with Forsyth on September 11, 1835, the Secretary asked if he was communicating an official document. Pageot replied that his directions were merely to read the letter and to offer a copy if requested. Forsyth listened to the reading, but, after placing emphasis on the propriety of official correspondence, he did not ask for a duplicate.[26] Though not explained to Pageot, reason for non-acceptance may be attributed to an expectation that the copy would have to be submitted to the Senate, where the opposition might use it in an attack on the administration's foreign policy.[27]

Pageot realized the importance of getting de Broglie's letter before Congress and the American public, where it would be interpreted as revealing a peaceful and moderate attitude on the part of the French government. Consequently on December 1 he wrote to the Secretary of State and enclosed a copy of the note. He stated that in view of the forthcoming annual message to Congress, he thought it desirable for the President to be in possession of all the facts; that Jackson could then form a true estimate of the pacific views held by the Louis Philippe government.[28]

Forsyth, however, was not deceived by the maneuver. He returned the de Broglie note to Pageot; accompanying it was a letter of rebuke. He referred the chargé to his previous statement concerning the reason for not requesting a copy of the dispatch: that, under the existing relationship between the two nations, the President thought it proper that all negotiations be conducted by direct communication. As to the assumption that the President had no knowledge of the note's contents, Forsyth stated that Jackson had been fully informed of the September interview and was in complete accord with the course adopted. Reprimanding Pageot for having revived the matter, Forsyth assured the Frenchman that any official communication would receive the proper consideration from the President.[29]

Within a few days, the Secretary received a sarcastic reply, in which Pageot wrote that he was astonished by the return of the document; that his intention had been to inform the President, Congress, and the American people of the French government's true disposition. The chargé regretted

that the misunderstanding between the two Governments, already so serious, should be kept up, not by weighty difficulties, which involve the interests and the dignity of the two countries, but by questions of form, as uncertain in their principles, as doubtful in their application.[30]

The issue concerning the de Broglie note was not concluded by the interchange of views between Forsyth and Pageot. Jackson's message to Congress, dated December 7, 1835, prepared the way for further developments. After a brief recapitulation of the controversial incidents, the President defended his own actions and criticized the French ministry for adhering to the conditional amendment. He contended that in his last message he had no intention of menacing or insulting France; that the charges were disavowed by Livingston and that subsequently he had approved the American Minister's conduct. Anxious for an early settlement, he had issued specific instructions to Thomas Pennant Barton, the United States chargé d'affaires in Paris. The latter was to ask for the French government's intentions pertaining to the payment of the indemnity; if not satisfied, Barton was to return to the United States. Jackson declared that unfortunately he had received no report from Paris; but as soon as the results were known he expected to send a special message to Congress.

A controversy between the two Washington journals, the *Globe* and the *National Intelligencer,* ensued over the presidential message. On December 13, the former paper, in defense of the Jacksonian policy, made the following statement:

We know the first Minister of France has himself expressly admitted that, taking each separate member of the [1834] message, and subjecting it to scrutiny, there is nothing in any portion of it to justify the offensive sense in which it has been interpreted.[31]

The *National Intelligencer* declared that it did not remember any such sentiments being expressed by de Broglie; that the *Globe* must have obtained its information through an official channel; that the contents of all important documents should be revealed to the American people. When the *Globe* replied that the source of its information was an unofficial letter from de Broglie to his correspondent in the United States, the *National Intelligencer* asked for the identity of the latter person and demanded that the communication be published.[32]

For several weeks, the Whig newspaper continued to emphasize what it termed "the suppressed letter." By January 5, it had reached the conclusion that a friendly overture from France had been repelled by the Jackson administration; it also called attention to the fact that the President, in his last message to Congress, had made no mention of such a proposal.[33] The New York *Times,* an administration paper, identified the "suppressed letter" as a private communication, to Pageot from his government, which the French chargé was instructed to read to Forsyth. The journal stated that the Secretary of State had not accepted a copy of the dispatch because of its private nature.

Commenting on this article, the *National Intelligencer* maintained that the letter was not private if Pageot officially offered a copy of it to Forsyth. By refusing to accept a duplicate, the cabinet member was accused of having "erred grossly not ignorantly . . . but from bad temper, bad taste, or cankered judgment . . . ."[34] Henry Clay advanced the opinion that "if Mr. Forsyth withheld the knowledge of that overture from the President, he ought to be dismissed or impeached. . . ."[35]

Meanwhile, the United States government had been unable to obtain a definite commitment from French officials as to payment of the spoliation claims. Insisting upon an apology from Jackson, de Broglie had informed Barton that there was nothing to add to the dispatch of June 17, which had been read to Forsyth by Pageot. As a consequence of the conversation, the American chargé had asked for his passports, claiming that he was withdrawing because the French had failed to execute the treaty. Barton arrived in Washington on January 14, 1836. Accompanied by Forsyth, Van Buren, and Livingston, Barton hurried to the White House and conferred with Jackson, who had delayed transmitting the special congressional message until he had had an opportunity to talk with Barton. In the preparation of this communication, Forsyth, Van Buren, and Livingston undoubtedly persuaded the President to adopt a somewhat moderate tone.[36]

The special message, dated January 15, was communicated to Congress three days later. Reviewing the de Broglie-Barton conference, Jackson was forced to explain Forsyth's rejection of the June 17 letter. He stated that since it was an unofficial dispatch, "the Secretary of State did not think proper to ask a copy, because he could have no use for it."[37] The *National Intelligencer*, in commenting on the report, was gratified to learn the history of the "suppressed letter," even though the document itself had not been produced. The newspaper spoke of the "blundering indiplomacy . . . ," and considered that the French overture had been "declined in all the forms of official repulsion."[38] A later issue of the Whig periodical declared:

Negotiators and Diplomatists should ever beware of confounding dignity and superciliousness, self-respect and false pride. Inexperienced Ministers are prone to this mistake; but, though the President may not be supposed to be familiar with all the practices which have become law in the intercourse between Nations, the experience of our Secretary of State . . . ought to have advised the President (if he did not) to make the just distinction in the case before us.[39]

On January 2, 1836, Forsyth received a communication from Pageot informing him that the chargé had been recalled by the French government. Before his departure from the United States, however, the Frenchman was successful in placing de Broglie's letter of June 17, 1835, before the American public. On January 19, 1836, it appeared in the New York *Star* and the New York *Journal of Commerce*; it was immediately identified as the famous "suppressed letter" and republished in both the *Globe* and the *National Intelligencer*.

There was much speculation as to who was responsible for the original publication. Forsyth reported that a New York postal employee had made a deposition to the effect that the letter was furnished to the newspapers by a member of the French legation. The New York *Times* thought that the blame should be placed on Pageot, regardless of who was the actual agent; it reported that Pageot's secretary had been seen in the city just prior to the publication, but that the French consul had denied taking any part in the affair. The editorial considered it highly improper that a foreign power should make an appeal to the American people, in opposition to the actions of their own government.[40] The *National Intelligencer* voiced a similar opinion, provided such was the true motive for the publication. Nevertheless, the Whig paper could not justify the omission in the President's annual message of the fact that France had made a friendly overture to the United States.

When Henry Clay, chairman of the Senate Foreign Relations Committee, inquired if the published note was the same as de Broglie's dispatch to Pageot, Forsyth reminded him that he had not retained a copy of the communication. The Secretary of State was of the opinion that the published letter did not substantially "differ from the translation read to . . ." him by the chargé.[41]

The truth of the matter was that Pageot, under direct orders from the French government, was responsible for furnishing the note to the New York newspapers.[42] He was suspected and denounced by the Washington *Globe*. The newspaper contended that Forsyth was justified in not asking for a copy of the ambiguous letter; that since it was not addressed to him it did not require an answer; therefore, he had no use for it. The *National Intelligencer,* disagreeing, maintained that the friendly French gesture had been rebuffed in such a manner as to discourage future attempts to effect a settlement of the controversy. One New York newspaper regretted that Forsyth had not accepted a copy of the letter, which the editor considered moderate and conciliatory. Another claimed that the Duke de Broglie was more desirous for a peaceful arrangement than was Forsyth.[43] The Albany *Evening Journal,* an opposition newspaper, judged that Forsyth had been correct in his treatment of the dispatch; that the meaning of the note was obscure.

The Secretary of State was defended in the United States Senate by James Buchanan of Pennsylvania. The Senator contended that if Forsyth had asked for a copy of the letter, he would have been required to answer it. Since the administration could not acquiesce in the conditions imposed by the French government, a reply would only have aggravated the situation. According to Buchanan, there was further justification of the Secretary's conduct:

The President intended, in his annual message, voluntarily to declare that he had never intended to menace France, or to impeach the faith of the French Government. . . . Had Mr. Forsyth taken a copy of this dispatch, and placed it among the archives of the Government, how could the President have made, consistently with his principles, the disclaimer which he has done? A demand for an explanation would thus have been interposed by a foreign Government, which would have compelled the President to remain silent. The refusal of Mr. Forsyth to ask a copy of the dispatch left the controversy in its old condition; and, so far as our Government was concerned, left this letter from the Duc de Broglie to M. Pageot as if it never had been written. The President, therefore, remained at perfect liberty to say what he thought proper in his message.[44]

During the controversy which resulted from the publication of the de Broglie letter, there were rumors that Great Britain had offered to act as a mediator in adjusting the dispute between the United States and France. The Washington *Globe* hoped that mediation would re-establish friendly diplomatic relationships between the two countries. On the other hand, the Washington *United States' Telegraph* announced that the cabinet was divided on acceptance of mediation, with Forsyth being among those opposing. The reported British action was initiated by Foreign Minister Henry John Temple, third Viscount Palmerston, who was anxious to prevent a war which would disturb the commerce of his country. Another reason for his interest was that England and France were allies in a movement to guarantee the integrity of the Ottoman Empire. Palmerston wanted his ally to be free in case of a war with Russia.[45]

On January 26, 1836, dispatches containing Palmerston's offer were delivered to Charles Bankhead, British chargé d'affaires, at the Forsyth home, where he was attending "a large evening party . . . ."[46] The following day, Bankhead wrote to Forsyth that he had been instructed to tender the good offices of his government for the mediation of the French controversy and that a similar note had been presented to the government of France. He stated that Great Britain desired to maintain peace throughout the world, and especially between the two powers with which she was united by close ties.

Bankhead's note of January 27 was answered by the Secretary of State on February 3. He expressed appreciation for the disinterested motives which caused Great Britain to offer to mediate. Forsyth refuted the contention suggested in Bankhead's note, that there was no question of national honor at issue. He claimed that no foreign state had the right to demand an explanation of a presidential message and to make that explanation a condition for the execution of a solemn treaty. This principle, said the

Secretary, could not be subjected to the authority of any mediating power. However, Forsyth asserted

that if, after the frank avowal of his sentiments upon the point last referred to, and the explicit reservation of that point, the Government of his Britannic Majesty shall believe that its mediation can be useful . . . the offer of mediation . . . is cheerfully accepted.[47]

On February 8, Jackson communicated a message to Congress announcing the British offer of mediation, and his acceptance, provided it did not compromise the national honor. The *National Intelligencer* commented that the arrangement and the tone of the message were an indication that Jackson had been influenced by the unanimous counsel of his cabinet.[48]

Formal mediation of the controversy by Great Britain soon became unnecessary. When Jackson's annual message of December 7, 1835, was received in Paris, his declaration that he had no intention of menacing or insulting France was considered by the Louis Philippe government to be a sufficient apology. In a note to the British government, the French signified their readiness to pay the American indemnity. This information was transmitted to Forsyth by Bankhead on February 15, 1836. In his acknowledgment of Bankhead's note, Forsyth stated that the President was entirely satisfied and anticipated a prompt resumption of friendly relations with France. Jackson's message to Congress on February 22 announced that the controversy had been settled. In a communication of May 10, 1836, the President informed Congress that France had paid, to the agent of the United States, the four installments of the indemnity which were due.

After France had agreed to make the indemnity payments, there remained other issues to be settled. Forsyth wanted the French government to repudiate Pageot's action in publishing the de Broglie letter. The Secretary of State instructed Aaron Vail, American chargé d'affaires in London, to suggest that Palmerston aid in obtaining the repudiation from the French. Palmerston showed no inclination to follow the suggestion; instead, he forwarded to Washington an explanation of the position of the government of France. The French contended that publication of the letter was justifiable in an effort to clarify the peaceful intentions of the Louis Philippe government. Furthermore, the French government could not disavow an express action in conformance with official instructions.[49] In reply, Forsyth informed Henry Stephen Fox, British Minister to the United States, that the President thought it proper for France to give an assurance that such a practice would not be repeated in the future. Such a deed would be misinterpreted by the American people, and the responsible agent would incur the displeasure of the United States government. The Secretary admitted that, under the circumstances, Pageot's "act cannot be disavowed, and therefore the subject had better rest as it is."[50]

A second point of issue was the unannounced arrival in Washington of Alphonse Pageot. Forsyth was angry with the Frenchman because of his participation in the de Broglie letter affair. He was also provoked because the State Department had not been consulted about or notified of Pageot's reappointment as chargé d'affaires. The Frenchman's return in his former capacity was accomplished through the artifice of his father-in-law, William B. Lewis, and Secretary of War Lewis Cass. The latter had a private conversation with Jackson and, upon the request of Lewis, sought to ascertain the President's sentiments toward Pageot. Jackson expressed his personal friendship and high regard for the ex-chargé.

According to Lewis, Cass then returned to the War Department and advised him of the presidential interview in such a manner as to indicate that Jackson desired the return of the young Frenchman. Lewis relayed the information in writing to Pageot, who showed a pertinent part of the letter to Louis Philippe. The reappointment followed, the French King acting under the impression that he was extending a friendly gesture toward Jackson. When the President learned the details of the matter, he was as indignant as was Forsyth.[51] Through the intervention of Fox, however, he eventually agreed to receive Pageot, who presented his credentials to the Secretary of State on November 19, 1836.

On one occasion, during the controversy with France, Forsyth left Washington for a visit to Georgia. His absence from the seat of the government, together with the absence of Cass, caused reports to be circulated that the two officials intended to resign from the cabinet because of the appointment of Amos Kendall as Postmaster General. The rumors were promptly denied. One newspaper declared that Forsyth had not only been consulted prior to the promotion, but that he had expressed his approval.[52] Another journal, denouncing the stories as without foundation, stated that both cabinet officers "have the entire confidence of the President, and they cherish for him . . . the warmest personal and political attachment."[53] A few months later, Jackson publicly showed his esteem for the Secretary of State by appointing John Forsyth, Junior, to the office of United States Attorney for the Southern District of Alabama.[54]

The older Forsyth was retained as Secretary of State by President Martin Van Buren. But shortly after the inauguration of the New Yorker, on March 9, the Secretary submitted his resignation, and also prepared to defend his action through publication of an address to the people of Georgia.

According to reports, the action was prompted by two incidents. The President, under the impression that Forsyth wished to become Minister to Austria, offered him that post. The Secretary immediately declined the offer, which he interpreted as an indication of his not being wanted in the new cabinet. A second reason for Forsyth's act was the result of a statement of policy, in which Van Buren spoke of the inexpediency of a presidential aspirant holding a cabinet position.[55]

Forsyth's letter of resignation brought a prompt reply from the President, with a request for reconsideration. Deploring all the misunderstandings, Van Buren gave an assurance that he had never had any intention of vacating Forsyth from the State Department unless the latter so desired.[56] With the matter clarified, Forsyth withdrew his resignation and suppressed publication of the address.

As secretary of state under two presidents, Forsyth became involved with various issues concerning the slave trade. Within two months of his accession to the office, he received a note on the subject from Charles Richard Vaughan, British Minister in Washington. The contents of the message revealed that the United States was invited to become a party to recently negotiated treaties between Great Britain and France for a more effective suppression of the nefarious traffic. Thus, the two European nations sought to alleviate the sensitive American opposition regarding search of vessels in time of peace.

Forsyth's reply indicated that the United States was in no mood to surrender what were considered her maritime rights. He stated that his government neither expected nor desired to exercise jurisdiction beyond the American continent. The United States, acting alone, was entirely capable of detecting and punishing those of her citizens who violated the laws. Any such plan as that proposed would cause innocent American nationals undue delay in their lawful pursuits; for, if suspected, they would be sent across the ocean to the United States for trial. French and British subjects would have access to courts near at hand and consequently would not suffer the same inconvenience and possible damage. Therefore, the Jackson administration would enter into no agreement for the establishment of an international police force off the coast of Africa and Madagascar for the purpose of searching suspected slave vessels.[57] Although his note to Vaughan was a reflection of the President's views, Forsyth undoubtedly was in complete accord. His views on an independent United States policy had not changed since he announced them in the House of Representatives in 1825.

The Van Buren administration followed a policy similar to that of its predecessor. In October, 1839, Forsyth received a communication from British Minister Henry S. Fox complaining of the deficiencies in the anti-slave trade laws of the United States. Declaring that all civilized nations were duty bound to unite in suppressing the traffic, he recommended that the United States agree to the mutual right of search. Forsyth replied that his government, as desirous as Great Britain of extinguishing the slave trade, had consistently pursued a course toward that objective. The fact that the slave trade continued to exist was due, not to inadequacy of American law, but to duplicity practised by those nations with which the British had contracted cooperative treaties. A faithful execution of the latter was more necessary than an Anglo-American convention.

Forsyth's note to Fox stated that a United States naval force had been stationed off the African coast "as a measure of precaution to protect American vessels from improper molestation . . . and also to detect those foreigners who may be found carrying, without proper authority, the flag of the United States."[58] Each of the problems mentioned was a source of controversy between the United States and Great Britain.

Forsyth was continually writing to Andrew Stevenson, the United States Minister in London, regarding American ships which had been stopped, searched, and detained by British vessels. Emphasizing that the United States was not a party to the treaties which permitted visit and search, he directed Stevenson to make representations to the British government for explanations and for punishment of the offenders. Stevenson complied with his instructions, but could obtain no satisfactory answer or promise of redress from Palmerston. Similar treatment was accorded claims of American citizens who were asking for indemnification for slaves shipwrecked near the Bahamas and liberated by the local authorities.

American suggestions for a treaty concerning disposal of shipwrecked slaves in the British West Indies and Bermuda came to naught when the London government refused to negotiate. On one occasion, a captured American vessel, the *Tigris,* was taken to Boston by a British warship. Forsyth informed Fox that the naval commander had admitted acting without official instructions. Consequently, the British government was requested to censure the responsible officer in such definite terms as to discourage others from following his example. In conclusion, the Secretary admonished that

> however strong and unchangeable may be the determination of this Government to punish any citizens of the United States who violate the laws . . . , it will not permit the exercise of any authority by foreign armed vessels in the execution of those laws.[59]

The British government denounced the protection afforded foreign slavers through unauthorized use of the American flag, and suggested, as remedies to arrest the evil, deployment of a combined Anglo-American fleet off the coast of Africa and strengthening of United States laws against the slave trade. The British complained also of the unusual leniency being granted American and Portuguese vessels leaving Havana for the African coast. Nicholas Philip Trist, United States Consul at the Cuban port, was charged with encouraging the slave trade by failure to exercise the proper vigilance when issuing clearance papers. John Quincy Adams, arguing wholeheartedly with the British, declared that Trist was guilty of "either the vilest treachery or the most culpable indifference to his duties."[60]

Forsyth adopted a more amicable attitude toward the American Consul. The Secretary's endeavors to secure all evidence possessed by the British were indicative of a desire to give Trist every opportunity to justify his actions.[61] Meanwhile, Forsyth assured Fox that the grave charge would necessitate a thorough investigation, even though the President was confident of a complete vindication of the accused. Forsyth defended Trist's innocence when serving in the absence of a Portuguese consul and expressed a personal conviction that any unprejudiced person would arrive at the same conclusion.[62] But John Quincy Adams did not agree. The ex-President considered the Forsyth note one "which is palliative and excusatory. . . ."[63]

The *Amistad* case involved directly the slave trade but it was expanded to include the question of treaty obligations versus jurisdiction of a state of the United States. In June, 1839, the Spanish schooner *Amistad* sailed from Havana, bound for the Cuban port of Guanaga. Her cargo included approximately fifty Negroes who had been purchased in violation of Spanish laws: imported from Africa, they had been sold in Havana to Spaniards José Ruiz and Pedro Montez.

During the voyage between the Cuban ports, the Negroes seized control of the *Amistad,* murdered the captain, and ordered the two slave merchants to assist in navigating the ship to the coast of Africa. Under pretense of obeying the command, the white navigators altered the course in such a manner as to bring the vessel to the New York shore. There, on August 26, the schooner was captured by the United States warship *Washington* and conveyed to the port of New London, Connecticut, for investigation.[64] Ten of the Negroes died during the passage from Cuba; the remaining thirty-nine mutineers were taken to New Haven and placed in the county jail to await determination of their status.[65]

The Madrid government was of the opinion that, since the alleged crimes were committed on a Spanish vessel outside the limits of the United States, the United States had no jurisdiction over the Negroes. Consequently, the Spanish Minister in Washington, A. Calderon de la Barca, addressed a note to Forsyth on September 6, which contained a formal demand for the surrender of the *Amistad* and her cargo including the Negroes.

Forsyth informed the President, who was absent from the city, that he had consulted with Secretary of the Treasury Levi Woodbury, Attorney General Felix Grundy, and Postmaster General Amos Kendall. All had agreed with him that the Spanish request was legitimate as provided by the terms of the 1795 treaty between that nation and the United States. The correctness of the interpretation had been reaffirmed by the Attorney General who, subsequently, had conducted a careful investigation of the entire matter. Confident that the proper decision had been reached, Forsyth wrote to Calderon and to William S. Holabird, United States Attorney in the Connecticut District, for all evidence which would expedite compliance with the Spanish petition.[66]

The action taken by Forsyth was not destined to produce conclusive results. Complications arose when as a result of various
salvage and restitution claims filed by interested parties the ultimate decision was transferred from the executive branch of
the government to the judiciary. Moreover, abolitionist sympathizers were aroused, and they argued that regardless of their previous status, the Negroes could no longer be classified as slaves
once they had entered upon the free soil of Connecticut; under
the existing situation, state laws could not be superseded by a
federal treaty.[67] Secretary of the Treasury Woodbury, realizing that sectional feeling might endanger the administration, confided to Van Buren that "perhaps nothing is lost in point of public
policy by letting the Judiciary take all the responsibility . . . which
they may choose to exercise. . . ."[68] But Forsyth was of a different opinion. In emphatic terms, he maintained that settlement of the *Amistad* affair was a prerogative of the President,
who was under treaty obligation to return the vessel and cargo
to the Spanish authorities. According to Forsyth, the United
States had no right to question the legality of the slaves' ownership; therefore the case before the federal court constituted improper litigation.[69]

The case was scheduled for trial before the district court sitting
in New Haven, the session to begin on January 7, 1840. Forsyth
anticipated a decision sustaining the tenets of the administration, but there was the possibility of an appeal from the court's
pronouncement. To forestall any such legal maneuver on the part
of the abolitionists, he made preparations for a hasty removal of
the *Amistad* captives from the United States.[70] He arranged
with Secretary of the Navy James Kirke Paulding for a vessel to
be stationed near the port of New Haven.

Once the expected decision was rendered by the judiciary, the
Negroes and all pertinent evidence, including court records, were
to be transported to Cuba for delivery to the Spanish authorities.
The Secretary of State directed that Holabird cooperate with
the marshal and the naval commander in executing the plan,
provided no immediate appeal was instituted. Forsyth added
that the District Attorney was "not to take it for granted that
it [appeal] will be interposed. And, if, on the contrary, the decision of the court is different [favorable to the Negroes], you are
to take out an appeal. . . ."[71]

The district court, refusing to recognize the 1795 treaty as applicable to the case, dismissed the claim of the alleged owners and

ordered that the free Negroes be returned to Africa. Upon receipt of the information, Forsyth wrote to Holabird reiterating
instructions for the filing of an appeal. While the appeal was
pending, Forsyth received a note from Henry S. Fox which expressed British opposition to the Spanish demand for return of
the *Amistad* prisoners. The British government was represented
as being anxious for the President to take the necessary steps
which would insure freedom to the Negroes. Evidently in a petu-
lant mood, the Secretary replied that the case was being reviewed
by the federal judiciary and that no final decision had been rendered. He reminded Fox that "the Executive has neither the
power nor the disposition to control the proceedings of the legal
tribunals when acting within their appropriate jurisdiction."[72]

Forsyth retired from office before the final verdict was reached.
In a decision of March 9, 1841, the United States Supreme Court
declared that it could find no proof, under Spanish laws, whereby
the Negroes should be classified as slaves. As a consequence, the
tribunal ordered that they be given their freedom; no specification was made as to their being restored to their native land.
Prior to the final decree, the abolitionists had offered to provide
transportation to Africa.[73] Following the Supreme Court decision, the Negroes' friends experienced difficulty in raising funds
for the project; however, the objective was accomplished when
thirty-five of the Africans sailed from New York and were landed
in Sierra Leone on January 15, 1842.[74]

In his capacity as Secretary of State, Forsyth exhibited the energy and ability which had been characteristic of his legislative
career. A newspaper article of November 15, 1834, remarked that

he discovers more talent in his own office than has generally been
ascribed to him . . . [since] it was surmised that he could not apply
himself with much assiduity to the details of business. The officers of
the department are consequently agreeably disappointed in finding
out his industry and capacity.[75]

An official of the patent office had reason to regret the Secretary's diligence and attention to details. Forsyth's first departmental act was to dismiss Chief Clerk Alexander McIntyre for
an offense considered detrimental to government service. Mc-
Intyre was accused of securing positions for friends, and thereby
causing loss of employment to other clerks.[76]

Lewis Cass, United States Minister to France, was another recipient of Forsyth's vigilance. When Cass signified his intention

of leaving his post for a journey to Milan, the Secretary reminded him of a previous visit to the Mediterranean area which had lasted for seven months, and conveyed the President's disapproval of the Milan trip. On a different occasion, Forsyth observed that Cass's communications to the Paris government were written in French. Forsyth advised the Minister to write his notes in English so as to guard against errors in translation; if he considered it necessary, he could enclose an informal French version with the official message.[77] Cass assured Forsyth that future business would be conducted in the prescribed manner.

Forsyth discovered that a public official is likely in the performance of duty to incur the displeasure of persons adversely affected. A vigorous administrator, he had various criticisms directed at his conduct of governmental affairs. Criticism of Forsyth developed from the quarrel between the state of Ohio and the territory of Michigan concerning the boundary line.

In 1835, the Ohio legislature passed a law providing for extension of state jurisdiction over the disputed area. A serious conflict seemed imminent when the Acting Governor of Michigan, Stevens Thomson Mason, directed that the militia resist enforcement of the statute. Forsyth reported to Secretary of War Lewis Cass that Major Henry Whiting of the United States Army had assumed responsibility for the issuance of arms and munitions in the territory. Acting in the name of the President, Forsyth sought to avert the clash by appealing to Mason and to Governor Robert Lucas of Ohio. He requested William C. Rives to represent the administration in an attempt to prevent hostilities.[78]

Forsyth's communications to Mason, Lucas, and Rives gave no evidence as to his sympathies in the contest, but John Quincy Adams stated that Forsyth favored the Ohio claims.[79] Mason, who was removed from office because of his non-conciliatory attitude, was firmly convinced that the Secretary was active in the interest of Ohio. The fact that the new Acting Governor, John Scott Horner, owed his appointment to Forsyth's influence[80] was not conducive to a change of opinion on the part of the dismissed official. In an open letter, Mason denounced Forsyth:

The people of this country are unaccustomed to the tricks of diplomacy, and require plain and open dealing from their public agents. Intrigue may flourish for a while, but it will ultimately prove its own ruin. In public as in private life, the man who is once found a profligate, is ever after suspected. The two, your experience may inform you, are generally found in the same individual. Begin then anew,

and although you may not succeed in convincing the world that you
are an honest man, you may at least induce them to believe, that you
are not so base as you have been.[81]   :

Another disgruntled official was Cornelius Peter Van Ness,
United States Minister to Spain. Prior to Forsyth's appointment as
Secretary of State, Van Ness had been granted permission for a
temporary return to the United States, the leave to begin approximately April 1, 1832. Three years passed, with the Minister remaining in Spain. On March 6, 1835, Secretary Forsyth informed
Van Ness that a new minister was to be appointed and asked
for the date of his departure from Madrid. As interpreted by
Van Ness, the previous request for leave was being used to maneuver him from the Spanish post. He replied that his application for temporary leave was not unusual, and pointed out that
Forsyth himself had spent eight months in the United States
while occupying the ministerial position. Emphasizing that devotion to duty had been responsible for postponement of his
journey, Van Ness fixed October 1, 1835, as the latest date for
his departure. He also indicated the probability of his leaving before the arrival of his successor.[82]

On January 17, 1836, Forsyth received a dispatch from Madrid
dated the preceding November. In the message, Van Ness complained that he had not been officially notified of the name of
his replacement. He had learned that William T. Barry, the appointee, had died at Liverpool while en route to Spain. Because of
these circumstances, he had decided to retain control of the legation pending receipt of further instructions.

The Secretary wasted little time in addressing a reply. He
indicated his surprise at Van Ness's continuance in Madrid, especially since Legation Secretary Arthur Middleton had for some
months been the recipient of departmental instructions. He contended that the former Minister must have had official knowledge of Barry's appointment through Middleton; he expressed
doubt that Van Ness would receive any compensation for the
period which had elapsed since October 1, 1835.[83] The Georgian
advised Middleton that, to avoid confusion pending arrival of a
new minister, he was to receive the archives and transact legation
business as "was the expectation of the Department . . . since
the 1st.of October last."[84]

In spite of Forsyth's exhortation, Van Ness remained at the
post for approximately another year. A March dispatch from
Spain was designated a final one; in May, the Secretary received

notification from Van Ness that the archives would be delivered
to Middleton; in August, the latter advised that the recalled
official had not departed from Madrid. A communication from
Van Ness, dated December 17, 1836, stated that he had not been
informed of John H. Eaton's appointment; nevertheless, he would
retire from the legation in order "to relieve the Govt. from the
further payments of two Ministers Salaries. . . ."[85] Three days
later, he left the legation in charge of Middleton.

The following February, Van Ness dispatched a letter from
Madrid to President Van Buren, in which he ridiculed Middleton, Eaton, and the latter's wife. His main condemnation, however, was reserved for Forsyth, whom he accused of an unfriendly
attitude toward the writer. Claiming that his removal was
prompted by the Secretary's working in collusion with Middleton, Van Ness classified Forsyth's conduct as "a tissue of falsehood
and duplicity for the purpose of opening a place to thrust in for
the moment a personal and unworthy favorite. . . ."[86]

Van Ness finally relinquished his post. But Forsyth soon discovered that the new Minister, John H. Eaton, was no improvement. In March, 1837, the Secretary wrote to Eaton complaining of his delay in reaching Madrid and of the lack of correspondence from him extending over a period of eight months.
The Minister replied that disturbed conditions, caused by a
Spanish revolt, had been responsible for his late arrival from
Cadiz. His answer to the second complaint was that he had had
nothing of an official nature to communicate. He refused to admit
that a minister should report insignificant information, including
gossip, private conversations, and theories.[87]

Eaton later claimed that Forsyth had neglected to answer his
dispatches. While he indicated the possibility that letters might
have been intercepted by Spanish bandits, he attributed the failure chiefly to indifference and disinclination on the part of the
Secretary. Forsyth contended that instructions had not only
been sent, but had been received, as indicated by observations
contained in Eaton's messages. Eaton explained that he regarded
the instructions as "replies," but that they did not give satisfactory
answers to his inquiries.[88] Whereupon, Forsyth reminded him
that "the replies . . . were written to regulate your conduct, and
not to satisfy your judgment."[89]

Other disagreements between the two men related to financial
matters. An unauthorized expenditure by Eaton of the legation
contingent fund was charged to his private account. Eaton de-

fended his action by accusing the State Department of issuing contradictory directions. Forsyth was just as insistent that the instructions were "in perfect harmony."[90]

In December, 1838, Eaton received a directive from an auditor in the Treasury Department, S. Pleasonton, instructing him to submit reports concerning his salary and the contingent fund. The Minister indignantly advised Forsyth that he would transact no business with a clerk, and that he would acknowledge no orders save those from the Secretary of State. Insisting that the disposal of his personal funds was a subject over which the government had no authority, he promised to transmit an accounting of the contingent fund to the State Department.[91]

Forsyth's sharp reply was a reminder that the Treasury Department was charged with government monetary affairs. Hence there was no intention of inspecting private accounts. If Eaton had made a careful study of Pleasonton's letter, he would have understood that a draft for his salary was chargeable to the Minister until he had rendered an account claiming corresponding credit. With respect to the contingent fund, Eaton had failed to comply with that section of his instructions requiring quarterly reports of disbursements.[92]

By September, 1839, the difficulties involving Eaton had accumulated to such an extent that Forsyth advised Van Buren of the necessity for removing the recalcitrant official. Notifying Eaton of his recall, Forsyth stated that his duties would cease on May 1, 1840. In accordance with departmental policy, he added that the London bankers would be instructed to close the Minister's salary credit on that date and to transfer the contingent fund to the account of his successor.[93]

Eaton replied that he did not deny the President's right to replace foreign agents, even without cause. Resentful of Forsyth's instructions regarding finances, he declared that he knew "of no act of mine, which can authorize against me a Suspicion of being a Swindler; and which this direction clearly indicates."[94] On April 30, Eaton released the legation property, but neglected to take formal leave of the Spanish Foreign Minister; nor did he present Secretary Middleton to the Madrid government. In August, a Washington newspaper announced that Eaton and his family had recently arrived in the city.[95]

Forsyth devoted considerable time and energy toward improving efficiency within the State Department. His reorganization was considered so serviceable that, except for minor changes, it was continued until 1870. He retained the seven divisions and fourteen clerks, but reassigned functions in such capable fashion that the number of bureaus was reduced from seven to four. Dissatisfied with the prevalent pay scale, he sought an increase and equalization of salaries for department personnel. He demanded strict observance of security regulations and expected precise performance of individual duties.[96]

Forsyth brought to the State Department a valuable background of governmental service. He had gained administrative experience while governor, and had accumulated general knowledge of foreign affairs while minister and legislator. His diplomatic correspondence gives evidence of cogent reasoning and sincerity of purpose. Generally tactful, he did not hesitate to adopt a peremptory tone when the occasion seemed to demand such.

In the controversy with France over the spoliations claims, Forsyth performed his duties in a capable manner. In dealing with questions involving the African slave trade, Forsyth exhibited a distrust of British maritime practices coupled with a desire to avoid entangling alliances. He preferred that the United States follow a policy of unilateral action. He favored protection of slave property and was decidedly hostile to the abolition movement. He was prophetic when he wrote to Van Buren that, unless preventive action was taken against the agitators, "I should not be at all surprised at a decisive renewed movement to establish the Southern Confederacy."[97]

As Secretary of State under Jackson, Forsyth acted in the role of faithful subordinate. He was overshadowed by the President, of course, but he succeeded in placing a restraint upon the rash tendencies of Jackson. While he did not determine policy, his moderate views undoubtedly had some effect. Under no circumstances, however, could his influence with Jackson be compared with Van Buren's.

In Van Buren's administration, Forsyth approached his duties with a less restricted attitude. Perhaps this was due to his long personal friendship with the New Yorker, as well as to the fact that the two men were usually in accord on matters of national interest. During his exchange of caustic correspondence with Eaton, Forsyth once stated that he was sending "the remarks contained in the preceding pages without previously submitting them to the President for his examination and approval."[98] There is little likelihood that such action was ever considered when Jackson dominated affairs. Although President Van Buren granted Forsyth increased freedom in the exercise of his office, Forsyth recognized his subordinate status and gave his friend no cause to doubt his loyalty and cooperation. Under two presidents, Forsyth was an able though not an outstanding Secretary of State.

X

Diplomacy: Southwest and Northeast

As SECRETARY of State, John Forsyth devoted considerable attention to diplomatic affairs of the North American continent. His interest was sincere, for he was confronted with serious questions which tended to strain relations between the United States and her neighbors to the southwest and northeast. Great Britain, with possessions in the western hemisphere, was involved in several of the issues. Of the major problems, one of the first with which Forsyth had to contend was the controversy over the boundary line between the United States and Mexico. He was handicapped in dealing with the issue because of unorthodox attempts made by the Jackson administration for purchase of Texas. When the Mexican problem merged with the Texas question, Forsyth's efforts became those of a cautious tactician.

By the treaty of February 22, 1819, the boundary line between the United States and Spain's Mexican territory was fixed at the Sabine River. After Mexico became independent, she negotiated with the United States the treaties of January 12, 1828, and April 5, 1831, whereby the boundary of 1819 was confirmed. A dispute occurred when President Jackson contended that the Neches River was only a western branch of the Sabine and that the land between the two bodies of water belonged to the United States.[1] In a convention signed April 3, 1835, the United States and Mexico agreed to appoint a joint commission for the purpose of surveying the disputed territory and determining the exact boundary line. The American agent who signed the agreement was Colonel Anthony Butler.

Butler was the United States chargé d'affaires to Mexico when

Forsyth assumed the duties of secretary of state. His most intensive activity in Mexico appears to have been concerned with
efforts to purchase Texas for the United States. "His chief
object," wrote one historian, "seems to have been to prolong his
period of employment and to overcast his failure by deluding
the administration with false hopes."[2] On August 11, 1834, Forsyth received a request from Butler for permission to visit the
United States. He desired an interview with either the Secretary
or the President, "at which certain communications may be
made and opinions freely exchanged and compared which it is
impracticable to do by any other mode."[3] Forsyth recommended
that the leave be granted, but the chargé did not return to
Washington until the following June.

Soon after Butler's arrival Forsyth and Jackson conferred with
him. Following the conferences, Butler prepared a written record
of his plan to obtain Texas, which he submitted to the Secretary.
In substance, the scheme was based on a proposed bribe of
$500,000 to be paid to Ignacio Hernandez, priest and confidant
of Mexican President Antonio Lopez de Santa Anna.[4] On July
2, 1835, Forsyth wrote Butler that his letter had been presented
to the President who, preferring a "very desirable alteration in
our boundary with Mexico, . . . is resolved that no means
of even an equivocal character shall be used to accomplish it."[5]
He informed Butler that Jackson had no confidence in further
negotiations, but was agreeable to a continuance provided negotiations were completed in time to present the results to the next
session of Congress.

On November 9, 1835, Forsyth notified Butler that the State
Department had received no communication from him since his
July departure from Washington. At approximately the same
time, Butler, disregarding the usual diplomatic procedure, addressed a letter directly to the President. He expressed himself
as confident of obtaining Texas for the United States provided
he was permitted to remain at his post for an additional three
or four months. He claimed that Forsyth's instructions were
vague, because they appeared to place a limitation on his work
by ordering a return to Washington in December.[6]

On December 16, 1835, Forsyth addressed a note to Butler
informing him that since the time allotted for the completion of
the negotiations had elapsed, the President was nominating a
new man for the Mexican post. Butler made an angry reply. He
contended that the instructions of the preceding July had not

been delivered until just prior to his departure from Washington, and consequently he was not fully familiar with the contents until several days later; he would not have accepted the appointment if he had known that a limitation of time had been prescribed for his mission. He also maintained that the directions contradicted what had been said and implied in the conversations with Forsyth and with Jackson. Evidently referring to the Secretary of State, Butler said:

how far my failure in effecting the object may be attributed to the indiscretion of certain persons who affect to be in the Confidence of the President, and to retail his opinions and declare his purposes will be for after times to disclose: I am in possession of all the facts, and a precious collection they are.[7]

Butler's collection of data was related to a matter which for some time had been of particular concern to Forsyth. Prior to the recall, the Secretary had notified Butler that the State Department did not have a complete file of his legation correspondence. Forsyth urged him to transmit the missing documents, but Butler disregarded the instructions.[8] According to John Quincy Adams, Butler "carried off some of the most important documents of the negotiations."[9]

Meanwhile, Mexico protested that the United States government was not enforcing its neutrality, and that armed men from the United States were openly joining the Texans. As a result of these charges, Forsyth wrote to various district attorneys directing that they prosecute all violations of the neutrality laws.[10] Because of public opinion in the United States, however, nothing was done to apprehend the filibusters.

On March 24, 1836, Forsyth presented to President Jackson the Mexican Minister to the United States, Manuel Eduardo de Gorostiza. This individual soon became involved in an extended correspondence with the Secretary of State over what the Mexican government considered a breach of neutrality by the United States. The issue was the occupation of Nacogdoches by Major-General Edmund Pendleton Gaines.

By the treaty of April 5, 1831, the United States and Mexico had mutually agreed to "restrain by force all hostilities and incursions on the part of the Indian nations living within their respective boundaries. . . ."[11] On March 29, 1836, General Gaines wrote to Secretary of War Lewis Cass requesting authority to move troops into the disputed territory, provided the Indians on the opposite side of the river created such disorder as to menace the frontier. Cass replied that the President did not intend to take advantage of the unsettled conditions in Mexico to appropriate any part of Mexican territory. Should an advance become necessary, Gaines was to exercise discretion and under no circumstances to go farther than Nacogdoches. Gaines interpreted this to mean that he might enter any area claimed to be within the limits of the United States.

Several days before Cass's message was sent to Gaines, Forsyth conferred with Gorostiza. He informed the Mexican Minister that Gaines would be ordered to take precautionary measures in order to preserve the disputed area from Indian depredations, to defend the United States territory from disturbances by Mexicans, Texans, or Indians, and to protect the joint commission when the group began the survey of the boundary line. Should it become necessary for the troops, in the performance of duty, to proceed into the controversial territory, Mexico was not to consider the occupation as a hostile move. According to Forsyth, the occupancy would be of a temporary nature, and the troops would be withdrawn once the boundary limits were determined and the disturbances ceased.[12] Gorostiza opposed occupation of the disputed area by United States troops.

In June, the troops of General Gaines crossed the Sabine River and occupied Nacogdoches. During the next few months, Gorostiza wrote numerous letters to the State Department, asking if newspaper accounts of the occupation were accurate. Forsyth was evasive on the subject. In a note to the Minister, on August 31, 1836, he transmitted a copy of Jackson's disapproval of General Gaines's requisition for the use of militia. The Secretary wrote that he hoped this would suffice as an answer to the protests. Later, in an interview with Gorostiza, Forsyth stated that he had nothing more than indirect information that United States troops were at Nacogdoches. He then read extracts from letters written by Jackson to Gaines authorizing the occupation. Gorostiza immediately protested and threatened to ask for his passport unless he received a satisfactory reply.[13]

Personal business requiring his presence in Georgia, Forsyth departed from Washington in late September. Thereafter, Gorostiza's correspondence was with Asbury Dickins, Acting Secretary of State. On October 13, the Mexican Minister was informed that the President, after giving full consideration to the matter, had determined not to rescind the orders given to General Gaines.

Two days later Gorostiza replied with a detailed protest. Critical of Gaines's partiality toward the Texans, he claimed that the Indian danger was purely a figment of the imagination. The Minister mentioned Forsyth's refusal, under presidential orders, to explain pertinent aspects of the situation. Convinced that Mexico could expect little consideration from the United States, Gorostiza took personal responsibility for concluding his mission and asked for his passport.[14]

Before he left, Gorostiza prepared a pamphlet of his correspondence, prefaced by a long introduction in defense of the Mexican position. The Minister sent the manifesto to various members of the foreign diplomatic corps. In addition, newspaper editors obtained copies, from which extracts were published. The Washington *Globe* commented on the publication: "Gorostiza abandons his mission here, under pretence that we are false and perfidious."[15]

Forsyth was furious with Gorostiza, claiming that the pamphlet contained "Statements and Comments defamatory of the Government and people of the United States, and obviously intended to injure the character of both for honor and good faith in the eyes of the world."[16] He declared that should the Mexican authorities uphold Gorostiza, discontinuance of diplomatic relations would result. Subsequently, the Mexican government gave notice that it concurred with Gorostiza's views, and approved his withdrawal from Washington.

The disruption of relations with Mexico brought little relief to Forsyth in the performance of his duties, for the Texas issue had entered the crucial stage. At a general convention, the Texans, on March 2, 1836, had declared their independence of Mexico. During the remainder of his tenure in the State Department, the Secretary was concerned with the efforts of various Texas agents seeking recognition and possible annexation of the new republic. On March 19, the government of Texas appointed George C. Childress and Robert Hamilton as special commissioners to the United States. They were to be associated with three agents previously sent to Washington: Stephen Fuller Austin, Branch Tanner Archer, and William H. Wharton. On April 1, President David Gouverneur Burnet issued a similar commission to Samuel Price Carson.

A prominent historian observed:

General Jackson dominated everything so completely that it is not easy to determine the attitude or influence of any member of his cabinet, but Forsyth always seemed more reluctant than the President to facilitate the recognition of Texas or its annexation to the United States.[17]

The instructions to Childress and Hamilton indicated some apprehension regarding the Secretary's attitude. The commissioners were directed to engage in private conversations with administration officials and with congressmen, to obtain their objectives. If they found Forsyth reluctant to listen to them, Childress was to approach Jackson "through the medium of old acquaintance and personal Friendship. . . ."[18] In June, the two agents reported that, though their credentials had been presented to the State Department, they had not been recognized officially. Forsyth had talked with them informally, but they had not been able to learn the position of the government toward recognition of Texas.[19]

Actually, the administration was pursuing a cautious policy. In Jackson's annual message to Congress of December, 1835, he had emphasized the neutrality of the United States in the struggle between Texas and Mexico. Another problem involved was the sectional attitude caused by the slavery question. A contemporary noted that "the tables of the members [of Congress] have groaned with pamphlets written by the abolitionists for the purpose of injuring and calumniating Texas."[20]

On July 8, 1836, James Collinsworth and Peter W. Grayson arrived in Washington to supersede the Texas agents then in the United States. When they presented their credentials to Forsyth, he refused to accept them as valid because there was no seal attached. In an interview with the commissioners, the Secretary learned that their purpose was to engage in preliminary talks regarding terms acceptable for admission of Texas to the Union.[21]

Collinsworth and Grayson reported to their government that Forsyth had seemed "but little disposed to be communicative in anything," although he had admitted that Jackson favored the annexation of Texas "whenever it could be done with propriety."[22] In a subsequent letter, Grayson remarked that the Secretary had indicated his willingness to talk with them, but only in an informal capacity, since they were not accredited agents.[23]

After the constitutional government of Texas was established, William H. Wharton was appointed Minister to the United States and Memucan Hunt was commissioned special representative to work with him. Wharton arrived in Washington on December

19, 1836, and two days later had an informal interview with
Forsyth. The Secretary gave him no satisfaction except to indi-
cate that the President intended to communicate a message to
Congress on the subject of Texas.[24]

On December 21, 1836, Jackson transmitted to Congress his
special message concerning the political, military, and civil condition of Texas. He invited attention to resolutions, passed by
both houses at the previous session, which declared that Texas
independence should be recognized when it was ascertained that
a capable civil government was in operation. In the preamble to
the House resolution, according to Jackson, there was a distinct
intimation that Congress should make the decision. He concurred
in this view, but emphasized that it was not his purpose to avoid
responsibility. Based on available information, his opinion was
that recognition of Texas independence should be deferred.

Meanwhile, Forsyth was adhering to his strict rule of having
no official relations with the Texas government. When Wharton
submitted a formal protest concerning Texas exclusion from a
possible Mexican-United States treaty, the Secretary refused to
receive the note. He did, however, listen to an oral protest from
the unaccredited minister.[25] As late as February 20, 1837, Forsyth
wrote a relative: "I make no Communication of any sort to
Texas."[26]

The recognition of Texas was consummated just before the
end of the Jackson administration. In February, Wharton wrote
to a member of the Texas cabinet that the House Committee on
Foreign Affairs recommended immediate recognition and also an
appropriation for sending a minister to Texas. He added signifi-
cantly: "It being important to know who are friends and for
us, I communicate for your information that Mr. Forsyth was
opposed to the report of the Committee."[27] The Senate shortly
thereafter passed a resolution for recognition and the House of
Representatives agreed to an appropriation for ministerial expenses, provided the President decided to send someone to Texas.
On March 5, 1837, Wharton communicated to his government
that Jackson had concurred in the congressional resolutions for
recognition by appointing Alceé La Branche, of Louisiana as the
chargé d'affaires to Texas. According to Wharton, the President
"sent for Genl Hunt and myself and requested the pleasure of
a glass of wine, and stated that Mr. Forsyth would see us
officially on Monday."[28] At President Van Buren's inauguration,

the day following Jackson's conversation, Wharton was present with the diplomatic corps.

The Texas authorities, having attained one objective, began to intensify their efforts toward achieving annexation. They soon learned that change of status had no material effect on Forsyth's cautious approach to the second issue.

Forsyth's views on annexation were variously interpreted by Memucan Hunt, Texas Minister to the United States. On August 4, 1837, Hunt complied with instructions by submitting to Forsyth a formal proposal for Texas annexation. When forwarding a copy of the note to his government, he expressed the opinion that Forsyth, Secretary of War Joel R. Poinsett, and Postmaster General Amos Kendall favored the addition of Texas to the Union.[29] His report of August 11, however, declared:

. . . I have ascertained beyond a doubt, that Mr. Forsyth . . . is violently opposed to annexation!! I could not avoid proclaiming on hearing of it, "and you too Brutus" knowing it as I did to be "the unkindest cut of all"; for it proves him to be a traitor to the most delicate and deepest interests of those to whom he is indebted for the very power and influence which he is now attempting to exercise against them. But thanks to God, if matters terminate as it has been intimated to me they will, this ingratitude will bring about results for Texas, the South and himself precisely contrary to his expectations. . . . If I am successful, this Cabinet will not remain as it is.[30]

On August 25, Forsyth replied to Hunt's proposal for annexation. He pointed out two obstacles which would prevent United States acceptance. In the first place, he questioned the constitutionality of annexing a free and alien nation; second, the United States could not disregard obligations established by her treaty of amity with Mexico.[31]

The Secretary of State had an interview with Hunt in November, in which the latter thought he detected a more favorable attitude regarding his objective than had been previously evidenced. Forsyth remarked that he expected annexation to be accomplished provided there were no complications. The envoy informed his government that, in his revised opinion, Forsyth "is a warm advocate of the measure. . . ."[32] In January, 1838, Hunt stated that Forsyth and Van Buren desired annexation, but were hesitant to take the step because of the following factors: treaty obligations with Mexico, danger of involving the United

States in a war, opposition from the northern states, and fear of
jeopardizing the fortunes of their political party.[33] Several months
later, Forsyth advised Nicholas Biddle that he did "not think
the Chief Magistrate has any settled resolution on the subject of
Texas, so the Course of this Govt will be directed by
Events. . . ."[34]

Meanwhile, Forsyth had received information concerning a
reported decision by the Texas government. The officials planned
to withdraw their application for annexation if it did not receive
approval from the existing session of Congress; thereafter, independence would be maintained by alliances with Great Britain
and other European nations.[35] The petition was withdrawn.
Nicholas Biddle wrote Forsyth and Poinsett expressing apprehension that Van Buren might be offended by the action. Biddle, who
was conducting loan negotiations with the Texans, did not wish
to see the westerners antagonized. He suggested that the President
be advised to speak of the Houston government in cordial terms
in his forthcoming message to Congress.[36] Forsyth replied that
Biddle's letter had arrived too late for any changes to be made
in the President's message, which, however, contained no derogatory statements regarding Texas relations. He added that even
had the letter been received in time, he would not have complied with Biddle's request. In his opinion, "the times do not
permit any specially favorable notice of Texas."[37]

The annexation issue was not successfully concluded during
Forsyth's tenure of office, but the boundary question was
settled. Hunt was persistent in his requests for determination
of a line separating the United States and Texas. At first,
Forsyth refused to make a formal reply to the Minister's
notes; in informal conversations, he insisted that the eastern
boundary of Texas should be the Neches River. Hunt disagreed and, citing the Spanish treaty of 1819, contended that
Texas should extend to the Sabine River.[38] Finally, on April
25, 1838, they affixed their signatures to a treaty which recognized the Sabine River as a boundary; other limits were to
be determined at the convenience of the two contracting
nations.

Forsyth's duties concerning affairs to the northeast were no
less strenuous than his duties involving Mexico and Texas. He
inherited several problems involving Canadian relations, and
others were initiated during his supervision of the State

Department. Among the former was the northeastern boundary controversy, which originated because of the indefinite and inaccurate terminology contained in the Anglo-American treaty of 1783.

After repeated attempts at agreement, the United States and Great Britain referred the dispute to the King of the Netherlands, who, in 1831, recommended an arbitrary compromise line as the best solution. He suggested that 7,908 square miles of the contested territory be awarded to the United States, with the remaining 4,119 square miles going to Great Britain.[39] The United States Senate, recognizing the decision to be political rather than judicial, rejected the arbiter's recommendation. Instead, it passed a resolution advising the President to renew negotiations for settlement on the basis of the 1783 treaty.

Several months after Forsyth became Secretary of State, he received a note from Charles R. Vaughan, British Minister to Washington, concerning his government's reaction to Jackson's proposal for appointment of a new commission. Vaughan referred to the difference of opinion regarding the highlands, which the commissioners, if appointed, were to locate. According to the treaty, the hills were situated between rivers flowing into the St. Lawrence River and those emptying into the Atlantic Ocean. In disagreement with the United States, the British maintained that the treaty did not interpret rivers flowing into the Bay of Fundy as draining into the ocean. The Minister stated that Great Britain was agreeable to Jackson's suggestion provided the United States agreed with the British contention, which would, in effect, eliminate the St. John River from consideration.

On April 28, 1835, Forsyth replied to Vaughan's note. Pointing out that certain elevations north of the St. John River were identical with treaty description, he declared that the President's proposal was not made with the intention of weakening or abandoning United States claims. The recommendation was submitted for the purpose of selecting impartial agents, who would render a decision based on established facts and judicious interpretation of the treaty. Since the British condition would impose preliminary restrictions upon the commissioners, Jackson rejected the suggestion.[40]

On December 28, 1835, Forsyth received notification that

Great Britain, in view of United States rejection, had withdrawn her acceptance of the Dutch king's recommendation. Since the two nations were unable to agree upon a treaty line, the British proposed a compromise boundary which would represent an approximately equal division of the disputed territory. Forsyth replied that the British plan "could not be accepted without disrespect to the previous decisions and just expectations of Maine."[41] As a substitute measure, the President suggested a different compromise line; he was prepared to request Maine's consent for the establishment of the St. John River as her boundary. This counter-proposal received no encouragement from Charles Bankhead, British chargé d'affaires, and was subsequently rejected by the London government.

During the Van Buren administration, Forsyth and British Minister Henry S. Fox exchanged numerous notes in unsuccessful attempts to find a formula for determining the northeastern boundary. Eventually, the two governments established separate commissions, but the survey reports were of little value except as information to the respective disputants.[42]

The boundary question was complicated by the fact that, according to the political system of the United States, the federal government cannot deprive a state of any territory without the state's consent. Maine was not disposed to relinquish an area which she considered as having been granted to the United States by the treaty of 1783; consequently, the state officials were usually opposed to suggestions for establishment of a compromise line. Forsyth's lack of success in reaching an agreement with the British caused the impatient Maine authorities to look with disfavor upon his efforts. Charles Stewart Daveis, Maine's agent in Washington, was "utterly disgusted" with him.[43]

Dissatisfied with the situation, the New Englanders began to criticize the attitude of the federal government as being too complacent. In answer to these complaints, Forsyth explained the difficulties of international negotiations and recommended patience on the part of Maine. Declaring that negotiations were being pursued with diligence, the Secretary assured Governor Robert Pinckney Dunlap that Maine's interests would receive ample protection from the federal government. The following year, 1838, Forsyth wrote to Governor Edward Kent requesting Maine's approval to the establishment of a conventional line. To avoid misunderstanding, he summarized the existing negotiations and enclosed pertinent documents.[44] Maine refused to consent to the proposal; instead, she insisted upon a survey based on treaty description.

The political situation in Maine was a primary reason for the stubborn opposition to compromise. Since the two national parties were of approximately equal strength in the state, popular feeling restrained both Democratic and Whig politicians from adopting a conciliatory attitude on the boundary question.[45] Somewhat belatedly, Forsyth sought to overcome this obstacle by resorting to a bi-partisan decision. In May, 1839, he offered to visit Maine for a conference with Senator Reuel Williams and Governor John Fairfield (Democrats), together with ex-Governor Kent and Daveis (Whigs). The meeting took place in June at Portland, where Forsyth revealed the contents of a British plan for regulating the actions of a joint commission. Since the United States was preparing to make a counter-proposal, the Van Buren administration wished to ascertain the views of the New England state. Unanimous in their disapproval of the British offer, the Maine delegates complied with the Secretary's request by suggesting directives which were in accord with their state's contentions.[46] Although the United States proposition was subsequently rejected by the British government, Forsyth received favorable newspaper reaction for his effort to coordinate a bi-partisan policy acceptable to the Maine populace.[47]

Forsyth's journey to Maine was also prompted by events of a serious nature which threatened to erupt into armed conflict. Since both Maine and New Brunswick claimed jurisdiction over the disputed territory, border incidents in 1839 precipitated a bloodless crisis known as the Aroostook War. In February, Maine dispatched a posse, led by Land Agent Rufus McIntyre, into the Aroostook Valley for the purpose of expelling Canadians who were cutting timber in the disputed area. McIntyre and other leaders were captured by the lumberjacks; but the remaining Americans, after retreating some distance up the Aroostook River, established fortifications. Governor Fairfield immediately demanded the release of the prisoners and directed that reinforcements be sent to the posse. In retaliation, Lieutenant Governor Sir John Harvey ordered New Brunswick troops into the danger zone. When Fairfield called upon the federal government for aid, the United States Congress appropriated $10,000,000 and authorized the President to enlist fifty thousand volunteers.[48]

Prior to the congressional action, Forsyth received a demand from Fox that the federal government force withdrawal of the Maine militia from the Aroostook Valley. The Minister declared that Maine had violated an agreement which guaranteed exclusive British jurisdiction and possession of the disputed area pending final settlement of the question.[49] Forsyth replied that, in spite of Great Britain's previous arguments for sole jurisdiction over the territory, the United States had never agreed to even a temporary relinquishment of her rights. In defense of Maine's activities, he stated that there had been no intention of military occupation; that the posse was instructed to depart after removing the trespassers. Under the existing circumstances, the New Englanders could not be expected to withdraw until they had accomplished their objective.[50] The Secretary also wrote to Governor Fairfield denying the existence of any agreement such as that mentioned by the British. He affirmed the President's readiness to support Maine if necessary, but expressed confidence that an amicable adjustment of the boundary would be completed at an early date. He suggested, therefore, that Maine and New Brunswick come to a mutual understanding with regard to prevention of future depredations.[51]

Forsyth's strategy became evident on the day following transmission of his letter to Fairfield. On February 27, 1839, he and Fox signed a memorandum containing recommendations to the state and provincial authorities. The document first presented the opposing views held by the United States and Great Britain with respect to existing jurisdiction over the disputed area. Then followed a statement that the issue was subordinate to the general question of boundary determination, which the two nations expected to settle through friendly negotiation. Pending final settlement, Canadian troops should not attempt to expel the armed Americans; but the latter should withdraw, voluntarily and without delay, from the controversial region. Should there be future necessity for dispersal of trespassers or for protection of public property, the governments of Maine and New Brunswick should act jointly or separately, according to agreement. All civil officers in custody were to be released. The provisions of the memorandum were not to be interpreted as any

augmentation or reduction of either disputant's claim to ultimate possession of the territory.[52]

Forsyth forwarded copies of the document to Fairfield, asking
that one be sent to Harvey. Assuring the New Englander that the
terms were consistent with Maine's honor and interests, he cited
the President's desire that the state comply with the recommendations.[53] Harvey readily agreed to negotiate with Fairfield
on the basis of the suggestions contained in the memorandum.
The Maine governor, however, considered the arrangement unsatisfactory. He declared that his troops would not be withdrawn unless the Canadians departed from the region. In addition, he opposed the recommendation granting concurrent jurisdiction along the Aroostook River. Even should both militia
forces retire, he intended to keep a civil posse in the valley for
protective purposes.[54]

General Winfield Scott was ordered to the Maine frontier
where, in March, he succeeded in negotiating an agreement
which, with some modification, resembled the plan suggested
in the Forsyth-Fox memorandum. The adjustment provided for
temporary possession and jurisdiction over lands held by each of
the contestants, with neither relinquishing claims to the entire
territory. For the time being, the Aroostook Valley was to be
retained by Maine and the upper St. John Valley by New Brunswick.

The Scott agreement provided an uneasy truce. After an interval of a few months, Forsyth and Fox proceeded to exchange
charges and countercharges concerning alleged violations within,
and encroachments upon, the designated zones. Nothing of consequence was decided, although Forsyth intimated the possibility
of war between the United States and Great Britain. One southern
newspaper, commenting upon the bitter controversy between the
Secretary and the Minister, predicted that a crisis was near.
Others remarked that despite the belligerent attitude assumed
by both men, there was no need to be apprehensive of an actual declaration of hostilities.[55] During the course of the Forsyth-Fox correspondence, Maine sensed the fact that the federal
government would not resort to extreme measures. In 1840, Fairfield declared that the Van Buren administration exhibited no
sympathy for the state and that he was "disappointed and
grieved" with Forsyth.[56]

A problem of considerable importance in Canadian relations
was created by the breach of United States neutrality laws. In

1837, an abortive rebellion caused William Lyon Mackenzie and other Canadians to seek refuge in the United States. Once across the border, they began preparations for an invasion of their native land by appealing to American sympathizers for supplies and volunteers. In addition, they established a base on Navy Island, a Canadian possession located in the Niagara River. Forsyth had attempted to preserve American neutrality prior to the arrival of the rebel leaders. In notes to the governors and district attorneys in New York, Vermont, and Michigan, he cited the probability of American citizens participating in the insurrection. To guard against such an eventuality, he advised vigilance with respect to questionable movements, and prosecution of all persons suspected of neutrality violation.[57]

On several occasions, in 1838, Fox demanded that the federal government adopt measures for suppression of expeditions which were in the process of organizing for a Canadian invasion. Forsyth replied that the administration was doing everything in its power to fulfill treaty obligations. Meanwhile, he sent dispatches to federal officials in the border states, reiterating his previous instructions. He promised military aid if civil authority was insufficient. Unfortunately for United States integrity, Forsyth's orders were disobeyed. In regions sympathetic to the rebel cause, they were inadequately enforced.[58]

The insurgent base at Navy Island constituted a menace which loyal Canadians determined to remove. On the night of December 29, 1837, an armed force proceeded across the Niagara River to Schlosser, New York, where they seized the steamer *Caroline*. In the attack, one American citizen was killed and several others seriously wounded. The vessel, which had been employed in transporting men and supplies to Navy Island, was set afire and cast adrift, ultimately sinking in the vicinity of the falls. The incident aroused such bitter feeling in the border states that reprisals seemed imminent. To insure the maintenance of peace, the federal government called New York and Vermont militia into service and dispatched General Winfield Scott to command the forces.[59]

On January 5, 1838, Forsyth addressed a note to Fox in which he denounced the Canadian attack on American territory. He informed the Minister that the United States intended to demand redress from Great Britain. Fox replied that destruction of the *Caroline* was a precautionary measure dictated in the interests of self-preservation; therefore the Canadian action could be justified on the basis of international law. Forsyth disagreed, but refused to enter into a detailed discussion until sufficient data could be obtained for a formal complaint to London.[60] In the meantime, he had instructed Nathaniel S. Benton, United States District Attorney at Buffalo,

to collect without delay, all the evidence, within your reach, of the circumstances of that transaction—the value of the property destroyed, the names of the persons killed and wounded—the fate of those, who have been carried off—and especially the names and Official characters of the persons who were the perpetrators, or the instigators of these Acts of atrocity.[61]

In March, 1838, Forsyth transmitted the information to United States Minister Andrew Stevenson, with instructions that he present Lord Palmerston with a demand for prompt redress. Forsyth stated that the Canadian effort to justify the aggression "is so preposterous, that it cannot be presumed the Metropolitan Government will adopt or attempt to sustain it."[62] Stevenson complied with the directive, but informed Forsyth of an impression that reparation would not be made. In July, 1839, having received no answer to his note, the Minister asked if he should press the subject. Forsyth replied in the negative; from conversations with Fox, he expected British reference to the matter at an early date.[63] But on the day prior to Forsyth's retirement from office, Stevenson addressed a dispatch declaring that no official decision from the British government had been communicated to him.[64]

The tension created by the *Caroline* raid was increased by the arrest of a suspected participant on November 12, 1840. Apprehended at Lewiston, New York, on charges of murder and arson, Alexander McLeod was committed to prison pending trial. Fox demanded the Canadian's release. He insisted that legal proceedings could not be instituted against an individual who, acting in the public service of his government, was required to obey the orders of his superior officers.[65] Forsyth replied that the federal government had no power to intervene in a case which was under the exclusive jurisdiction of a state. He also took issue with Fox's argument. Since the British government had neglected to answer Stevenson's note, there was no official indication that the London authorities regarded the *Caroline* attack as a public act.[66]

During the few remaining months of the Van Buren administration, Forsyth and Fox were unable to agree on a solution to the impasse. Fox repeated his opinion concerning the legality of the *Caroline* assault and predicted dire consequences should any harm come to McLeod. Forsyth replied that the Minister's defense "would hardly have been hazarded, had you been possessed of the carefully collected testimony . . . in the case."[67]

The United States-Canadian fisheries controversy was an intermittent problem for Forsyth. In January, 1836, he received a complaint from Charles Bankhead about alleged encroachments on inshore fisheries of the Canadian maritime provinces. The complaint stated that certain Americans, fishing in St. Lawrence waters, had violated the three-mile limit established by the treaty of 1818. Without waiting to investigate the charges, Forsyth notified Bankhead that United States customs officials had been instructed "to enjoin upon those persons a strict observance of the limits assigned for taking, drying, and curing fish by the American fishermen. . . ."[68] Nova Scotia, in the same year, took action against American infringement by enacting laws providing for more stringent regulation of treaty stipulations.

In 1840, the United States was the complainant. On April 17, Forsyth directed Stevenson to present a remonstrance to the British government embodying three subjects: (1) the United States was dissatisfied with what was considered arbitrary seizure and detention of American fishing vessels by provincial authorities; (2) she was opposed to a Nova Scotia statute requiring payment of a light duty when ships passed through the Strait of Canso; (3) she denounced provincial officers for their lack of cooperation in apprehending American seamen guilty of desertion.[69] In his reply to Stevenson's note, Palmerston did not enter into a discussion of the first protest. He explained that all vessels, except those of Nova Scotia, were subject to payment of the Canso Strait light dues; therefore, no concession could be granted to the United States. Since the American deserters violated no British law, the provincial authorities were powerless to arrest them.[70]

Forsyth refused to accept dismissal of the unexplained topic. On February 20, 1841, he returned to the subject with instructions for another representation to the British government. He expressed the opinion that the 1836 Nova Scotia law was designed for restriction, and possible extermination, of American fisheries in the area. Reviewing pertinent provisions of the 1818 convention, he made the following assertion:

. . . the construction attempted to be put upon that instrument by the authorities of Nova Scotia is directly in conflict with its provisions, and entirely subversive of the rights and interests of our citizens. It is one which would lead to the abandonment, to a great extent, of a highly important branch of American industry, and cannot for one moment be admitted by this Government.[71]

No reply to Forsyth's vigorous note was received prior to his retirement from the State Department.

In a period abounding with frontier disputes, Forsyth was charged with enormous responsibility. He had to face criticism when his activities were not in accord with popular sentiment. Yet he was pledged to support neutrality laws and treaty obligations. Above all, his efforts were directed toward settlement of the problems without resort to war.

The Mexican situation presented an especially difficult problem for Forsyth. Butler's intrigues, together with his by-pass of Forsyth in correspondence with Jackson, produced a lack of coordination. Nevertheless, Forsyth was industrious in attempts to preserve neutrality, as was shown by his many letters instructing district attorneys to prosecute violators of the law. He followed the same procedure when there was danger of partisan invasion of Canada. His evasive replies to Mexican Minister Gorostiza's protests do not reflect credit upon Forsyth, but his conduct may be explained by the fact that he was acting under instructions from the President.

Forsyth's lack of enthusiasm for the Texans' cause may be attributed to several reasons in addition to recognition of Mexican treaty obligations. He was apprehensive lest the Texas question create a division in the Democratic party over the issue of supplementary pro-slavery territory. Besides being a loyal Democrat, he had personal reasons for wanting the party to remain intact. His friendship for Van Buren was well known. In his autobiography Van Buren consistently refers to the Georgian as his friend. And Forsyth aspired to a higher office; hence he was careful not to take sides in a bitter sectional and partisan controversy. Finally Forsyth, always an advocate of exact diplomatic procedure, was technically correct in his refusal to receive communications from the unaccredited Texas agents.

Forsyth was sincere in his desire to solve the northeastern boundary controversy, but negotiations were retarded by the uncompromising attitude of Maine. In addition, he was forced to deal with the aggressive Lord Palmerston. The Aroostook War might have produced bloodshed but for the Forsyth-Fox memorandum which, issued at a critical moment, provided the basis for the Scott agreement. The partisan raids on Canada, the *Caroline* affair, and the McLeod incident provided opportunities for Forsyth to make contribution to a peaceful settlement. He may certainly be considered among the political leaders referred to by historians who said, "That it [the period] did not result in war is decidedly creditable to those political leaders who braved the anger of the mob in order to preserve international peace. . . ."[72]

In the management of diplomatic affairs, Forsyth's ability as a tactician was subjected to an exacting test. He could no longer rely upon his forensic talent as a primary weapon. Instead, he was required to compete with skilled diplomats through the media of consultation and formal correspondence. The fact that he aquitted himself in a capable manner is a tribute to his resourceful characteristics.

XI

The Curtain Falls

JOHN FORSYTH'S adult life, almost without interruption, was spent in the arena of practical politics. With the passage of time, he received positions of increasing importance. His long service and his prominence among party leaders eventually resulted in his being considered as candidate for the vice-presidency of the United States. An ambitious man, Forsyth was not averse to the idea.

President Andrew Jackson dictated the selection of Democratic candidates for the presidential election of 1836; consequently, Forsyth was forced to hold his personal ambitions in abeyance. He was unable, however, to conceal his disappointment in not being chosen with Martin Van Buren. When he was invited to attend a New York testimonial for the vice-presidential nominee, Richard Mentor Johnson, he dispatched a curt refusal.[1]

Several weeks prior to the election, Forsyth notified President Jackson that his private business necessitated a brief return to Georgia. Though his stay at home was ostensibly to attend to personal affairs, he took advantage of the situation to advance the cause of Van Buren. He was quoted as predicting the election of Van Buren by an overwhelming majority. His opponents were quick to seize upon the political implications of the visit. One editorial, referring to his alleged political activities in Georgia, declared that federal government interference with elections was intolerable and should be prohibited.[2] Another remarked that Forsyth was "politic enough to kill two birds with one stone, and while attending to his own affairs, he will doubtless put in a good word for his master, should opportunity occur."[3]

Several of Forsyth's friends in Baldwin County addressed a

letter to him asking to be informed of Van Buren's views on the
abolition question. As slaveholders, they inquired whether southern interests would be protected under a Van Buren administration. In his reply, Forsyth made the unqualified assertion that the
New Yorker's feelings toward the abolitionists were similar to
those held by every honest Southerner. If he had any doubt
concerning Van Buren's sincerity on the matter, he would be
in opposition to the New Yorker's election despite their long
friendship.[4]

The Milledgeville *Federal Union* praised Forsyth's letter as
one which should dispel all mistrust of the Democratic presidential nominee. In disagreement, the Augusta *Chronicle* said Van
Buren was an equivocator, and the exchange of messages between
Forsyth and his constituents was a political scheme to win votes.
But in spite of Forsyth's efforts, Georgia cast her eleven electoral
votes for Hugh Lawson White and John Tyler.

Prior to the 1840 campaign, rumors were current that Vice-
President Richard M. Johnson would not seek re-election. As a
consequence, there was much speculation concerning a candidate for the position, with Forsyth's name being among those
most prominently mentioned. On November 22, 1838, a group of
Union Democrats, composed of state legislators and private citizens, assembled in Milledgeville and adopted a resolution nominating Forsyth as the southern candidate for the vice-presidency.
The action was endorsed by the Athens *Southern Banner,* which
predicted enthusiastic response from other states. The Milledgeville *Federal Union,* although favorable to Forsyth, labeled the
resolution premature. Until Johnson's intentions were definitely
known, the newspaper could see no reason for a move which
might endanger party unity.[5]

On December 17, 1838, Georgia's Union Democrats held a
formal session in Milledgeville. Declaring their action to be in
the interests of national party harmony, they decided against the
adoption of the resolution passed by the unofficial group in November. Instead, they recommended Van Buren and Forsyth
"to our Republican brethren throughout the United States, as
suitable candidates. . . ."[6]

The trend of events was detrimental to Forsyth's hopes. In June
the New York Democratic Committee approved a resolution nominating Johnson. Coming from Van Buren's home state, the action
was a decided rebuff to the Georgia recommendation. In December, the Harrisburg Whig convention chose General William

Henry Harrison and John Tyler as candidates for president and vice-president respectively. The consensus was that Johnson, a military personality, would be renominated in order to counteract Harrison's popularity in the West.[7] Consequently, the Augusta *Constitutionalist* expressed concern over the political situation. After reviewing the prospects of various candidates, it reached the conclusion that Johnson could win the support of neither the West nor the South. The pro-Forsyth journal suggested that the Democrats "bear in mind that we have a strong Virginia State Rights man to contend with on the opposition ticket for Vice-President, and that unless we meet him *on his own ground,* we have but little hope in the contest."[8]

When the Democratic convention met in Baltimore on May 5, 1840, Van Buren was nominated for the presidency. However, the convention failed in its efforts to designate a vice-presidential candidate and adjourned with the announcement that selection should be made by the respective states.

A few days later, the Washington *Globe* published an open letter in which Forsyth declared that he did not wish to be considered a candidate for the vice-presidency. Dissatisfied with the convention's negative approach to the problem, he prophesied injury to the party through lack of concentration. Under the existing situation, no friend of the administration could expect popular election to the vice-presidency. Since it would be necessary for the United States Senate to make the decision, the winning candidate would occupy the position knowing that he was not the choice of the majority of the people. Forsyth asserted that he had never held office under such circumstances, nor did he have any desire to do so.[9]

The Whigs, in an attempt to exploit Forsyth's letter, declared that it was evidence of dissension within administration ranks. Forsyth's partisans, characterizing the message as explicit and commendable, accused the opposition of deliberate misinterpretation.[10] A personal friend explained Forsyth's statement regarding lack of popular support for administration adherents: since four of them were candidates, a split vote would be the inevitable result.[11]

Georgia's Union Democrats assembled in Milledgeville for celebration of the Fourth of July, 1840. In addition to the usual toasts and speeches, letters were read from prominent members who were unable to attend. Forsyth had been invited, but had declined with the explanation that official duties required his presence in Washington. In his letter, the Secretary of State admitted that his acquaintance with Harrison had been pleasant over a period of years. He had no desire to question the General's intentions or ability. However, Harrison had not received Georgia's vote in 1836 and he had done nothing since to warrant a change in the state's attitude.[12] Commenting on the message, the opposition press contended that Forsyth, through contact with Harrison, had become convinced of the General's worthy qualities.[13]

On September 2, 1840, the Union Democrats held a Van Buren rally at Indian Springs to which Forsyth was invited. He accepted but, after departing from Washington, had to cancel the trip when he became ill in Fredericksburg, Virginia. Since he could not be present to lend assistance to the cause, he addressed a circular letter to the people of Georgia. He asked that the voters examine the important issues of the day and compare the positions taken by the two presidential candidates. Van Buren's opinions were prompt and unequivocal; Harrison's were given with reluctance, and were often contradictory. Harrison was portrayed as the nominee of a coalition with only one common interest—hatred for the administration. Nothing would be so disastrous to the South as having this heterogeneous party in power. Forsyth declared that he was confident concerning voter reaction, for "when the spirit of inquiry is awakened, the people are not to be turned from the pursuit of facts by processions and parades, by travelling orators and ballad singers, by fiddlings and revelries."[14]

Forsyth's address received commendation from the Milledgeville *Federal Union*,[15] but it elicited considerable criticism from other sources. The Whig press criticized the style and content of the document as the weakest effort of Forsyth's career. He had made no attempt to defend the administration against direct charges preferred against it. Instead, his cunning and invidious treatment was filled with misrepresentations concerning a devoted patriot. He was accused of being a self-seeking politician who had feigned illness rather than face the Georgians in a hopeless cause.[16]

During the final days of the 1840 campaign, Forsyth continued to be a favorite target for Whig attack. He was criticized for violation of the franking privilege when he sent copies of the Washington *Globe* to inferior courts in Georgia.[17] A report was circulated that he had had a quarrel with the President over the

conditions of Minister John H. Eaton's recall from Spain.[18] The
bitter assault upon Forsyth may have had some influence in
the campaign, for Harrison and Tyler carried the state in 1840.
Other factors influencing the result in Georgia were the popularity of the Whig candidates and "the strenuous labor of the Whig
leaders in the State. . . ."[19]

Forsyth's public service ended with the inauguration of Harrison. On March 13, 1841, he and Joel R. Poinsett accompanied
Van Buren to Baltimore, where they spent a few days before the
ex-President proceeded to Philadelphia with the expectation of
arriving in New York on March 23. Forsyth rejoined Van Buren
in New York, where, despite a torrential rain, they were wel-
comed at the Battery and escorted by a large procession to Tam-
many Hall. After Forsyth's return to Washington, he wrote to Van
Buren of President Harrison's critical physical condition. With
reference to presidential responsibilities, he did not "suppose the
Genl. thinks so, but his death at this moment would be the fortunate conclusion of a fortunate life."[20] The following day, both
Forsyth and Poinsett informed the New Yorker of Harrison's
death.

Forsyth was one of four Van Buren cabinet members who were
among the honorary pallbearers for the deceased President.[21]
The account of the funeral rites which Forsyth gave Van Buren
provided him with an opportunity for some interesting reflec-
tions. He decided that the responsibilities and mortifications of
office caused a president to pay a high price for his honors and
power. Any person was "both fool and madman . . ." who would
injure body, mind, reputation, and soul in order to attain the
position. He declared that, while all superficial proprieties were
observed at the funeral, those present seemed to have forgotten
the deceased and to be occupied with matters of personal interest.
According to speculation, there was the probability of Whig party
disruption. As the Whigs had little confidence in Tyler, Forsyth
predicted a struggle between Daniel Webster, Henry Clay, and
Henry Alexander Wise for the Whig leadership.[22]

Forsyth continued to reside in Washington, where he had purchased a home in 1839. He made no public announcement concerning his plans for the future, but there is little doubt that
he anticipated a return to the United States Senate. His adherents
in Georgia sought to make that possible. The Athens *Southern
Banner* noted that Alfred Cuthbert's name was not listed in any of
the votes taken during the senatorial session and suggested that if

he was unable to represent the state he should resign. Another journal remarked that Cuthbert had no ambition for the legislative position which he had accepted merely from a sense of duty. Praising Forsyth's senatorial achievements, the paper declared that Cuthbert's resignation in favor of his predecessor would be regarded as an act of patriotism.[23]

Forsyth's actions and words indicate that he was in a receptive mood. He arrived in Milledgeville on May 3, 1841, and the following day addressed the convention of Democratic Young Men of Georgia. The speech was criticized by "some of the Log Cabin luminaries. . . ,"[24] but was described by his party's organ as eloquent, appropriate, and impressive.[25] Forsyth was invited to address the citizens of Mobile, Alabama. He declined the invitation, but gave assurance

that no exertions of mine . . . shall be wanting to alarm and enlighten the public mind, should unwise, unprincipled or dangerous propositions be made by those into whose hands the power of the federal government has recently dropped.[26]

The Democratic plan to return Forsyth to the United States Senate came to an abrupt end with his untimely death. After an illness of approximately four weeks, Forsyth died at his home in Washington on October 21, 1841. J. L. Martin wrote Van Buren, as follows:

I snatch the pen to communicate to you, the distressing intelligence of the death of Mr. Forsyth, which took place last evening at a little before nine. This illness was a relapsed remittent fever, under which the system would not react, & which after many fluctuations, finally eventuated in death. I did not leave him, an hour, for the last four days & nights, & had the melancholy satisfaction of closing his eyes, & decently imposing his limbs.[27]

On October 23, 1841, funeral services were conducted by the Reverend William Hawley, rector of St. John's Episcopal Church, assisted by the Reverend Doctor Butler of the same denomination. In attendance were many private citizens, the commanding general of the United States Army, foreign diplomats, cabinet members, and numerous government officials. President John Tyler was not among them.[28] Forsyth was buried in the congressional cemetery at Washington.

Forsyth's death evoked expressions of profound regret by those newspapers which had supported him. They were profuse in their tributes to his abilities and services. But the eulogies were not restricted to his supporters. The Washington *National Intelligencer* remarked that "he possessed qualities which placed him above the level of the mass of mankind."[29] The Milledgeville *Southern Recorder* said:

Differing for years as we have with Mr. Forsyth in politics, we scruple not to pay to his memory its deserved meed of applause; for the mental qualities of this gentleman justly merit at the hands even of an opponent, the highest praise that can be awarded to them.[30]

The Georgia legislature, by unanimous vote, passed an official resolution of respect to his memory.

In the field of practical politics, Forsyth emerged as a tactician of the first order. His natural abilities predestined him to a political career. Living as he did in an era when gifted oratory was considered a prerequisite to political success, and possessing superior forensic talents, he had an advantage which opponents found difficult to overcome. His proficient analyses of the opposition's strategy gave him the opportunity to make effective use of obstructionist tactics. His keen intellect enabled him not only to master details, but to maintain them in proper perspective. Added to his general competence, was a devotion to duty that reached the point of compulsiveness.

In attempts to disparage Forsyth's acumen, his political adversaries resorted to attacks on his integrity. Despite their intensive efforts in this direction, there is adequate reason to evaluate him as an individual who acted in what he considered the best interests of his nation and state. If he was sometimes guilty of errors of judgment, he was always honest in purpose. As governor and legislator, his qualities of leadership were outstanding.

Forsyth recognized the necessity of compromise and alternatives. This should not be interpreted as a weakness, but rather as a practical approach to the complexities of the governmental and party systems as represented in the United States. As an expert politician, Forsyth knew that the successful operation of government was dependent upon the ability of lawmakers to reconcile their differences in the interest of positive legislation. He accepted the fact and adopted the policy of meeting his colleagues halfway, provided there was no loss of principle.

Party regularity was characteristic of Forsyth. He was a loyal and indefatigable party member. On occasion, he exhibited independence; furthermore, he did not compromise his integrity.

Nevertheless, he understood the value of conformity within party ranks. He realized that divided counsel diminished the chances of success in politics and endangered the very life of the party. Therefore, Forsyth generally followed the dictates of the political organization.

Forsyth's concern with politics was both idealistic and realistic. Possessing a deep interest in public affairs, he had the opportunity of rendering valuable service by contributing his talents to the development of a better nation and state. In a practical sense, Forsyth looked upon politics as representing a means of livelihood, with pleasant associates, gracious living, and prestige among his contemporaries.

No detraction should be attached to the Georgian for his efforts to move up the ladder of political prominence, for he would have been lacking in qualities which constitute a leader in any field had he been content to rest on his laurels. Undeniably, he sought to align himself with influential persons whose views coincided with his own. As a practical and ambitious politician, he was anxious to improve his position and, as a tactician, he made steady progress without surrendering principle or individualism. He performed his services in a competent manner, regardless of the responsibilities involved.

Forsyth was dissatisfied as governor because he preferred the Washington limelight. He considered himself naturally fitted for national politics. Nevertheless, his inclination for efficiency, honesty, and economy resulted in an administration of pronounced success.

Since Forsyth wished to advance in his chosen profession, he was careful not to become involved in the acrimonious sectional dispute. The fact that he was scrupulous in his endeavors to avoid sectionalism is further indication that he was a realistic tactician. He was striving for the personal satisfaction to be gained from higher office; in addition, he was seeking to avoid being considered an extremist. In the role of a moderate, he would be in a more favorable position to use his influence should sectional controversy endanger the preservation of the Union. Such reasoning was to be expected from Forsyth, who made no secret of his desire for continuance of a united nation.

Forsyth's early congressional career indicates that he was first and foremost a nationalist. However, he did not desert the cause of state rights. After some years, state rights gained ascendancy with him and provided considerable motivation for his activities.

While governor, Forsyth was closely associated with Georgia's problems. He was duty bound to direct his efforts toward solution of them; and, in seeking his objective, he was often required to resort to state rights. He thus displayed a desirable attribute of political leadership: the ability to adapt to environment and exigency. After Forsyth's return to Washington, he reverted to his original character of being primarily an exponent of nationalism. Because of his extended contact with the federal government and his frequent absences from Georgia, he became more identified with national matters as time progressed. Georgia's affairs continued to receive his attention; but, where there was a divergence of interests, his attachment to the Union was paramount.

Forsyth was a strict constitutionalist. Whether in the capacity of state executive, national legislator, or federal administrator, his efforts were employed within the framework of precise legality. In executing his duties, as leader or subordinate, he demonstrated courage and resourcefulness. He did not evade the issue when in his opinion the interests of Georgia or of the Union were threatened. He took a positive, though tactful, position for his state on the question of Indian removal. Yet he invited criticism and insult when he favored the federal government during the nullification crisis. With regard to Texan and Canadian problems, he attempted to enforce neutrality laws despite the opposition of partisans within the United States.

Forsyth's political activities were facilitated by an enviable private life. He bestowed an ardent affection upon his family, which was reciprocated. There is no indication that he was other than a model husband and father. His humor and gentility were recognized by those with whom he came in contact. Political differences seldom affected his tranquility or his associations; his conciliatory nature tended to reduce the number of his adversaries. His manner toward his opponents contributed to his effectiveness as a master tactician. In the social sphere, his conduct was impeccable: he was charming, gracious, and entertaining. Forsyth's personable characteristics commanded respect from his contemporaries and gained for him popularity from the fashionable clique.

Forsyth achieved success in both public and private life, but his potentialities were never fully realized. Various factors contributed to his failure to reach the pinnacle of genuine greatness. His meticulous devotion to duty, although laudable, resulted in a restriction upon further exploitation of his talents. In addition, his social activities were far too extensive for a man of his position. Consequently, Forsyth had little time to concentrate upon that extra effort which would have assured him a more prominent place in the annals of his country. He was often lacking in sustained aggressiveness. He could be aroused into diligent support of a cause, but it was only a matter of time before his naturally calm disposition became predominant. Another factor which was injurious to Forsyth was his failure to establish a close association with the populace. He was a political aristocrat whose course was determined by the theory that experienced officials should formulate and direct public opinion. While he gave strong support to the interests of his constituents, he did not mingle with the masses. Therefore, he was seldom identified with the popular agitations of his generation. Several of the characteristics which were of value to Forsyth in other respects proved to be handicaps in his bid for true greatness.

The fact remains, however, that, excluding the Spanish mission, Forsyth served his state and his nation in a commendable manner, and left a favorable imprint upon the pages of American history.

Notes

CHAPTER I

1. Jennie Forsyth Jeffries, *A History of the Forsyth Family*, 49.

2. Frederic Gregory Forsyth de Fronsac, *Memorial of the Family of Forsyth de Fronsac*, 35. (Hereinafter cited as *Memorial*.)

3. Jeffries, *A History of the Forsyth Family*, 49; Gaius Marcus Brumbaugh (ed.), *Revolutionary War Records*, I (Virginia), 96, 302, 341, 431; John Forsyth to Arthur Shaaff, October 26, 1832, Forsyth Papers, Princeton University Library.

4. Abstract, Robert Forsyth to Agent of Supplies in Virginia, December 6, 1780, *Calendar of Virginia State Papers*, I, 394-95; Robert Forsyth to Benjamin Harrison, December 14, 1781, *ibid.*, II, 658.

5. Christopher Febiger to Colonel Davies, January 23, 1782, *ibid.*, III, 44-45.

6. De Fronsac, *Memorial*, 31-36, Jeffries, *A History of the Forsyth Family*, 49-50. Fanny Forsyth had a daughter by her previous marriage; Sarah (Sally) became the wife of James Armstrong of Richmond County, Georgia. After the death of Sarah's husband in 1800, John Forsyth's half sister lived with her mother. *Historical Collections of the Georgia Chapters, Daughters of the American Revolution*, II, 12, 72; Clara Forsyth to Julia Austin, January 23, 1803, Forsyth Papers.

7. *Biographical Directory of the American Congress, 1774-1927*, 980; Lucian Lamar Knight, *Reminiscences of Famous Georgians Embracing Episodes and Incidents in the Lives of the Great Men of the State*, II, 80-81.

8. George H. Aubrey, "Robert Forsyth," William Jonathan Northen (ed.), *Men of Mark in Georgia*, I, 97; "Political Portraits with Pen and Pencil, (No. VII): John Forsyth," *United States Magazine and Democratic Review*, II (June, 1838), 273. (Hereinafter cited as "Political Portraits: Forsyth.")

9. Augusta *Georgia State Gazette or Independent Register*, November 25, December 9, 1786; April 21, 1787; November 29, 1788.

10. Augusta *Chronicle and Gazette of the State*, May 8, 1790.

11. Joseph R. Lamar, *Trustees of Richmond Academy, Augusta, Georgia; Their Work during the Eighteenth Century in the Management of a School, a Town and a Church*, 3.

12. Augusta *Georgia State Gazette or Independent Register*, December 2, 1786.

13. *Annals of the Congress of the United States, 1789-1824*, 1 Congress,

223

1 Session, I, 87-89, 91, 93. (Hereinafter cited as *Annals of Congress.*)

14. Augusta *Chronicle and Gazette of the State,* April 7, 1792.

15. Robert Forsyth to Richard Call, July 1, 1790, Miscellaneous Letters.

16. Savannah *Georgia Journal; and Independent Federal Register,* January 15, 1794; Augusta *Southern Sentinel, and Gazette of the State,* January 16, March 6, 1794.

17. Augusta *Chronicle and Gazette of the State,* March 1, 8, June 21, 1794.

18. Augusta *Southern Sentinel, and Gazette of the State,* January 16, 1794; Lucian Lamar Knight, *Georgia's Landmarks, Memorials, and Legends,* II, 314.

19. *Annals of Congress,* 3 Congress, 1 Session, IV, 74 and *passim*; "Political Portraits: Forsyth," 273.

20. Stephen Francis Miller, *The Bench and Bar of Georgia: Memoirs and Sketches,* II, 13; George White, *Historical Collections of Georgia. . . ,* 233. (Hereinafter cited as *Historical Collections.*)

21. *General Catalogue of Princeton University, 1746-1906,* n. p. (preface), 110, 112; "Political Portraits: Forsyth," 273; White, *Historical Collections,* 233; Miller, *The Bench and Bar of Georgia,* II, 13.

22. John Forsyth Account Book and Diary of Voyage, May 12, 1823, MSS, Library of Congress. The Savannah *Georgia Gazette,* May 27, 1802, published an announcement of the marriage, but erroneously cited the date as May 13, 1802.

23. Clara Forsyth to Julia Austin, January 23, 1803, Forsyth Papers. Julia Austin later became the wife of Clara's brother, Henry Meigs.

24. Genealogy chart, Forsyth Papers. John Forsyth to Henry Meigs, December 6, 1824, *ibid.*

25. John Forsyth to Henry Meigs, May 15, 1806, *ibid.;* Clara Forsyth to Julia Austin, January 23, 1803, *ibid.*

26. John Forsyth to Henry Meigs, August 20, 1802, *ibid.;* cf. Clara Forsyth to Henry Meigs, April 3, 1804, *ibid.*

27. John Forsyth to Horatio Marbury, April 8, 1802, Forsyth Papers, Georgia Department of Archives and History, Atlanta. (Hereinafter cited as GDAH.)

28. Augusta *Chronicle,* July 25, 1807.

29. *Ibid.,* August 15, 1807.

30. Clara Forsyth to Henry Meigs, April 3, 1804, Forsyth Papers.

31. Clara Forsyth to Henry Meigs, September 29, 1804, *ibid.*

32. Clara Forsyth to Henry Meigs, December 23, 1804, *ibid.*

33. John Forsyth to Henry Meigs, May 15, 1806, *ibid.*

34. Clara Forsyth to Henry Meigs, December 23, 1804, *ibid.*

35. Minutes of the Executive Department of the State of Georgia, November 16, 1809, 9, GDAH. (Hereinafter cited as Executive Minutes.)

36. *Ibid.,* May 19, 1808, 85.

37. Ellis Merton Coulter, *Georgia, A Short History,* 219-20.

38. "Political Portraits: Forsyth," 273.

39. Athens *Foreign Correspondent & Georgia Express,* June 16, July 14, 28, 1810.

40. Josiah Meigs to Editor of the *Monitor,* August 14, 1810, in Washington, Georgia, *Monitor,* August 25, 1810.

41. Milledgeville *Georgia Journal,* September 3, 1827.

42. Henry Stuart Foote, *Casket of Reminiscences,* 100.

43. Athens *Georgia Express,* January 10, 1812.

44. Augusta *Chronicle,* October 30, 1812, May 14, 1813.

CHAPTER II

1. *Niles' Register,* LXI (November 6, 1841), 151.

2. Miller, *The Bench and Bar of Georgia,* II, 50.

3. Margaret Harrison Smith to Jane Bayard Kirkpatrick, March 13, 1814, Mrs. Samuel Harrison Smith Papers, IX.

4. John Forsyth to Nicholas Biddle, January 29, 1818, Biddle Papers, unbound.

5. Nicholas Biddle to John Forsyth, February 19, 1827, Biddle Papers, XVI.

6. John Forsyth to Nicholas Biddle, March 7, 1827, *ibid.*

7. Lawton Bryan Evans, "Historic Spots in Summerville," *The Georgia Historical Quarterly,* I (June, 1917), 135-39. Other noted residents of Summerville, at various times, were Thomas and Alfred Cumming, John Milledge, Richard Henry Wilde, and Charles Jones Jenkins.

8. John Forsyth to Nicholas Biddle, June 25, 1818, Biddle Papers, V.

9. John Forsyth to Nicholas Biddle, July 30, 1818, *ibid.*

10. *Niles' Register,* X (August 17, 1816), 445; Henry Adams, *History of the United States during the Administrations of Jefferson and Madison,* IX, 135-38; John Bach McMaster, *A History of the People of the United States from the Revolution to the Civil War,* IV, 357-62.

11. Athens *Gazette,* September 19, 1816; Charles Maurice Wiltse, *John C. Calhoun, Nationalist, 1782-1828,* 125.

12. John Forsyth to Members of the Georgia General Assembly, October 7, 1818, in Augusta *Chronicle & Georgia Gazette,* October 24, 1818.

13. John Forsyth to Nicholas Biddle, December 4, 1818, Biddle Papers, V.

14. Roberta Florence Cason, "The Public Career of John Forsyth, 1813-1834," 6, unpublished M.A. thesis, Emory University Library.

15. John Forsyth to Richard Henry Wilde, October 13, 1814, Personal Miscellany Papers.

16. John Forsyth to Richard Henry Wilde, February 4, 1815, Forsyth Papers.

17. Washington *National Intelligencer,* February 24, 1814.

18. *Annals of Congress,* 13 Congress, 2 Session, XXVII, 1605-06.

19. *Ibid.,* 1609.

20. *Ibid.,* 14 Congress, 1 Session, XXIX, 940-48.

21. *Ibid.,* 15 Congress, 1 Session, XXXI, 409-10.

22. *Ibid.,* 406, 408.

23. John Forsyth to Nicholas Biddle, February 15, March 2, 11, June 25, August 8, 1818, Biddle Papers, V.

24. James Daniel Richardson (ed.), *A Compilation of the Messages and Papers of the Presidents, 1789-1897,* II, 13 and *passim.* (Hereinafter cited as *Messages and Papers.*)

25. John Forsyth to Nicholas Biddle, March 29, 1818, Biddle Papers, V.

26. *Annals of Congress,* 15 Congress, 1 Session, XXXII, 1466.

27. *Ibid.,* 1748.

28. Nicholas Biddle to Edward Everett, March 10, 1832, "President's Letter Book," IV, 213, Biddle Papers; Ralph Charles Henry Catterall, *The Second Bank of the United States,* 117.

29. Adams, *History of the United States,* IX, 134-35.

30. *Annals of Congress,* 14 Congress, 2 Session, XXX, 558.

31. *Ibid.,* 15 Congress, 1 Session, XXXI, 592 and *passim.*

32. *Ibid.,* 416-17, 422-23.

33. Savannah *Georgian,* March 4, 1826; *The Register of Debates in the Congress of the United States,* 19 Congress, 1 Session, II Part I, 1419-21. (Hereinafter cited as *Register of Debates.*)

34. *Annals of Congress,* 15 Congress, 1 Session, XXXI, 1103.

35. *Register of Debates,* 18 Congress, 2 Session, I, 582.

36. *Ibid.,* 19 Congress, 2 Session, III, 546-47; Milledgeville *Southern Recorder,* January 2, 1827.

37. *Annals of Congress,* 18 Congress, 1 Session, XLII, 2431 and *passim.*

38. Charles Francis Adams (ed.), *Memoirs of John Quincy Adams, Comprising Portions of His Diary from 1795 to 1848,* VI, 308. (Hereinafter cited as *Memoirs.*)

39. *Annals of Congress,* 18 Congress, 1 Session, XLII, 2661.

40. *Ibid.,* 2915.

41. Ninian Edwards to James Monroe, June 22, 1824, Elihu Benjamin Washburn (ed.), *The Edwards*

Papers; Being a Portion of the Collection of the Letters, Papers, and Manuscripts of Ninian Edwards, 224-29.

42. Charles Sackett Sydnor, *The Development of Southern Sectionalism, 1819-1848,* 157-66.

43. Washington *National Intelligencer,* February 16, 1824.

44. Milledgeville *Georgia Journal,* March 16, April 27, 1824.

45. Adams, *Memoirs,* VI, 372-73.

46. John Forsyth to Martin Van Buren, September 20, 1824, Van Buren Papers, VI.

47. John Forsyth to Bartlett Yancey, September 4, 1824, Bartlett Yancey Papers.

48. John Forsyth to Henry Meigs, February 9, 1825, Forsyth Papers.

49. John Forsyth to Henry Meigs, March 24, 1825, *ibid.*

50. Fifth Census, 1830, Population, Georgia, XVII, 93.

51. Sixth Census, 1840, Population, District of Columbia, I, 1.

52. *Register of Debates,* 19 Congress, 2 Session, III, 565.

53. *Ibid.,* 18 Congress, 2 Session, I, 739.

54. *Ibid.,* 19 Congress, 2 Session, III, 1353-63.

55. Adams, *Memoirs,* IV, 31.

56. *Annals of Congress,* 13 Congress, 3 Session, XXVIII, 1275-80, Appendix, 1943-44.

57. *Annals of Congress,* 14 Congress, 1 Session, XXIX, 419 and *passim.*

58. *American State Papers, Documents, Legislative and Executive of the United States, Foreign Relations,* V, No. 332, 1-11. (Hereinafter cited as *American State Papers.*)

59. *Ibid.,* No. 398, 585-87; Richardson, *Messages and Papers,* II, 257-58.

60. *Annals of Congress,* 14 Congress, 2 Session, XXX, 477 and *passim.*

61. *Register of Debates,* 19 Congress, 1 Session, II Part II, 2009 and *passim.*

62. *American State Papers, Foreign Relations,* V, No. 422, 829-30.

63. Augusta *Constitutionalist,* September, 25, 1827.

CHAPTER III

1. Washington *National Intelligencer,* February 25, 1819.

2. Hunter Miller (ed.), *Treaties and Other International Acts of the United States of America,* III, 3-7, 18. (Hereinafter cited as *Treaties.*)

3. Adams, *Memoirs,* IV, 287-91.

4. *Ibid.;* John Quincy Adams to John Forsyth, March 10, 1819, unnumbered, Instructions, Spain, VIII, 310-11.

5. Louisville, Georgia, *American Advocate,* April 25, 1816.

6. John Forsyth to Nicholas Biddle, December 15, 1818, Biddle Papers, V; cf. *Niles' Register,* XV (January 30, 1819), 431.

7. John Forsyth to Nicholas Biddle, September 3, October 13, 29, December 4, 1818, February 14, 1819, Biddle Papers, V; John Forsyth to William Lowndes, October 6, 1818, William Lowndes Papers.

8. Adams, *Memoirs,* IV, 194, 263.

9. *Ibid.,* 521-22.

10. James Barbour to William Rabun, February 18, 1819, Forsyth Papers, GDAH.

11. John Forsyth to Nicholas Biddle, January 31, March 4, 1819, Biddle Papers, V.

12. Philadelphia *Franklin Gazette,* n.d., in Savannah *Columbian Museum and Savannah Daily Gazette,* March 22, 1819.

13. Savannah *Georgian,* June 3, 1819.

14. John Quincy Adams to John Forsyth, March 8, 10, 1819, unnumbered, Instructions, Spain, VIII, 304-11.

15. John Forsyth to John Quincy Adams, March 15, 1819, No. 1, Despatches, Spain, XVII.

16. John Quincy Adams to John Forsyth, March 26, 1819, No. 5, Instructions, Spain, VIII, 314-15.

17. John Forsyth to John Quincy Adams, June 17, 1819, private letter, Despatches, Spain, XVII.

18. "John Forsyth Journal, 1819-1820," Forsyth Papers.

19. *Ibid.;* cf. "Logbook of the USS Hornet, March 26, 1819 to March 25, 1821," 4-11.

20. "John Forsyth Journal, 1819-1820," Forsyth Papers.

21. *Ibid.;* John Forsyth to John Quincy Adams, April 18, 1819, No. 2, Despatches, Spain, XVII.
22. John Forsyth to John Quincy Adams, June 10, 1819, No. 3, *ibid.*
23. "John Forsyth Journal, 1819-1820," Forsyth Papers.
24. *Ibid.*
25. *Ibid.;* "Logbook of the USS Hornet, March 26, 1819 to March 25, 1821," 15, 41.
26. John Forsyth to the Marquis of Casa Yrujo, May 18, 1819, Despatches, Spain, XVII.
27. John Forsyth to John Quincy Adams, June 10, 1819, No. 3, *ibid.*
28. John Forsyth to John Quincy Adams, June 17, 1819, No. 4, *ibid.*
29. Manuel Gonzales Salmon to John Forsyth, June 19, 1819, *ibid.*
30. John Forsyth to Manuel Gonzales Salmon, June 21, 1819, *ibid.*
31. Adams, *Memoirs,* IV, 404-07, 411-12, 419.
32. John Quincy Adams to John Forsyth, August 18, 1819, No. 8, Instructions, Spain, VIII, 343-54.
33. Manuel Gonzales Salmon to John Forsyth, August 10, 1819, Despatches, Spain, XVII.
34. John Forsyth to Manuel Gonzales Salmon, August 12, 1819, *ibid.*
35. Manuel Gonzales Salmon to John Forsyth, August 19, 1819, *ibid.*
36. John Forsyth to Manuel Gonzales Salmon, August 21, 1819, *ibid.*
37. John Forsyth to John Quincy Adams, August 22, 1819, No. 6, *ibid.*
38. John Forsyth to John Quincy Adams, October 28, 1819, No. 7, *ibid.*
39. John Forsyth to the Duke of San Fernando and Quiroga, October 18, 1819, *ibid.*
40. The Duke of San Fernando and Quiroga to John Forsyth, November 12, 1819, *ibid.*
41. John Forsyth to the Duke of San Fernando and Quiroga, November 20, 1819, *ibid.*
42. John Forsyth to John Quincy Adams, November 27, 1819, No. 10, *ibid.*
43. The Duke of San Fernando and Quiroga to John Forsyth, December 16, 1819, *ibid.*
44. John Forsyth to John Quincy Adams, January 3, 1819 [1820], No. 11, *ibid.*
45. Philadelphia *Daily Advertiser,* n.d., in Savannah *Daily Georgian,* May 5, 1820.
46. Milledgeville *Southern Recorder,* April 25, 1820, in Savannah *Daily Georgian,* May 5, 1820.
47. Adams, *Memoirs,* IV, 521.
48. John Quincy Adams to John Forsyth, February 11, 1820, No. 11, Instructions, Spain, IX, 3.
49. John Forsyth to John Quincy Adams, March 9, 1820, No. 14, Despatches, Spain, XVII.
50. John Forsyth to John Quincy Adams, March 30, 1820, No. 15, XVIII, *ibid.*
51. John Forsyth to John Quincy Adams, May 20, 1820, No. 18, *ibid.*
52. John Forsyth to John Quincy Adams, August 27, 1820, private letter, *ibid.*
53. John Forsyth to John Quincy Adams, October 5, 1820, *ibid.*
54. John Forsyth to John Quincy Adams, October 24, 1820, No. 22, Despatches, *ibid.*
55. Evaristo Perez de Castro to John Forsyth, October 24, 1820, *ibid.*
56. Philip C. Brooks, *Diplomacy and the Borderlands, The Adams-Onis Treaty of 1819,* 185.

CHAPTER IV

1. "John Forsyth Journal, 1819-1820," Forsyth Papers.
2. John Forsyth to Nicholas Biddle, June 19, 1819, Biddle Papers, VI.
3. John Forsyth to John Quincy Adams, August 22, 1819, private letter, Despatches, Spain, XVII.
4. John Forsyth to Nicholas Biddle, May 10, 1820, Biddle Papers, unbound.
5. John Forsyth to John Quincy Adams, April 13, 1820, No. 16, Despatches, Spain, XVIII.
6. John Forsyth to Thomas L. L.

Brent, April 15, 1820, *ibid.;* Thomas L. L. Brent to John Quincy Adams, April 20, 1820, No. 1, *ibid.;* John Forsyth to John Quincy Adams, May 10, 1820, No. 17, *ibid.*

7. John Forsyth to Nicholas Biddle, May 10, 1820, Biddle Papers, unbound.

8. "John Forsyth Journal, 1819-1820," Forsyth Papers.

9. William H. Crawford to James Monroe, July 8, 1820, Monroe Papers, XXIX.

10. John Forsyth to Nicholas Biddle, May 10, 1820, Biddle Papers, unbound; John Forsyth to John Quincy Adams, May 10, 1820, No. 17, Despatches, Spain, XVIII.

11. John Forsyth to Evaristo Perez de Castro, November 5, 1820, *ibid.*

12. John Forsyth to John Quincy Adams, November 12, 1820, No. 23, *ibid.*

13. John Forsyth to Evaristo Perez de Castro, November 25, 1820, Notes to Spanish Government of Minister John Forsyth. (Hereinafter cited as Forsyth Notes, Spain.)

14. Josiah Meigs to Richard Henry Wilde, October 11, 1819, Richard Henry Wilde Papers; Margaret Harrison Smith to Jane Bayard Kirkpatrick, September 18, 1820, Mrs. Samuel Harrison Smith Papers, X.

15. John Forsyth to James Monroe, March 20, 1821, Monroe Papers, XXX.

16. Adams, *Memoirs,* V, 320.

17. Margaret Harrison Smith to Susan H. Smith, March 19, 1821, Mrs. Samuel Harrison Smith Papers, X.

18. Augusta *Chronicle,* March 1, April 2, 9, 1821.

19. John Forsyth to Henry Meigs, March 18, 1821, Forsyth Papers.

20. John Forsyth to John Quincy Adams, August 23, 1821, No. 26, Despatches, Spain, XIX; John Forsyth to Eusebio de Bardaxi y Azara, August 18, 1821, *ibid.*

21. Clara Forsyth to Henry Meigs, February 10, June 17, 1822, Forsyth Papers.

22. Clara Forsyth to Henry Meigs, February 10, 1822, *ibid.*

23. John Forsyth to Evaristo Perez de Castro, September 17, 1820, Forsyth Notes, Spain.

24. John Forsyth to Francisco Martinez de la Rosa, n.d., *ibid.*

25. John Forsyth to Evaristo San Miguel, October 13, 1822, Despatches, Spain, XXI.

26. John Forsyth to John Quincy Adams, January 2, 1822, No. 31, XX.

27. John Quincy Adams to John Forsyth, May 30, 1822, No. 22, Instructions, Spain, IX, 123.

28. John Forsyth to John Quincy Adams, July 11, 1822, No. 43, Despatches, Spain, XX.

29. John Forsyth to John Quincy Adams, June 10, 1819, No. 3, XVII, *ibid.;* John Forsyth to John Quincy Adams, August 22, 1819, No. 6, *ibid.*

30. John Forsyth to John M. Hall, September 6, 1819, United States Legation, Madrid, Official Papers, 1815-1824.

31. John Forsyth to the Duke of San Fernando and Quiroga, September 21, 1819, Despatches, Spain, XVII.

32. Juan Jabat to John Forsyth, April 12, 1820, *ibid.*

33. Circular, John Forsyth to the Consuls, April 13, 1820, United States Legation, Madrid, Official Papers, 1815-1824.

34. John Quincy Adams to John Forsyth, August 18, 1820, No. 15, Instructions, Spain, IX, 17.

35. John Forsyth to John Quincy Adams, November 12, 22, 1820, No. 23, Despatches, Spain, XVIII. This is one letter, the first part written on November 12, and the final paragraph dated November 22.

36. John Forsyth to Evaristo Perez de Castro, November 25, 1820, Forsyth Notes, Spain.

37. John Forsyth to John Quincy Adams, November 10, 1821, No. 28, Despatches, Spain, XIX.

38. John Forsyth to Eusebio de Bardaxi y Azara, November 16, 1821, *ibid.*

39. John Forsyth to John Quincy Adams, December 17, 1821, No. 30, *ibid.*

40. Francisco Martinez de la Rosa and John Forsyth became such personal

friends that Forsyth later named one of his twin daughters, Rosa, for the Spaniard. After de la Rosa lost favor with the Spanish government, Forsyth provided him with refuge by hiding him in his home.

41. John Forsyth to Francisco Martinez de la Rosa, April 9, 1822, Despatches, Spain, XIX.

42. John Forsyth to John Quincy Adams, November 12, 22, 1820, No. 23, XVII, *ibid.*

43. John Forsyth to John Quincy Adams, November 10, 1821, No. 28, XIX, *ibid.*

44. John Quincy Adams to Hugh Nelson, April 28, 1823, unnumbered, Instructions, Spain, IX, 233-34.

45. John Forsyth to Eusebio de Bardaxi y Azara, October 4, 1821, Despatches, Spain, XIX.

46. John Forsyth to John Quincy Adams, December 17, 1821, No. 30, *ibid.*

47. Eusebio de Bardaxi y Azara to John Forsyth, December 17, 1821, *ibid.*

48. John Forsyth to Eusebio de Bardaxi y Azara, December 25, 1821, *ibid.*

49. Ramon Lopez Pelegrin to John Forsyth, January 23, 1822, XX, *ibid.*

50. John Forsyth to Ramon Lopez Pelegrin, January 31, 1822, *ibid.*

51. John Forsyth to Evaristo San Miguel, December 19, 1822, XXI, *ibid.*

52. John Forsyth to Eusebio de Bardaxi y Azara, September 1, 1821, XIX, *ibid.*

53. John Forsyth to Eusebio de Bardaxi y Azara, October 2, 1821, *ibid.*

54. John Quincy Adams to John Forsyth, May 30, 1822, No. 22, Instructions, Spain, IX, 123-24.

55. John Forsyth to Evaristo San Miguel, August 20, 1822, No. 44, Despatches, Spain, XX.

56. John Forsyth to Evaristo San Miguel, December 19, 1822, XXI, *ibid.*

57. John Quincy Adams to Hugh Nelson, April 28, 1823, unnumbered, Instructions, Spain, IX, 231.

58. John Forsyth to John Quincy Adams, May 20, 1822, No. 39, Despatches, Spain, XX.

59. John Quincy Adams to John Forsyth, December 17, 1822, No. 28, Instructions, Spain, IX, 158-59.

60. John Forsyth to John Quincy Adams, January 10, 12, 1823, No. 54, Despatches, Spain, XXI.

61. John Forsyth to Evaristo San Miguel, February 25, 1823, *ibid.*

62. Copy of speech of John Forsyth to the King of Spain, March 2, 1823, inclosed with despatch, John Forsyth to John Quincy Adams, March 3, 1823, No. 60, *ibid.*

63. "Political Portraits: Forsyth," 279; Washington *National Intelligencer*, May 5, 1823; Savannah *Georgian*, May 14, 1823.

64. John Forsyth to John Quincy Adams, March 3, 1823, No. 60, Despatches, Spain, XXI.

65. George Dangerfield, *The Era of Good Feelings*, 154.

CHAPTER V

1. Ulrich Bonnell Phillips, *Georgia and State Rights, American Historical Association, Annual Report, 1901,* II, 90-93; Coulter, *Georgia, A Short History,* 239-40; Richard Harrison Shryock, *Georgia and the Union in 1850,* 90-91; Amanda Johnson, *Georgia as Colony and State,* 179-80.

2. Augusta *Chronicle and Sentinel*, October 23, 1837.

3. Paul Murray, *The Whig Party in Georgia, 1825-1853*, 2.

4. Phillips, *Georgia and State Rights*, 98.

5. Augusta *Constitutionalist*, July 25, 1826.

6. Savannah *Georgian*, August 15, 29, September 9, 1826.

7. Augusta *Constitutionalist*, August 22, 25, September 5, 1826.

8. Macon *Telegraph*, December 26, 1826.

9. Duncan G. Campbell to Matthew Talbot, July 23, 1827, in Augusta *Constitutionalist*, July 31, 1827.

10. John Forsyth to William C. Rives, October 16, 1827, William Cabell Rives Papers, unbound, Library of

Congress; William Drayton to John Forsyth, October 21, 1827, in Milledgeville *Georgia Journal*, November 26, 1827; Michael Hoffman to John Forsyth, November 8, 1827; in Milledgeville *Georgia Journal*, November 26, 1827.

11. Macon *Telegraph*, March 12, 26, April 16, July 9, September 4, 1827; Savannah *Georgian*, September 20, 1827.

12. Milledgeville *Georgia Journal*, September 3, 1827.

13. Augusta *Constitutionalist*, August 31, 1827.

14. Savannah *Georgian*, October 6, 9, 1827; *Niles' Register*, XXXIII (October 27, 1827), 129.

15. Macon *Telegraph*, October 16, 23, 1827.

16. John Forsyth to George M. Troup, October 13, 1827, Forsyth Papers, GDAH.

17. Executive Minutes, November 7, 1827, 396, GDAH; Augusta *Constitutionalist*, November 13, 1827.

18. Executive Minutes, December 18, 1828, 582-83, GDAH.

19. George R. Gilmer to his constituents, in Athens *Athenian*, January 27, March 3, and 18, 1829.

20. John Forsyth to his constituents, January 22, 1829, in Athens *Athenian*, February 3, 1829; John Forsyth to his constituents, March 5, 1829, in Athens *Athenian*, March 17, 1829; George R. Gilmer to John Clark, November 11, 1820, in Milledgeville *Georgia Journal*, January 26, 1829. Forsyth stated that a report to his constituents was necessary; otherwise, his silence would be construed as admitting to the accuracy of Gilmer's statements.

21. West Chester (Pa.) *Village Record*, n.d., in Washington *National Intelligencer*, June 9, 1829.

22. William H. Holt to John Forsyth, November 30, 1829, in Washington *National Intelligencer*, December 19, 1829.

23. George R. Gilmer to the People of Georgia, May 9, 1829, in Athens *Athenian*, May 26, 1829.

24. John Forsyth to Wilson Lumpkin, November 19, 1828, "Governors' Letter Book," 585, GDAH; John Forsyth to Wilson Lumpkin, December 14, 1828, *ibid.*, 589.

25. John Forsyth to William Wimbush, May 11, 1829, *ibid.*, 626; John Forsyth to Josiah Freeman, May 11, 1829, *ibid.*, 627; John Forsyth to Josiah Freeman, May 16, 1829, *ibid.*, 628; John Forsyth to R. L. Simms, July 2, 1829, *ibid.*, 640; John Forsyth to Ernest L. Young, October 9, 1829, *ibid.*, 655.

26. Executive Minutes, December 17, 1828, 581, GDAH.

27. *Ibid.*, November 3, 1829, 9; John Forsyth to the Mayor, Aldermen, and Council of Savannah, February 23, 1829, "Governors' Letter Book," 610-11, GDAH; John Forsyth to William T. Williams, February 23, 1829, *ibid.*, 611.

28. John Forsyth to William B. Barnett, July 30, 1829, *ibid.*, 644.

29. John Forsyth to the Georgia House of Representatives, November 12, 1827, in Milledgeville *Georgia Journal*, November 15, 1827.

30. Warren Grice, *The Georgia Bench and Bar*, I, 301, 306; Albert Berry Saye, *A Constitutional History of Georgia, 1732-1945*, 246-47.

31. *Ibid.*, 185-86; Ethel Kime Ware, *A Constitutional History of Georgia*, 93, 98; Grice, *The Georgia Bench and Bar*, I, 266-67.

32. John Forsyth to the Governor of New York, February 11, 1828, "Governors' Letter Book," 533, GDAH.

33. Athens *Athenian*, December 2, 1828, January 6, 1829. Prior to the enactment, the Georgia penitentiary officials had been elected by the General Assembly.

34. Executive Minutes, November 3, 1829, 5, GDAH.

35. Porter Lee Fortune, Jr., "George M. Troup: Leading State Rights Advocate," 161-64, unpublished Ph. D. dissertation, University of North Carolina Library.

36. Executive Minutes, November 15, 1827, 403, GDAH; John Forsyth to

Alexander Telfair, November 15, 1827, "Governors' Letter Book," 513, GDAH.

37. John Forsyth to Alexander Telfair, James H. Couper, and George W. McAllister, November 21, 1827, "Governors' Letter Book," 514-15, GDAH.

38. Executive Minutes, December 1, 1827, 416, GDAH; cf. John Forsyth to Alexander Telfair, James H. Couper, and George W. McAllister, December 1, 1827, "Governors' Letter Book," 517, GDAH.

39. Executive Minutes, December 20, 1828, 593, GDAH.

40. *Acts of the General Assembly of the State of Georgia* (1828), 34-41; Athens *Athenian,* January 6, 13, September 15, 1829; Executive Minutes, January 1, 1829, 597, GDAH; *ibid.,* January 14, 1829, 605; Thomas P. Govan, "Banking and the Credit System in Georgia, 1810-1860," *Journal of Southern History,* IV (May, 1933), 172; Ulrich Bonnell Phillips, *A History of Transportation in the Eastern Cotton Belt to 1860,* 311. (Hereinafter cited as *History of Transportation.*)

41. Executive Minutes, November 3, 1829, 6-9, GDAH.

42. John Forsyth to Hamilton Fulton, March 28, 1828, "Governors' Letter Book," 542, GDAH; John Forsyth to Sowell Woolfolk, March 28, 1828, *ibid.,* 541.

43. Fletcher Melvin Green, "Georgia's Board of Public Works, 1817-1826," *The Georgia Historical Quarterly,* XXII (June, 1938), 133-34, 137.

44. The Georgians principally responsible for the Board's recommendation were: George M. Troup, Wilson Lumpkin, James H. Couper, and Hamilton Fulton.

45. Executive Minutes, November 3, 1829, 9, GDAH.

46. Phillips, *History of Transportation,* 120-21; Coulter, *Georgia, A Short History,* 252.

47. John Forsyth to Georgia Senators and Representatives in the Congress

of the United States, March 18, 1828, "Governors' Letter Book," 540, GDAH.

48. John Forsyth to John Taylor, November 12, 1828, *ibid.,* 585; Executive Minutes, November 14, 1828, 557, GDAH.

49. *Ibid.,* 557-58.

50. Johnson, *Georgia as Colony and State,* 381. Wright was Governor of East Florida.

51. Johnson, *Georgia as Colony and State,* 382.

52. Executive Minutes, November 28, 1827, 410, GDAH.

53. Augusta *Constitutionalist,* December 7, 1827.

54. John Forsyth to Georgia Senators and Representatives in the Congress of the United States, December 11, 1827, "Governors' Letter Book," 521, GDAH. Forsyth erroneously refers to an act of 1825; obviously, the reference should be to the measure which was signed on May 4, 1826. For the latter law, see *Register of Debates,* 19 Congress, 1 Session, II Part II, Appendix, 12.

55. John Forsyth to John Quincy Adams, December 29, 1827, "Governors' Letter Book," 526, GDAH.

56. Wilson Lumpkin to John Forsyth, March 4, 1834, in Wilson Lumpkin, *The Removal of the Cherokees from Georgia,* I, 248.

57. John Forsyth to Georgia Representatives in the Congress of the United States, April 7, 1828, "Governors' Letter Book," 544-46, GDAH.

58. Executive Minutes, November 4, 1828, 539-40, GDAH.

59. *Ibid.,* November 3, 1829, 5.

60. John Forsyth to Churchill Caldom Cambreleng, June 14, 1828, Miscellaneous Letters; John Forsyth to Arthur Schaaff, May 25, 1829, Forsyth Papers.

61. John Forsyth to Fellow Citizens, July 30, 1829, in Athens *Athenian,* August 11, 1829.

62. Augusta *Chronicle and Georgia Advertiser,* September 26, 1829; Athens *Athenian,* September 1, 1829.

63. Augusta *Constitutionalist*, September 29, 1829.
64. Athens *Athenian*, November 17, 1829.

65. Augusta *Chronicle and Georgia Advertiser*, November 12, 1828.
66. Milledgeville *Georgia Journal*, November 17, 1828.

CHAPTER VI

1. *American State Papers, Public Lands,* I, No. 69, 125-26.
2. Charles J. Kappler (ed.), *Indian Affairs: Laws and Treaties,* II, 107-10, 155-56, 195-97. (Hereinafter cited as *Indian Affairs.*)
3. Coulter, *Georgia, A Short History,* 223-27.
4. *Journal of the House of Representatives of the State of Georgia* (1823), 223-34. (Hereinafter cited as *Georgia House Journal.*)
5. George M. Troup to Georgia Senators and Representatives in the Congress of the United States, January 6, 1824, "Governors' Letter Book," 176, GDAH.
6. The Georgia Senators and Representatives in the Congress of the United States to George M. Troup, March 17, 1824, in Milledgeville *Georgia Journal,* April 20, 1824. The four Cherokee chiefs were John Ross, George Lowrey, Major Ridge, and Elijah Hicks.
7. Adams, *Memoirs,* VI, 262.
8. The Georgia Senators and Representatives in the Congress of the United States to President James Monroe, March 10, 1824, in Milledgeville *Georgia Journal,* April 20, 1824.
9. Richardson, *Messages and Papers,* II, 235.
10. *Annals of Congress,* 18 Congress, 1 Session, XLII, 2348-57; *American State Papers, Indian Affairs,* II, No. 207, 495-98.
11. *The Statutes at Large of the United States, 1789-1893,* IV, 36. (Hereinafter cited as *Statutes at Large.*)
12. *Niles' Register,* XXVII (December 4, 1824), 223-24; *American State Papers, Indian Affairs,* II, No. 222, 564-75; Duncan G. Campbell to John C. Calhoun, January 8, 1825, *United States House Report No. 98,* 19 Congress, 2 Session, III, 86-91. (Here-

inafter cited as *House Report No. 98.*)
13. Kappler, *Indian Affairs,* II, 214-17, 583-84; *House Report No. 98,* 19 Congress, 2 Session, III, 133-36.
14. *Register of Debates,* 18 Congress, 2 Session, I, 410.
15. *House Report No. 98,* 19 Congress, 2 Session, III, 123-25.
16. George M. Troup to Duncan G. Campbell and James Meriwether, February 12, 1825, "Governors' Letter Book," 260, GDAH.
17. John Forsyth to James Barbour, March 9, 1825, Forsyth Papers, GDAH.
18. Kappler, *Indian Affairs,* II, 284-85; Adams, *Memoirs,* VII, 362.
19. *American State Papers, Indian Affairs* II, No. 249, 747.
20. *Register of Debates,* 19 Congress, 1 Session, II Part II, 2607-17, 2625.
21. *Ibid.,* 2670-78.
22. Richardson, *Messages and Papers,* II, 370-73.
23. *Register of Debates,* 19 Congress, 2 Session, III, 935-37, 1038-51.
24. Lumpkin, *The Removal of the Cherokee Indians from Georgia,* I, 42-43; *Niles' Register,* XXXIII (January 19, 1828), 346. For the text of the Cherokee Constitution, see *United States House Executive Document No. 91,* III, 23 Congress, 2 Session, 10-19.
25. *United States Senate Document No. 80,* 20 Congress, 1 Session, III, 13.
26. John Forsyth to the President of the United States, January 16, 1828, Letters Received, Bureau of Indian Affairs.
27. John Forsyth to Samuel Houston, December 12, 1827, "Governors' Letter Book," 521, GDAH; John Forsyth to John Quincy Adams, January 26, 1828, *ibid.,* 530.
28. John Forsyth to Hugh Montgomery, May 21, 1828, *ibid.,* 549.

29. Executive Minutes, November 4, 1828, 540-41, GDAH.

30. John H. Eaton to the Cherokee Delegation, April 18, 1829, in Athens *Athenian*, June 9, 1829.

31. John Forsyth to John H. Eaton, May 23, 1829, "Governors' Letter Book," 630, GDAH.

32. Executive Minutes, November 3, 1829, 4-5, GDAH.

33. John Forsyth to Hugh Montgomery, June 12, 1828, "Governors' Letter Book," 551, GDAH.

34. John Forsyth to Hugh Montgomery, August 25, 1828, *ibid.*, 567.

35. John Forsyth to John H. Eaton, May 19, 1829, *ibid.*, 629-30.

36. Samuel A. Wales to John Forsyth, May 12, 1829, Letters Received, Bureau of Indian Affairs; Hugh Montgomery to John H. Eaton, May 9, 1829, *ibid.*

37. Samuel A. Wales to Hugh Montgomery, May 13, 1829, *ibid.*

38. John Forsyth to John H. Eaton, May 23, 1829, "Governors' Letter Book," 631, GDAH.

39. John H. Eaton to Hugh Montgomery, October 9, 1829, "Letter Book," VI, 107, Bureau of Indian Affairs.

40. John H. Eaton to John Forsyth, September 15, 1829, *ibid.*, 86; Executive Minutes, November 3, 1829, 3, GDAH.

41. John H. Eaton to John Forsyth, October 14, 1829, "Letter Book," VI, 113-19, Bureau of Indian Affairs; Executive Minutes, November 3, 1829, 3, GDAH.

42. *Ibid.*, 3-4.

43. Act of the Georgia General Assembly, December 20, 1828, inclosed in letter, John Forsyth to the President of the United States, March 11, 1829, Letters Received, Bureau of Indian Affairs.

44. John Forsyth to James Barbour, November 29, 1827, Letters Received, Bureau of Indian Affairs.

45. John Forsyth to John Crowell, November 29, 1827, *ibid.*

46. Thomas L. McKenney to Peter B. Porter, October 6, 1828, "Letter Book," V, 147-48, Bureau of Indian Affairs.

47. John Forsyth to John Crowell, September 29, 1828, "Governors' Letter Book," 579, GDAH; John Forsyth to Sowell Woolfolk, September 29, 1828, *ibid.*; John Forsyth to Peter B. Porter, September 18, 1828, *ibid.*, 576-77.

48. John Forsyth to John H. Eaton, September 7, 1829, "Governors' Letter Book," 651, GDAH.

49. John Forsyth and Richard Henry Wilde to the Governor of Georgia, February 9, 1830, Forsyth Papers, GDAH.

50. *Register of Debates*, 21 Congress, 1 Session, VI Part I, 8.

51. *Register of Debates*, 23 Congress, 1 Session, X Part II, 1772 and *passim.*

52. Macon *Georgia Telegraph*, November 28, 1832. Forsyth's name was also given to the county seat of Monroe County which, in 1821, was created out of lands acquired from the Creeks.

CHAPTER VII

1. Claude Gernade Bowers, *The Party Battles of the Jackson Period*, 56.

2. For example, see John Forsyth to Martin Van Buren, February 25, 1828, Van Buren Papers, VII.

3. Washington *United States' Telegraph*, July 25, 1832.

4. James Parton, *Life of Andrew Jackson*, II, 463-80, 506-07; John Spencer Bassett, *The Life of Andrew Jackson*, I, 254-64.

5. *Ibid.*, 281-82, 288-89; Adams, *Memoirs*, IV, 239-40.

6. John Forsyth to William Lowndes, October 6, 1818, William Lowndes Papers.

7. John Forsyth to Nicholas Biddle, December 21, 1818, Biddle Papers, V, L.C.

8. *Ibid.*, December 15, 1818.

9. Adams, *Memoirs*, IV, 239-41.

10. *Ibid.*, 245.

11. John Forsyth to Martin Van Buren, February 25, 1828, Van Buren Papers, VII, LC.

12. John Forsyth to Arthur Shaaff, May 25, 1829, Forsyth Papers.

13. James A. Hamilton to the public, February 22, 1831, in Washington *United States' Telegraph*, February 28, 1831; Narrative by William B. Lewis, October 25, 1859, in Parton, *Life of Andrew Jackson*, III, 315-18. A duplication of the correspondence connected with the entire Crawford letter affair may be found in *Niles' Register*, XL (March 5, 1831), 11-24, XL (March 12, 1831), 37-40, XL (March 19, 1831), 41-45. The Washington *United States' Telegraph* and the Washington *Globe* also contain copies.

14. William H. Crawford to John Forsyth, April 30, 1830, Jackson Papers, IV (2nd. series).

15. John Forsyth to the editor, February 19, 1831, in Washington *United States' Telegraph*, February 22, 1831.

16. John C. Calhoun to the editor, February 24, 1831, in Washington *United States' Telegraph*, February 25, 1831.

17. John C. Calhoun to Andrew Jackson, May 29, 1830, Jackson Papers, LXXV (1st. series).

18. *Ibid.*; John C. Calhoun to James Henry Hammond, February 16, 1831, James H. Hammond Papers, II.

19. John Forsyth to John C. Calhoun, May 31, 1830, Jackson Papers, LXXV (1st series).

20. John C. Calhoun to John Forsyth, June 1, 1830, *ibid.*

21. Washington *United States' Telegraph*, February 28, March 24, 1831, February 20, 1832.

22. John Forsyth to the editor, February 19, 1831, in Washington *United States' Telegraph*, February 22, 1831.

23. Martin Van Buren to the editor, February 25, 1831, in Washington *United States' Telegraph*, February 26, 1831.

24. Thomas Hart Benton, *Thirty Years' View; or, A History of the Working of the American Government for Thirty Years, from 1820 to 1850...*,

I, 214. (Hereinafter cited as *Thirty Years' View*.) *Register of Debates*, 22 Congress, 1 Session, VIII Part I, 1309; Andrew Jackson to Martin Van Buren, December 17, 1831, John Spencer Bassett (ed.), *Correspondence of Andrew Jackson*, IV, 385.

25. Benton, *Thirty Years' View*, I, 215.

26. Benton, *Thirty Years' View*, I, 216; *Register of Debates*, 22 Congress, 1 Session, VIII Part I, 1314 and *passim*.

27. Washington *United States' Telegraph*, February 20, 1832.

28. John Forsyth to Martin Van Buren, January 28, 1832, Van Buren Papers, XIV.

29. John Forsyth to John Branch, February 7, 1832, in *Niles' Register*, XLI (February 11, 1832), 430.

30. William Henry Sparks, *The Memories of Fifty Years...*, 56.

31. Andrew Jackson to Martin Van Buren, December 17, 1831, Bassett, *Correspondence of Andrew Jackson*, IV, 385; Andrew Jackson to Martin Van Buren, February 12, 1832, *ibid.*, 405.

32. Martin Van Buren to Andrew Jackson, February 20, 1832, *ibid.*, 407-08; *Niles' Register*, XLII (July 14, 1832), 355.

33. John Forsyth to Martin Van Buren, January 28, 1832, Van Buren Papers, XIV.

34. Augusta *Chronicle*, June 2, 1832.

35. *Register of Debates*, 23 Congress, 1 Session, X Part I, 344.

36. Arthur Meier Schlesinger, Jr., *The Age of Jackson*, 74-78, 88.

37. Benton, *Thirty Years' View*, I, 235-36; *Register of Debates*, 22 Congress, 1 Session, VIII Part II, 1846. Although Senator Benton was the instigator, the proposal for a house investigating committee was made by Representative Augustin S. Clayton of Georgia.

38. Benton, *Thirty Years' View*, I, 236.

39. Thomas Cadwalader to Nicholas Biddle, December 21, 1831, Reginald Charles McGrane (ed.), *The Correspondence of Nicholas Biddle Dealing with National Affairs, 1807-1844*, 149; Thomas Cadwalader

to Nicholas Biddle, December 23, 1831, *ibid.*, 152.

40. Andrew Jackson to Reverend Hardy M. Cryer, April 7, 1833, Bassett, *Correspondence of Andrew Jackson*, V, 53.

41. *Register of Debates*, 23 Congress, 1 Session, X Part IV, Appendix, 59-68.

42. Bowers, *The Party Battles of the Jackson Period*, 323.

43. *Register of Debates*, 23 Congress, 1 Session, X Part I, 37. The original resolution had been modified so as to omit the demand for presidential verification of the letter.

44. *Ibid.*, 342-72, records the date of Forsyth's address as January 27, 1834. However, Washington *National Intelligencer*, January 29, 1834, reported that the speech was not concluded until the following day.

45. New York *Journal of Commerce*, n.d., in Macon *Georgia Telegraph*, February 13, 1834.

46. *Register of Debates*, 23 Congress, 1 Session, X Part I, 365.

47. Washington *United States' Telegraph*, February 1, 6, 1834; Washington *Examiner*, n.d., in Macon *Georgia Telegraph*, February 13, 1834; Charleston *Mercury*, n.d., in Augusta *Chronicle*, February 8, 1834.

48. Augusta *Georgia Constitutionalist*, February 11, 1834.

49. Benton, *Thirty Years' View*, I, 423.

50. *Register of Debates*, 23 Congress, 1 Session, X Part II, 1400.

51. *Ibid.*, 1420 and *passim*.

52. *Ibid.*, 1650.

53. *Ibid.*, X Part I, 626.

54. Washington *United States' Telegraph*, March 1, 3, 1834; Milledgeville *Southern Recorder*, March 12, 1834; Alexandria (Va.) *Gazette*, n.d., in Augusta *Chronicle*, March 15, 1834.

55. *Journal of the Senate of the United States of America*, February 28, 1834, in Washington *United States' Telegraph*, March 3, 1834.

56. *Register of Debates*, 23 Congress, 1 Session, X Part II, 1914 and *passim*.

57. *Ibid.*, 2075-76, 2120.

58. *Annals of Congress*, 14 Congress, 2 Session, XXX, 933-34. The Bonus Bill provided that the bonus which the federal government would receive from the Bank of the United States, together with the annual dividends of stock, should be used as a fund for internal improvements.

59. *Annals of Congress*, 18 Congress, 1 Session, XLI, 1041-42, 1468-69. The General Survey Bill directed the President of the United States to cause the survey and estimate of those roads and canals which were considered of importance for defense, commercial, or postal purposes.

60. *Register of Debates*, 21 Congress, 1 Session, VI Part I, 342.

61. Washington *Globe*, June 4, 1834.

62. John Forsyth to Andrew Jackson, June 20, 1831, Jackson Papers, LXXVIII (1st. Series).

63. William Stickney (ed.), *Autobiography of Amos Kendall*, 421-22.

CHAPTER VIII

1. Ellis Merton Coulter, "The Nullification Movement in Georgia," The *Georgia Historical Quarterly*, V (March, 1921), 4-37.

2. Phillips, *Georgia and State Rights*, 124-32, 143-46.

3. *Annals of Congress*, 14 Congress, 1 Session, XXIX, 1240.

4. *Ibid.*, 1263.

5. Executive Minutes, November 4, 1828, 547-48, Georgia Department of Archives and History, Atlanta.

6. *Niles' Register*, XXXV (November 22, 1828), 195; Washington *National Intelligencer*, November 18, 1828.

7. Columbia (S.C.) *Telescope*, November 21, 1828, in Athens *Athenian*, December 9, 1828.

8. Executive Minutes, November 3, 1829, 10, GDAH.

9. *Register of Debates*, 22 Congress, 1 Session, VIII Part I, 55 and *passim*.

10. *Ibid.*, 106.

11. *Ibid.*, 107.

12. *Ibid.*, 624-25.

13. *Ibid.*, 626.

14. *Ibid.*, 1290.

15. Milledgeville *Recorder,* n.d., in Macon *Telegraph,* August 1, 1832; Macon *Telegraph,* August 8, 1832.

16. Milledgeville *Federal Union,* August 16, 1832.

17. Augusta *Chronicle,* August 25, 1832.

18. Phillips, *Georgia and State Rights,* 130; Augusta *Georgia Constitutionalist,* August 31, September 4, 21, 25, 28, October 2, 9, 1832.

19. Athens *Southern Banner,* n.d., in Macon *Telegraph,* August 8, 1832; Washington *National Intelligencer,* August 13, 1832; Athens *Gazette,* August 3, 1832, in Macon *Telegraph,* August 8, 1832.

20. Macon *Telegraph,* September 5, 12, 1832.

21. *Proceedings of the Anti-Tariff Convention of the State of Georgia, Held in Milledgeville, 1832,* 10. (Hereinafter cited as *Convention Proceedings.*)

22. Milledgeville *Journal of the Times,* n.d., in Macon *Georgia Telegraph,* November 21, 1832.

23. *Convention Proceedings,* 12.

24. Macon *Georgia Telegraph,* November 21, 1832; Macon *Georgia Messenger,* November 15, 1832; Miller, *The Bench and Bar of Georgia,* II, 31, 35.

25. Milledgeville *Georgia Journal,* November 15, 1832; *Niles' Register,* XLIII (December 1, 1832), 221.

26. Miller, *The Bench and Bar of Georgia,* II, 32.

27. Milledgeville *Federal Union,* November 22, 1832.

28. *Convention Proceedings,* 14; Augusta *Chronicle,* November 21, 1832.

29. Macon *Georgia Telegraph,* November 21, 1832; Baltimore *American,* n.d., in Washington *United States' Telegraph,* November 28, 1832. The opposition denied that more than twenty counties had failed to elect

delegates. Milledgeville *Georgia Journal,* November 19, 1832.

30. *Convention Proceedings,* 15-20.

31. *Ibid.,* 26-27; Macon *Georgia Messenger,* November 15, 22, 1832.

32. Macon *Georgia Telegraph,* November 21, 28, 1832.

33. *Niles' Register,* XLIII (December 1, 1832), 231.

34. John Forsyth to Martin Van Buren, November 23, 1832, Van Buren Papers, XVII.

35. *Register of Debates,* 22 Congress, 2 Session, IX Part I, 592-93.

36. Georgia required all white persons living among the Cherokees to obtain a permit prior to March 1, 1831. Certain missionaries, hostile toward Georgia's treatment of the Indians, refused to abide by the law. Samuel A. Worcester and Elizur Butler accepted imprisonment rather than conform. In the case of *Worcester vs. Georgia,* the court upheld the missionary's contention that the state law was unconstitutional. President Jackson refused to enforce the decision and, consequently, the two missionaries remained in prison until they petitioned for clemency. They were pardoned by Governor Gilmer on January 10, 1833.

37. *Register of Debates,* 22 Congress, 2 Session, IX Part I, 595.

38. Washington *United States' Telegraph,* July 19, 1833.

39. Augusta *Chronicle,* July 10, 1833.

40. Washington *National Intelligencer,* April 16, 1833.

41. John Forsyth to Jacob Wood *et al.,* November 11, 1833, in Augusta *Georgia Constitutionalist,* November 15, 1833.

42. *Register of Debates,* 22 Congress, 2 Session, IX Part I, 473, 476, 480.

43. *Ibid.,* 805.

44. *Register of Debates,* 23 Congress, 1 Session, X Part II, 1600-05.

CHAPTER IX

1. John Forsyth to Andrew Jackson, June 20, 1831, Jackson Papers, LXXVIII (1st. series); Martin Van Buren to Andrew Jackson, November 29, 1832, in Fitzpatrick, *The Autobiography of Martin Van Buren,* 598, 606; Martin Van Buren to Andrew Jackson, December 22,

1832, Van Buren Papers, XVII, LC;
Martin Van Buren to Andrew
Jackson, February 6, 1833, *ibid.*,
XVIII; John Forsyth to Martin Van
Buren, November 29, 1833, *ibid.*,
XIX.

2. John Forsyth to Martin Van Buren,
December 30, 1832, *ibid.*, XVII.

3. John Forsyth to Martin Van Buren,
March 29, 1833, *ibid.*, XIX. Because
of the difficulty of reading Forsyth's
handwriting, this letter is catalogued
incorrectly as having been written
on November 29, 1833 ("March"
being mistaken for "Novb").

4. Andrew Jackson to Martin Van
Buren, April 25, 1833, Van Buren
Papers, XVIII.

5. John Forsyth to Martin Van Buren,
August 4, 1833, *ibid.*; Andrew Jack-
son to Martin Van Buren, August
16, 1833, *ibid.*; John Forsyth to Louis
McLane, April 18, 1834, Jackson
Papers, LXXXVI (1st. series).

6. Washington *National Intelligencer,*
June 20, 1834.

7. Allan Nevins (ed.), *The Diary of
Philip Hone, 1828-1851,* I, 204.

8. Fitzpatrick, *The Autobiography of
Martin Van Buren,* 613.

9. Nicholas Biddle to John Forsyth,
July 11, 1834, "President's Letter
Book," V, 253, Biddle Papers, LC.

10. Washington *National Intelligencer,*
July 15, 1834.

11. Harriet Martineau, *Retrospect of
Western Travel,* I, 235.

12. Richard Aubrey McLemore, "The
French Spoliation Claims, 1816-1836:
A Study in Jacksonian Diplomacy,"
Tennessee Historical Magazine, II
(July, 1932), 234-42.

13. Louis Serurier to Count de Rigny,
October 22, 1834, in Washington
Globe, March 12, 1835.

14. Louis Serurier to Count de Rigny,
November 20, 1834, in Washington
Globe, March 12, 1835.

15. John Forsyth to Martin Van Buren,
September 30, 1834, Van Buren
Papers, XX.

16. Henry Alexander Wise, *Seven Decades of the Union,* 145-46.

17. Washington *National Intelligencer,*
December 4, 8, 1834.

18. Washington *Globe,* January 5, 1835.

19. John Forsyth to Louis Serurier,
February 23, 1835, *United States
House Executive Document No. 174,*
23 Congress, 2 Session, IV, 14.

20. Louis Serurier to John Forsyth,
February 23, 1835, *ibid.*

21. Pageot's wife was a frequent visitor
at the White House and his son
was named for the president.

22. John Forsyth to Andrew Jackson,
February 28, 1835, Bassett, *Correspondence of Andrew Jackson,* V,
329.

23. Andrew Jackson to Amos Kendall,
July 19, 1835, *ibid.*, 357.

24. Duke de Broglie to Alphonse Pageot, June 17, 1835, in Washington
Globe, January 22, 1836.

25. Andrew Jackson to John Forsyth,
September 6, 1834 [1835], Jackson
Papers, XCI (1st. series).

26. *United States House Executive
Document No. 67, 24* Congress,
1 Session, III, 2-3.

27. Charles Kingsley Webster, "British
Mediation between France and the
United States in 1834-6," *The English Historical Review,* XLII (January, 1927), 65.

28. Alphonse Pageot to John Forsyth,
December 1, 1835, *United States
House Executive Document No. 67,*
24 Congress, 1 Session, III, 12-13.

29. John Forsyth to Alphonse Pageot,
December 3, 1835, *ibid.*, 13-14.

30. Alphonse Pageot to John Forsyth,
December 5, 1835, *ibid.*, 14-15.

31. Washington *Globe,* December 13,
1835.

32. Washington *National Intelligencer,*
December 14, 16, 1835.

33. *Ibid.,* January 5, 1836.

34. *Ibid.,* January 7, 1836.

35. Henry Clay to Nicholas Biddle,
January 6, 1836, Biddle Papers, LVII.

36. Richard Aubrey McLemore, *Franco-
American Diplomatic Relations,
1816-1836,* 196.

37. *United States House Executive
Document No. 67, 24* Congress, 1
Session, III, 2-3.

38. Washington *National Intelligencer,*
January 19, 1836.

39. *Ibid.,* January 21, 1836.

40. New York *Times,* n.d., in Washington *Globe,* February 3, 1836.

41. John Forsyth to Henry Clay, January 28, 1836, in Washington *National Intelligencer,* February 12, 1836.

42. William B. Lewis to Alphonse Pageot, July 6, 1836, Jackson Papers, XCV (1st. series); Alphonse Pageot to Henry S. Fox, November 17, 1836, Notes from Great Britain, XIX; Henry S. Fox to John Forsyth, November 18, 1836, *ibid.;* John Forsyth to Lewis Cass, December 10, 1836, No. 7, Instructions, France, XIV, 222.

43. New York *Gazette,* January 20, 1836, in Washington *National Intelligencer,* January 23, 1836; New York *American,* January 20, 1836, in Washington *National Intelligencer,* January 23, 1836.

44. *Register of Debates,* 24 Congress, 1 Session, XII Part I, 353.

45. Webster, "British Mediation between France and the United States in 1834-6," 60-61.

46. Isaac McKim to William C. Rives, January 31, 1836, William Cabell Rives Papers, Box XIV.

47. John Forsyth to Charles Bankhead, February 3, 1836, *United States House Executive Document No. 116,* 24 Congress, 1 Session, IV, 7.

48. Washington *National Intelligencer,* February 9, 1836.

49. Henry S. Fox to John Forsyth, n.d. [received at the State Department on June 9, 1836], Notes from Great Britain, XIX.

50. John Forsyth to Henry S. Fox, June 9, 1836, Notes to British Legation, VI, 60.

51. Lewis Cass to William B. Lewis, June 13, 1836, Bassett, *Correspondence of Andrew Jackson,* V, fn., 436-37; Andrew Jackson, "Memorandum Respecting A. Pageot," November 15, 1836, *ibid.,* 436-37.

52. New York *Journal of Commerce,* May 30, 1835, in Washington *National Intelligencer,* June 4, 1835.

53. Washington *Globe,* June 9, 1835.

54. Andrew Jackson to John Forsyth [Sr.], September 29, 1835, Appointment Papers of the Department of State: Applications and Recommendations for Office, 1829-1836.

55. *Niles' Register,* LII (March 18, 1837), 33; *ibid.,* LII (March 25, 1837), 50; Macon *Georgia Messenger,* March 23, 1837; W. B. Hodgson to William C. Rives, May 27, 1839, William Cabell Rives Papers, Box XVI.

56. Martin Van Buren to John Forsyth, March 9, 1837, Van Buren Papers, XXVI.

57. John Forsyth to Charles R. Vaughan, October 4, 1834, Notes to British Legation, VI, 6-8.

58. John Forsyth to Henry S. Fox, February 12, 1840, *ibid.,* 152.

59. John Forsyth to Henry S. Fox, March 1, 1841, *ibid.,* 195.

60. Adams, *Memoirs,* X, 255.

61. John Forsyth to Andrew Stevenson, January 25, 1840, No. 65, Instructions, Great Britain, V, 11-12; Andrew Stevenson to John Forsyth, February 29, 1840, No. 88, Despatches, Great Britain, VI, 162-64; Andrew Stevenson to John Forsyth, August 12, 1840, No. 103, *ibid.,* 226.

62. John Forsyth to Henry S. Fox, February 12, 1840, Notes to British Legation, VI, 154-58.

63. Adams, *Memoirs,* X, 255.

64. Official correspondence concerning the issue is in *United States House Executive Document No. 185,* 26 Congress, 1 Session, IV, 1-69.

65. New York *Journal of Commerce,* n.d., in Washington *Globe,* September 5, 1839.

66. John Forsyth to Martin Van Buren, September 18, 1839, Van Buren Papers, XXXVI, Library of Congress; John Forsyth to Martin Van Buren, September 23, 1839, *ibid.*

67. Carl Brent Swisher, *Roger B. Taney,* 417.

68. Levi Woodbury to Martin Van Buren, September 22, 1839, Van Buren Papers, XXXVI.

69. New York *Courier and Enquirer,* November 18, 1839, in Washington *National Intelligencer,* November 22, 1839.

70. William S. Holabird to John For-

syth, December 20, 1839, Miscellaneous Letters.

71. John Forsyth to William S. Holabird, January 12, 1840, Domestic Letters, XXX, 520.

72. John Forsyth to Henry S. Fox, February 1, 1841, Notes to British Legation, VI, 191.

73. S. Wilkeson to Martin Van Buren, January 17, 1840, Miscellaneous Letters; Lewis Tappan to Martin Van Buren, January 20, 1840, *ibid.*

74. *Niles' Register,* LXI (October 30, 1841), 144; *ibid.,* (December 4, 1841), 224; *ibid.,* LXII (March 12, 1842), 17; *ibid.* (April 23, 1842), 128.

75. Charleston *Courier,* November 15, 1834, in Macon *Georgia Telegraph,* December 4, 1834.

76. Macon *Georgia Telegraph,* July 17, 1834.

77. John Forsyth to Lewis Cass, July 14, 1838, No. 24, Instructions, France, XIV, 244; John Forsyth to Lewis Cass, January 21, 1840, No. 42, *ibid.,* 259-60.

78. John Forsyth to Robert Lucas, March 14, 1835, in Washington *United States' Telegraph,* June 27, 1835; John Forsyth to William C. Rives, March 17, 1835, William Cabell Rives Papers, Box D-G.

79. Adams, *Memoirs,* IX, 229.

80. Kent Sagendorph, *Stevens Thomson Mason: Misunderstood Patriot,* 207-08.

81. Stevens T. Mason to John Forsyth, November 26, 1835, Detroit *Journal,* n.d., in *Niles' Register,* XLIX (December 26, 1835). 292-93.

82. Cornelius P. Van Ness to John Forsyth, May 15, 1835, No. 100, Despatches, Spain, XXXII.

83. John Forsyth to Cornelius P. Van Ness, January 20, 1836, unnumbered, Instructions, Spain, XIV, 75-76.

84. John Forsyth to Arthur Middleton, January 20, 1836, *ibid.,* 77.

85. Cornelius P. Van Ness to John Forsyth, December 17, 1836, No. 127, Despatches, Spain, XXXII.

86. Cornelius P. Van Ness to Martin Van Buren, February 10, 1837, Van Buren Papers, XXVI.

87. John H. Eaton to John Forsyth, May 6, 1837, unnumbered, Despatches, Spain, XXXII.

88. John H. Eaton to John Forsyth, July 12, 1839, No. 10, *ibid.*

89. John Forsyth to John H. Eaton, October 12, 1839, No. 27, Instructions, Spain, XIV, 101.

90. *Ibid.*

91. John H. Eaton to John Forsyth, December 27, 1838, No. 7, Despatches, Spain, XXXII.

92. John Forsyth to John H. Eaton, March 7, 1839, No. 26, Instructions, Spain, XIV, 98-99.

93. John Forsyth to Martin Van Buren, September 23, 1839, Van Buren Papers, XXXVI; John Forsyth to John H. Eaton, December 24, 1839, No. 29, Instructions, Spain, XIV, 105-07.

94. John H. Eaton to John Forsyth, March 21, 1840, unnumbered, Despatches, Spain, XXXII.

95. Washington *National Intelligencer,* August 5, 1840.

96. Graham Henry Stuart, *The Department of State: A History of Its Organization, Procedure, and Personnel,* 82-83; John Forsyth, State Department circular, November 30, 1836, in Gaillard Hunt, *The Department of State of the United States, Its History and Functions,* 211-18.

97. John Forsyth to Martin Van Buren, August 5, 1835, in William Allen Butler, *A Retrospect of Forty Years, 1825-1865,* 79.

98. John Forsyth to John H. Eaton, October 12, 1839, No. 27, Instructions, Spain, XIV, 105.

CHAPTER X

1. Eugene Campbell Barker, "President Jackson and the Texas Revolution," *The American Historical Review,* XII (July, 1907), 794.

2. Bassett, *The Life of Andrew Jackson,* II, 675.

3. Anthony Butler to Louis McLane, July 1, 1834, Despatch No. 72, Jack-

son Papers, LXXXVI (1st series).

4. Anthony Butler to John Forsyth, June 17, 1835, William Ray Manning (ed.), *Diplomatic Correspondence of the United States: Inter-American Affairs, 1831-1860,* VIII (Mexico), 289-96. (Hereinafter cited as *Diplomatic Correspondence.*)

5. John Forsyth to Anthony Butler, July 2, 1835, No. 94, Instructions, Mexico, XV, 49.

6. Anthony Butler to Andrew Jackson, [October ?, 1835], Bassett, *Correspondence of Andrew Jackson,* V, 376-77.

7. Anthony Butler to John Forsyth, January 15, 1836, Manning, *Diplomatic Correspondence,* VIII (Mexico), 307.

8. John Forsyth to Anthony Butler, June 26, 1835, No. 92, Instructions, Mexico, XV, 47-48; John Forsyth to Powhatan Ellis, July 20, 1836, No. 16, *ibid.,* 81; John Forsyth to Powhatan Ellis, September 1, 1836, No. 21, *ibid.,* 86.

9. Adams, *Memoirs,* XI, 349.

10. John Forsyth to Benjamin F. Linton, November 4, 1835, *United States House Executive Document No. 256,* 24 Congress, 1 Session, VI, 36.

11. Miller, *Treaties,* III, 622.

12. Confirmatory memorandum, John Forsyth to Manuel Eduardo de Gorostiza, April 20, 1836, Manning, *Diplomatic Correspondence,* VIII (Mexico), 45-46.

13. Manuel Eduardo de Gorostiza to the Department of Relations of Mexico, October 4, 1836, *United States Executive Document No. 190,* 25 Congress, 2 Session, VII, 105-09.

14. Asbury Dickins to Manuel Eduardo de Gorostiza, October 13, 1836, *United States Senate Document No. 1,* 24 Congress, 2 Session, I, 92-95; Manuel Eduardo de Gorostiza to Asbury Dickins, October 15, 1836, *ibid.,* 95-105.

15. Washington *Globe,* February 2, 1837.

16. John Forsyth to Powhatan Ellis, December 10, 1836, No. 24, Instructions, Mexico, XV, 97.

17. Eugene Irving McCormac, "John Forsyth," Samuel Flagg Bemis (ed.), *The American Secretaries of State and their Diplomacy,* IV, 323.

18. Samuel P. Carson to George C. Childress and Robert Hamilton, April 1, 1836, George Pierce Garrison (ed.), *Diplomatic Correspondence of the Republic of Texas, American Historical Association, Annual Report, 1907,* II Part I, 77. (Hereinafter cited as *Texan Correspondence.*)

19. George C. Childress and Robert Hamilton to David G. Burnet, June 10, 1836, *ibid.,* 99-100.

20. William H. Wharton to Stephen F. Austin, January 15, 1837, *ibid.,* 176.

21. John Forsyth to Andrew Jackson, July 15, 1836, Jackson Papers, XCV (1st. series).

22. James Collinsworth and Peter W. Grayson to David G. Burnet, July 15, 1836, Garrison, *Texan Correspondence,* 110.

23. Peter W. Grayson to David G. Burnet, August 2, 1836, *ibid.,* 117.

24. William H. Wharton to Stephen F. Austin, December 22, 1836, *ibid.,* 157-58.

25. William H. Wharton to Thomas J. Rusk, [February 16, 1837], *ibid.,* 192.

26. John Forsyth to Henry Meigs, February 20, 1837, Forsyth Papers.

27. William H. Wharton to Thomas J. Rusk, [February 16, 1837], Garrison, *Texan Correspondence,* 194.

28. William H. Wharton to James Pinckney Henderson, March 5, 1837, *ibid.,* 201.

29. Memucan Hunt to R. A. Irion, August 10, 1837, *ibid.,* 252, 255.

30. Memucan Hunt to R. A. Irion, August 11, 1837, *ibid.,* 255-56.

31. John Forsyth to Memucan Hunt, August 25, 1837, *Register of Debates,* 25 Congress, 1 Session, XIV Part II, Appendix, 121-22.

32. Memucan Hunt to R. A. Irion, November 15, 1837, Garrison, *Texan Correspondence,* 268.

33. Memucan Hunt to R. A. Irion, January 31, 1838, *ibid.,* 284-85.

34. John Forsyth to Nicholas Biddle, September 9, 1838, Biddle Papers,

LXXX.

35. Alcée La Branche to John Forsyth, March 13, 1838, No. 7, Despatches, Texas, I.

36. Nicholas Biddle to John Forsyth, November 27, 1838, "President's Letter Book," VII, 9-10, Biddle Papers; Nicholas Biddle to Joel R. Poinsett, November 27, 1838, *ibid.*, 10-13.

37. John Forsyth to Nicholas Biddle, November 29, 1838, Biddle Papers, LXXXII.

38. Memucan Hunt to R. A. Irion, January 31, 1838, Garrison, *Texan Correspondence,* 287.

39. Hugh Llewellyn Keenleyside and Gerald Saxon Brown, *Canada and the United States: Some Aspects of Their Historical Relations,* 140-45.

40. John Forsyth to Charles R. Vaughan, April 28, 1835, Notes to British Legation, VI, 29.

41. John Forsyth to Charles Bankhead, February 29, 1836, *ibid.,* 55.

42. McCormac, "John Forsyth," Bemis, *The American Secretaries of State and their Diplomacy,* IV, 335-36.

43. Adams, *Memoirs,* X, 21.

44. John Forsyth to Robert P. Dunlap, August 17, 1837, Domestic Letters, XXIX, 158-62; John Forsyth to Edward Kent, March 1, 1838, *ibid.,* 336-66.

45. Thomas LeDuc, "The Maine Frontier and the Northeastern Boundary Controversy," *American Historical Review,* LIII (October, 1947), 39-40.

46. Washington *National Intelligencer,* June 24, 1839; Augusta (Maine) *Age,* June 25, 1839, in Athens *Southern Banner,* July 12, 1839; Augusta (Maine) *Journal,* June 27, 1839, in Milledgeville *Southern Recorder,* July 9, 1839.

47. Washington *National Intelligencer,* July 2, 8, 1839; Athens *Southern Banner,* July 12, 1839.

48. John Fairfield to Martin Van Buren, February 22, 1839, Miscellaneous Letters; *Niles' Register,* LVI (March 9, 1839), 18.

49. Henry S. Fox to John Forsyth, February 23, 1839, Notes from Great Britain, XIX.

50. John Forsyth to Henry S. Fox, February 25, 1839, Notes to British Legation, VI, 100-104.

51. John Forsyth to John Fairfield, February 26, 1839, Domestic Letters, XXX, 173-74.

52. Memorandum signed by John Forsyth and Henry S. Fox, February 27, 1839, Notes to British Legation, VI, 104-06.

53. John Forsyth to John Fairfield, February 27, 1839, Domestic Letters, XXX, 176-77.

54. Sir John Harvey to John Fairfield, March 7, 1839, in Washington *Globe,* March 16, 1839; Boston *Daily Advertiser,* March 12, 1839, in Washington *National Intelligencer,* March 18, 1839.

55. Charleston *Courier,* March 21, 1840, in Augusta *Constitutionalist,* March 26, 1840; Columbus *Enquirer,* April 8, 1840; Milledgeville *Federal Union,* April 28, 1840.

56. John Fairfield to Martin Van Buren, January 8, 1840, Van Buren Papers, XXXVII.

57. John Forsyth to William Learned Marcy, December 7, 1837, Domestic Letters, XXIX, 250; John Forsyth to Daniel Kellogg, December 7, 1837, *ibid.,* 250-51.

58. Keenleyside and Brown, *Canada and the United States: Some Aspects of Their Historical Relations,* 88.

59. Joel R. Poinsett to William L. Marcy, January 5, 1838, Miscellaneous Letters.

60. Henry S. Fox to John Forsyth, February 6, 1838, Notes from Great Britain, XIX.

61. John Forsyth to Nathaniel S. Benton, January 6, 1838, Domestic Letters, XXIX, 278.

62. John Forsyth to Andrew Stevenson, March [12], 1838, No. 34, Andrew Stevenson Letter Book, 94.

63. John Forsyth to Andrew Stevenson, September 11, 1839, No. 58, Instructions, Great Britain, IV, 311.

64. Andrew Stevenson to John Forsyth, March 3, 1841, William Ray Manning (ed.), *Diplomatic Correspondence of the United States: Canadian Relations, 1784-1860,* III, 613.

65. Henry S. Fox to John Forsyth, December 13, 1840, Notes from Great Britain, XX.
66. John Forsyth to Henry S. Fox, December 26, 1840, Notes to British Legation, VI, 187-89.
67. John Forsyth to Henry S. Fox, December 31, 1840, *ibid.*, 190.
68. John Forsyth to Charles Bankhead, January 18, 1836, *ibid.*, 41.
69. John Forsyth to Andrew Stevenson, April 17, 1840, No. 71, Andrew

Stevenson Letter Book, 205-08.
70. Lord Palmerston to Andrew Stevenson, November 10, 1840, Manning, *Diplomatic Correspondence of the United States: Canadian Relations, 1784-1860*, III, 596-98.
71. John Forsyth to Andrew Stevenson, February 20, 1841, No. 89, Andrew Stevenson Letter Book, 245.
72. Keenleyside and Brown, *Canada and the United States: Some Aspects of Their Historical Relations*, 91.

CHAPTER XI

1. John Forsyth to the Committee in New York, September 24, 1835, in Milledgeville *Georgia Journal*, November 10, 1835.
2. Macon *Georgia Messenger*, October 20, 1836; Augusta *Chronicle*, November 5, 1836; Alexandria (Va.) *Gazette*, n.d., in Milledgeville *Southern Recorder*, November 18, 1836.
3. Macon *Georgia Messenger*, October 20, 1836.
4. John Forsyth to Thomas Moughon *et al.*, October 28, 1836, in Milledgeville *Federal Union*, November 1, 1836.
5. Milledgeville *Federal Union*, November 22, 27, 1838; Athens *Southern Banner*, December 8, 1838.
6. Milledgeville *Federal Union*, December 25, 1838.
7. Augusta *Constitutionalist*, January 22, 1840.
8. *Ibid.*, February 11, 1840.
9. Letter signed by John Forsyth, n.d., in Washington *Globe*, May 8, 1840.
10. Milledgeville *Southern Recorder*, May 19, 1840; Augusta *Constitutionalist*, May 21, 1840; Macon *Georgia Telegraph*, June 2, 1840.
11. Letter signed "A Georgian," May 13, 1840, in Augusta *Constitutionalist*, May 21, 1840.
12. John Forsyth to William A. Tennille *et al.*, June 25, 1840, in Athens *Southern Banner*, July 17, 1840.
13. Washington *Madisonian*, n.d., in Washington *National Intelligencer*, July 29, 1840; Columbus *Enquirer*, August 19, 1840.

14. John Forsyth to the People of Georgia, August 29, 1840, in Athens *Southern Banner*, September 18, 1840.
15. Milledgeville *Federal Union*, September 15, 1840.
16. Augusta *Tri-Weekly Chronicle & Sentinel*, September 10, 24, 1840; Milledgeville *Southern Recorder*, September 15, October 6, 1840; Washington *National Intelligencer*, September 26, 1840.
17. Columbus *Enquirer*, September 30, 1840.
18. William S. Ashe to John Forsyth, October 12, 1840, in Washington *Globe*, November 4, 1840.
19. Phillips, *Georgia and State Rights*, 147.
20. John Forsyth to Martin Van Buren, April 3, 1841, Van Buren Papers, XLII.
21. Adams, *Memoirs*, X, 460. The other Van Buren advisers who participated in the funeral were Poinsett, James Kirke Paulding, and Henry Dilworth Gilpin.
22. John Forsyth to Martin Van Buren, April 10, 1841, Van Buren Papers, XLII.
23. Athens *Southern Banner*, June 18, July 2, 1841.
24. Macon *Georgia Telegraph*, May 25, 1841.
25. Milledgeville *Federal Union*, May 11, 1841.
26. John Forsyth to Mr. Sanford *et al.*, May 24, 1841, in Augusta *Georgia Constitutionalist*, June 1, 1841.
27. J. L. Martin to Martin Van Buren,

October 22, 1841, Van Buren Papers, XLIII.

28. Washington *National Intelligencer,* October 25, 1841.

29. Washington *National Intelligencer,* October 23, 1841.

30. Milledgeville *Southern Recorder,* November 2, 1841.

Bibliography

I. PRIMARY SOURCES

A. MANUSCRIPTS

1. *Official Collections in Division of State Department Archives, National Archives, Washington, D. C.*

Appointment Papers of the Department of State: Applications and Recommendations for Office, 1829-1836.

Despatches, France, Vols. XXVII-XXIX (June 1, 1833-March 7, 1843).

Despatches, Great Britain, Vols. V-VI (May 14, 1836-Jan. 3, 1842).

Despatches, Mexico, Vols. VI-X (September 10, 1832-May 19, 1842).

Despatches, Spain, Vols. XVII-XXI (March 15, 1819-March 3, 1823), and XXXII-XXXIII (July 26, 1834-August 1, 1842).

Despatches, Texas, Vol. I (July 18, 1836-July 5, 1842).

Domestic Letters, Vols. XXVI-XXXI (July 5, 1833-August 6, 1841).

Instructions, France, Vol. XIV (July 20, 1829-April 12, 1844).

Instructions, Great Britain, Vols. III-V (August 3, 1831-July 28, 1841).

Instructions, Mexico, Vol. XV (May 29, 1833-March 29, 1845).

Instructions, Spain, Vols. VIII-IX (Nov. 2, 1815-July 15, 1823), and XIV (March 12, 1833-Dec. 27, 1852).

Instructions, Texas, Vol. I (Dec. 20, 1836-Dec. 30, 1844).

Miscellaneous Letters, unbound collection (Sept. 2, 1837-March 31, 1841).

Notes to British Legation, Vol. VI (July 1, 1834-April 4, 1844).

Notes from Great Britain, Vols. XVIII-XX (June 29, 1834-April 25, 1842).

Notes to Spanish Government of Minister John Forsyth (May 12, 1819-Nov. 20, 1822).

United States Legation, Madrid, Official Papers, 1815-1824 (July 17, 1815-Nov. 30, 1824).

2. *Other Official Collections*

"Letter Book," Vols. IV-VI (April 1, 1827-July 30, 1830). Contains important War Department letters to Forsyth and to Indian agents relative to Creek and Cherokee matters in Georgia. Bureau of Indian Affairs, Division of Interior Department Archives, National Archives, Washington, D. C.

Letters Received, unbound collection (January 1, 1827-Dec. 31, 1830). Includes valuable information concerning Creek and Cherokee affairs in Georgia. *Ibid.*

Letters Received, Vols. XI-LVII (January 1, 1818-Dec. 31, 1841). Division of War Department Archives, National Archives, Washington, D. C.

"Logbook of the USS *Hornet,* March 26, 1819 to March 25, 1821." Division of Navy Department Archives, National Archives, Washington, D. C.

Fifth Census, 1830, Population, Georgia, Vol. XVII; Sixth Census, 1840, Population, District of Columbia, Vol. I. Bureau of the Census Archives, National Archives, Washington, D. C.

Andrew Stevenson Letter Book (May 19, 1836-July 28, 1841). Manuscript Division, Library of Congress, Washington, D. C.

"Governors' Letter Book" (Nov. 22, 1821-Nov. 30, 1829). Georgia Department of Archives and History, Atlanta, Georgia.

Minutes of the Executive Department of the State of Georgia (Feb. 19, 1808-Sept. 1, 1832). *Ibid.*

3. *Unofficial Collections*

John McPherson Berrien Papers. Letters, manuscripts, and maps giving valuable information concerning the controversial Georgia-Florida boundary. Southern Historical Collection, University of North Carolina Library.

Nicholas Biddle Papers. 113 volumes, 4 boxes of unbound papers, and 7 letter books. The last named are entitled "President's Letter Book." Letters, reports, extracts and newspaper clippings. Manuscript Division, Library of Congress, Washington, D. C.

John Floyd Papers. 1 box of unbound papers. *Ibid.*

Peter Force Papers. 32 volumes. Letters and manuscripts, many of which provide information concerning political affairs in Georgia during the 1830's. Five letters from Forsyth are of little value. *Ibid.*

John Forsyth Account Book and Diary of Voyage. Contains an account of the ministerial expenses between September 10, 1819 and March 3, 1823; also a journal, dated April 28-May 30, 1823, of Bordeaux to New York voyage aboard the *Othello*. *Ibid*.

John Forsyth Papers. 13 items. Unbound letters and hand-written documents extending over the period 1802-1835, dealing primarily with Forsyth's participation in official matters corncerning the state of Georgia. Georgia Department of Archives and History, Atlanta, Georgia.

John Forsyth Papers. A valuable collection of letters and one manuscript entitled "John Forsyth Journal, 1819-1820." The letter group consists of approximately 70 items written by Forsyth during the years 1802-1840; 18 written by his wife, Clara Forsyth, dated 1803-1851; and 1 by his son, John Forsyth, Jr., written on August 15, 1829. Manuscript Division, Princeton University Library.

"Georgia Autographs." A volume of correspondence, documents, and portraits of prominent Georgians. Two Forsyth letters are included, one from Madrid in 1820 and the other from Washington in 1840. Georgia Historical Society, Savannah, Georgia.

Duff Green Papers. 2 volumes; 3 boxes and 2 portfolios of unbound material. Manuscript Division, Library of Congress, Washington, D. C.

James Henry Hammond Papers. 33 volumes and an unbound collection of scrapbooks, notebooks, plantation manuals, account books, and slave lists. Many letters discuss Georgia politics and how that state might be induced to co-operate with South Carolina on the issue of nullification. *Ibid*.

William Henry Harrison Papers. 8 volumes and an unbound collection of correspondence. *Ibid*.

Andrew Jackson Papers. 119 volumes (1st series); 8 volumes (2nd series); 2 boxes of unbound manuscripts; 23 additional volumes of letters, orders, memoranda, and journals; 13 volumes of military papers. *Ibid*.

William Jones Papers. A small unbound collection of letters and documents. Georgia Historical Society, Savannah, Georgia.

William Lowndes Papers. An unbound collection of correspondence and manuscript material. Southern Historical Collection, University of North Carolina Library.

Miscellaneous Letters. Four Forsyth letters are included in the collection. Manuscript Division, Duke University Library.

James Monroe Papers. 37 volumes. Manuscript Division, Library of Congress, Washington, D. C.

Nathan Morse Papers. 18 items. *Ibid*.

Personal Miscellany Papers. A large unbound collection of miscellaneous documents and letters written by various political leaders of the United States. *Ibid.*

James Knox Polk Papers. 86 volumes (1st series) and 52 volumes (2nd series) of letters, memoranda, drafts of speeches and campaign material. *Ibid.*

William Cabell Rives Papers. 194 boxes of unbound letters and manuscripts. *Ibid.*

Mrs. Samuel Harrison Smith Papers. 16 volumes; 1 box of unbound letters. *Ibid.*

Martin Van Buren Papers. 76 volumes and an unbound collection of letters and manuscripts. *Ibid.*

Richard Henry Wilde Papers. A small, unbound collection of correspondence and manuscript material. Manuscript Division, Duke University Library.

Levi Woodbury Papers. 60 volumes. An extensive collection of letters, drafts, reports, memoranda, and newspaper clippings. Manuscript Division, Library of Congress, Washington, D. C.

Bartlett Yancey Papers. An unbound collection of correspondence and manuscripts relating to personal and political affairs, 1817-1828. Southern Historical Collection, University of North Carolina Library.

B. PUBLIC DOCUMENTS

1. *United States*

American State Papers, Documents, Legislative and Executive of the United States, 38 volumes, Washington: Gales and Seaton, 1832-1861.

Annals of the Congress of the United States, 1789-1824, 42 volumes. Washington: Gales and Seaton, 1834-1856.

Biographical Directory of the American Congress, 1774-1949. Washington: Government Printing Office, 1950.

Garrison, George Pierce (ed.), *Diplomatic Correspondence of the Republic of Texas, American Historical Association, Annual Report, 1907,* volume II part I. Washington: Government Printing Office, 1908.

Kappler, Charles J. (ed.), *Indian Affairs: Laws and Treaties,* 2 volumes. Washington: Government Printing Office, 1904.

Manning, William Ray (ed.), *Diplomatic Correspondence of the United States: Canadian Relations, 1784-1860,* 4 volumes. Washington: Carnegie Endowment for International Peace, 1940-1945.

————————, *Diplomatic Correspondence of the United States: Inter-American Affairs, 1831-1860,* 10 volumes. Washington: Carnegie Endowment for International Peace, 1932-1938.

Miller, Hunter (ed.), *Treaties and Other International Acts of the United States of America,* 8 volumes. Washington: Government Printing Office, 1931-1948.

The Register of Debates in the Congress of the United States, 14 volumes. Washington: Gales and Seaton, 1825-1837.

Richardson, James Daniel (ed.), *A Compilation of the Messages and Papers of the Presidents, 1789-1897,* 10 volumes. Washington: Government Printing Office, 1896-1899.

The Statutes at Large of the United States, 1789-1893, 27 vols. Boston: Little, Brown, and Company, 1845-1873. Washington: Government Printing Office, 1875-1893.

United States House Executive Documents, various ones for sessions of Congress, 1829-1839 (see Notes).

United States House Report, various ones for sessions of Congress, 1827-1836 (see Notes).

United States Senate Documents, various ones for sessions of Congress, 1828-1836 (see Notes).

2. *Georgia*

Acts of the General Assembly of the State of Georgia (1825-1841). Milledgeville: State Printers, 1825-1841.

Journal of the House of Representatives of the State of Georgia (1800-1841). *Ibid.* Milledgeville: State Printers, 1800-1841.

Journal of the Senate of the State of Georgia (1800-1841). *Ibid.* Milledgeville: State Printers, 1801-1841.

3. *Virginia*

Brumbaugh, Gaius Marcus (ed.), *Revolutionary War Records,* volume I (Virginia). Washington: Lancaster Press, Inc., 1936.

Calendar of Virginia State Papers, 11 volumes. Richmond: (printer varies), 1875-1893.

C. NEWSPAPERS AND PERIODICALS

Athens *Athenian,* 1828-1832.

Athens *Gazette,* 1814-1817.

Athens *Georgia Express,* 1808-1809, 1812-1813. Title varies: Athens *Foreign Correspondent & Georgia Express,* 1809-1810.

Athens *Southern Banner,* 1833-1842.

Augusta *Constitutionalist,* 1825-1841. Title varies: Augusta *Georgia Constitutionalist* (scattered issues).

Augusta *Georgia State Gazette or Independent Register,* 1786-1789. Title varies: Augusta *Chronicle and Gazette of the State,* 1789-1805; Augusta *Chronicle,* 1807-1836 (broken file); Augusta *Chronicle & Georgia Gazette,* 1818; Augusta *Chronicle and Georgia Advertiser,* 1823, 1828-1829; Augusta *Chronicle & Sentinel,* 1837; Augusta *Tri-Weekly Chronicle & Sentinel,* 1838-1841.

Augusta *Southern Sentinel and Universal Gazette*, 1793. Title varies: Augusta *Southern Sentinel and Gazette of the State*, 1793-1799.

Columbus *Enquirer*, 1838-1841.

Louisville *American Advocate*, 1816.

Macon *Advertiser and Agricultural and Mercantile Intelligencer*, 1831-1832.

Macon *Georgia Messenger*, 1830-1841.

Macon *Telegraph*, 1826-1841. Title varies: Macon *Georgia Telegraph* (scattered issues).

Milledgeville *Federal Union*, 1830-1846.

Milledgeville *Georgia Journal*, 1820-1836.

Milledgeville *Georgia Patriot*, 1824-1825.

Milledgeville *Southern Recorder*, 1823-1841.

Niles' Register, 76 volumes. Baltimore, 1811-1849.

Savannah *American Patriot*, 1812.

Savannah *Columbian Museum & Advertiser*, 1798, 1804, 1806-1812.

Savannah *Daily Republican*, 1841.

Savannah *Gazette*, 1817. Title varies: Savannah *Columbian Museum and Daily Gazette*, 1817-1820; Savannah *Columbian Museum and Gazette* (scattered issues).

Savannah *Gazette of the State of Georgia*, 1783-1788. Title varies: Savannah *Georgia Gazette*, 1788-1793, 1797-1802.

Savannah *Georgia Journal: and Independent Federal Register*, 1793-1794.

Savannah *Georgia Republican*, 1806-1807.

Savannah *Georgia Republican & State Intelligencer*, 1803-1805.

Savannah *Georgian*, 1818-1841. Title varies: Savannah *Georgian and Evening Advertiser*, 1821; Savannah *Daily Georgian* (scattered issues).

Savannah *Museum*, 1822.

Savannah *Public Intelligencer*, 1807-1809.

Savannah *Republican*, 1825.

Savannah *Republican; and Evening Ledger*, 1807-1813.

Savannah *Royal Georgia Gazette*, 1781.

Savannah *Southern Patriot*, 1806. Title varies: Savannah *Patriot and Commercial Advertiser*, 1806-1807.

Washington *Globe*, 1830-1841.

Washington *Monitor*, 1809-1810, 1813. Title varies: Washington *Friend and Monitor*, 1815.

Washington *National Intelligencer*, 1811-1841.

Washington *United States' Telegraph*, 1826-1837.

D. CONTEMPORARY WORKS

Adams, Charles Francis (ed.), *Memoirs of John Quincy Adams, Comprising Portions of His Diary from 1795 to 1848,* 12 volumes. Philadelphia: J. B. Lippincott and Company, 1847-1877.

Bassett, John Spencer (ed.), *Correspondence of Andrew Jackson,* 7 volumes. Washington: Carnegie Institute of Washington, 1926-1935.

Benton, Thomas Hart, *Thirty Years' View; or, A History of the Working of the American Government for Thirty Years, from 1820 to 1850. Chiefly Taken from the Congress Debates, the Private Papers of General Jackson, and the Speeches of Ex-Senator Benton, with His Actual View of Men and Affairs: With Historical Notes and Illustrations, and Some Notices of Eminent Deceased Cotemporaries* [sic], 2 volumes. New York: D. Appleton and Company, 1854, 1856.

McGrane, Reginald Charles (ed.), *The Correspondence of Nicholas Biddle Dealing with National Affairs, 1807-1844.* Boston: Houghton Mifflin Company, 1919.

Martineau, Harriet, *Retrospect of Western Travel,* 3 volumes. London: Saunders and Otley, 1838.

Nevins, Allan (ed.), *The Diary of Philip Home,* 1828-1851, 2 volumes. New York: Dodd, Mead and Company, 1927.

"Political Portraits with Pen and Pencil (No. VII): John Forsyth," *United States Magazine and Democratic Review,* II (June, 1838), 273-281.

Proceedings of the Anti-Tariff Convention of the State of Georgia, Held in Milledgeville, 1832. Milledgeville: Times Office, 1832.

Washburn, Elihu Benjamin (ed.), *The Edwards Papers; Being a Portion of the Collection of the Letters, Papers, and Manuscripts of Ninian Edwards.* Chicago: Fergus Printing Company, 1884.

II. SECONDARY WORKS

A. AUTOBIOGRAPHIES AND MEMOIRS

Butler, William Allen, *A Retrospect of Forty Years, 1825-1865.* New York: Charles Scribner's Sons, 1911.

Fitzpatrick, John Clement (ed.), *The Autobiography of Martin Van Buren, American Historical Association, Annual Report,* 1918, volume II. Washington: Government Printing Office, 1920.

Foote, Henry Stuart, *Casket of Reminiscences.* Washington: Chronicle Publishing Company, 1874.

Miller, Stephen Francis, *The Bench and Bar of Georgia: Memoirs and Sketches,* 2 volumes. Philadelphia: J. B. Lippincott and Co., 1858.

Sparks, William Henry, *The Memoirs of Fifty Years: Containing Brief Biographical Notices of Distinguished Americans, and Anecdotes of Remarkable Men; Interspersed with Scenes and Incidents Occurring During a Long Life of Observation Chiefly Spent in the Southwest*. Macon: J. W. Burke Company, 1870.

Stickney, William (ed.), *Autobiography of Amos Kendall*. Boston: Lee and Shepard, 1872.

Wise, Henry Alexander, *Seven Decades of the Union*. Philadelphia: J. B. Lippincott and Company, 1881.

B. BIOGRAPHIES, MONOGRAPHS, AND SPECIAL STUDIES

Aubrey, George H., "Robert Forsyth," *Men of Mark in Georgia*, 7 volumes. Edited by William Jonathan Northen (Atlanta: A. B. Caldwell, 1907-1912), I, 97.

Bowers, Claude Gernade, *The Party Battles of the Jackson Period*. Boston: Houghton Mifflin Company, 1922.

Brooks, Philip Coolidge, *Diplomacy and the Borderlands, The Adams-Onis Treaty of 1819*. Berkeley: University of California Press, 1939.

Brooks, Robert Preston, "John Forsyth," *Dictionary of American Biography*, 21 volumes. Edited by Allen Johnson and Dumas Malone (New York: Charles Scribner's Sons, 1928-1937), VI, 533-35.

Cason, Roberta Florence, "The Public Career of John Forsyth, 1813-1834." Unpublished M.A. thesis, Emory University Library, 1935.

Catterall, Ralph Charles Henry, *The Second Bank of the United States*. Chicago: The University of Chicago Press, 1903.

Chadwick, French Ensor, *The Relations of the United States and Spain, Diplomacy*, 3 volumes. London: Chapman and Hall, Ltd., 1911.

Chappell, Absalom H., *Miscellanies of Georgia, Historical, Biographical, Descriptive, etc*. Atlanta: James F. Meegan, 1874.

Dangerfield, George, *The Era of Good Feelings*. New York: Harcourt, Brace and Company, 1952.

De Fronsac, Frederic Gregory Forsyth, *Memorial of the Family of Forsyth de Fronsac*. Boston: Press of S. J. Parkhill and Company, 1903.

Evans, Lawton Bryan, "John Forsyth," *Men of Mark in Georgia*, 7 volumes. Edited by William Jonathan Northen (Atlanta: A. B. Caldwell, 1907-1912), II, 289-94.

Historical Collections of the Georgia Chapters, Daughters of the American Revolution, 4 volumes. Atlanta: C. P. Byrd, 1926-1931.

Hunt, Gaillard, *The Department of State of the United States, Its History and Functions*. New Haven: Yale University Press, 1914.

Jeffries, Jennie Forsyth, *A History of the Forsyth Family*. Indianapolis: William H. Burford, 1920.

Keenleyside, Hugh Llewellyn, and Gerald Saxon Brown, *Canada and the United States: Some Aspects of Their Historical Relations.* New York: Alfred A. Knopf, 1952.

Knight, Lucian Lamar, *Georgia's Landmarks, Memorials and Legends,* 2 volumes. Atlanta: The Byrd Printing Company, 1913-1914.

——————, *Reminiscences of Famous Georgians Embracing Episodes and Incidents in the Lives of the Great Men of the State,* 2 volumes. Atlanta: Franklin-Turner Company, 1907-1908.

Lamar, Joseph R., *Trustees of Richmond Academy, Augusta, Georgia; Their Work During the Eighteenth Century in the Management of a School, a Town and a Church.* Augusta: [no publisher indicated], 1910.

Lumpkin, Wilson, *The Removal of the Cherokee Indians from Georgia,* 2 volumes. New York: Dodd, Mead and Company, 1907.

Lynch, William Orlando, *Fifty Years of Party Warfare.* Indianapolis: The Bobbs-Merrill Company, 1931.

McCormac, Eugene Irving, "John Forsyth," *The American Secretaries of State and their Diplomacy,* 10 volumes. Edited by Samuel Flagg Bemis (New York: Alfred A. Knopf, 1927-1929), IV, 301-43.

McLemore, Richard Aubrey, *Franco-American Diplomatic Relations, 1816-1836.* Baton Rouge: Louisiana State University Press, 1941.

Murray, Paul, *The Whig Party in Georgia, 1825-1853.* Chapel Hill: University of North Carolina Press, 1948.

Parton, James, *Life of Andrew Jackson,* 3 volumes. New York: Mason Brothers, 1860.

Phillips, Ulrich Bonnell, *Georgia and State Rights, American Historical Association, Annual Report, 1901,* volume II. Washington: Government Printing Office, 1902.

——————, *A History of Transportation in the Eastern Cotton Belt to 1860.* New York: Columbia University Press, 1908.

Sagendorph, Kent, *Stevens Thomson Mason: Misunderstood Patriot.* New York: E. P. Dutton and Company, 1947.

Schlesinger, Arthur Meier, Jr., *The Age of Jackson.* Boston: Little, Brown and Company, 1946.

Shryock, Richard Harrison, *Georgia and the Union in 1850.* Durham: Duke University Press, 1926.

Stuart, Graham Henry, *The Department of State: A History of Its Organization, Procedure, and Personnel.* New York: The Macmillan Company, 1949.

Swisher, Carl Brent, *Roger B. Taney.* New York: The Macmillan Company, 1935.

Sydnor, Charles Sackett, *The Development of Southern Sectionalism, 1819-1848* (volume V of Wendell Holmes Stephenson and Ellis Merton Coulter, eds., *A History of the South*). Baton Rouge: Louisiana State University Press, 1948.

White, George, *Historical Collections of Georgia: Containing the Most Interesting Facts, Traditions, Biographical Sketches, Anecdotes, etc. Relating to Its History and Antiquities, From Its First Settlement to the Present Time*. New York: Pudney and Russell, 1854.

Wiltse, Charles Maurice, *John C. Calhoun, Nationalist, 1782-1828*. Indianapolis: The Bobbs-Merrill Company, 1944.

——————, *John C. Calhoun, Nullifier, 1829-1839*. Indianapolis: The Bobbs-Merrill Company, 1949.

C. NATIONAL AND STATE HISTORIES

Adams, Henry, *History of the United States during the Administrations of Jefferson and Madison*, 9 volumes. New York: Charles Scribner's Sons, 1889-1891.

Coulter, Ellis Merton, *Georgia, A Short History*. Chapel Hill: University of North Carolina Press, 1947.

Johnson, Amanda, *Georgia as Colony and State*. Atlanta: Walter W. Brown, 1938.

McMaster, John Bach, *A History of the People of the United States from the Revolution to the Civil War*, 8 volumes. New York: D. Appleton and Company, 1884-1900.

Saye, Albert Berry, *A Constitutional History of Georgia, 1732-1945*. Athens: The University of Georgia Press, 1948.

Ware, Ethel Kime, *A Constitutional History of Georgia*. New York: Columbia University Press, 1947.

D. PERIODICAL ARTICLES

Barker, Eugene Campbell, "President Jackson and the Texas Revolution," *The American Historical Review*, XII (July, 1907), 788-809.

Coulter, Ellis Merton, "The Nullification Movement in Georgia," *The Georgia Historical Quarterly*, V (March, 1921), 3-39.

Evans, Lawton Bryan, "Historic Spots in Summerville," *The Georgia Historical Quarterly*, I (June, 1917), 135-41.

Govan, Thomas Payne, "Banking and the Credit System in Georgia, 1810-1860," *The Journal of Southern History*, IV (May, 1938), 164-84.

Green, Fletcher Melvin, "Georgia's Board of Public Works, 1817-1826," *The Georgia Historical Quarterly*, XXII (June, 1938), 117-37.

Le Duc, Thomas, "The Maine Frontier and the Northeastern Boundary Controversy," *The American Historical Review*, LIII (October, 1947), 30-41.

McLemore, Richard Aubrey, "The French Spoliation Claims, 1816-1836: A Study in Jacksonian Diplomacy," *Tennessee Historical Magazine,* II (July, 1932), 234-54.

Webster, Charles Kingsley, "British Mediation between France and the United States in 1834-6," *English Historical Review,* XLII (January, 1927), 58-78.

Index

Abisval, Count, 49-50
Adams, John, 10, 85
Adams, John Quincy, 18, 30, 35, 37-38, 61, 68, 80, 130, 188, 196; 1824 presidential campaign, 31-33; Panama Congress, 38-39; Adams-Onis treaty, 42-43; complains of Forsyth appointment, 44; first instructions to Forsyth, 45-47; Forsyth reports from Spain, 50, 52, 54, 59, 60, 63, 66, 67, 71, 72, 74, 77, 79, 80; additional instructions to Forsyth, 56, 78, 79; Georgia-Florida boundary dispute, 99-100; Indian removal, 108, 109-12; Cherokee constitution, 114; denounces Trist, 184-85
Alagon, Duke of, 43, 52, 59
Albany *Evening Journal*, 178
Algiers, 35
Allen, Beverly, 4
Allen, William, 4
Altamaha River, 92, 95, 105
Ambrister, Robert C., 129
American Colonization Society, 34-35
Amistad affair, 185-87
Anderson, John, 26
Appleton, John James, 71, 79
Arbuthnot, Alexander, 129
Archer, Branch Tanner, 198
Armstrong, Mrs. Sarah, half sister of John Forsyth, 8
Aroostook War, 205-07, 211
Athens, 6, 8, 156
Athens *Athenian*, 101
Athens *Georgia Express*, 11
Athens *Southern Banner*, 214, 217
Aubrey, William P., son-in-law of John Forsyth, 6

Augusta, 2, 3, 4, 5, 6, 7, 11, 15, 68, 80, 102, 156
Augusta *Chronicle*, 68, 214; opposes Forsyth for governor, 83
Augusta *Constitutionalist*, 101, 215; supports Forsyth for governor, 83
Austin, Julia, 6
Austin, Stephen Fuller, 198

Bacon, John, 3
Baldwin, Abraham, 5
Baltimore and Ohio Railroad Company, 148
Bank of Darien, 92-93
Bank of the United States, 21-25, 169; war on, 137-46; spoliation claims, 170
Bankhead, Charles, 179-80, 204, 210
Barbour, James, 45; Indian removal, 109-11
Barca, A. Calderon de la, 185
Bardaxi y Azara, Eusebio de, 69, 74, 75; Florida claims records, 76; Havana archives, 78
Baring Brothers and Company, 45
Barnett, William, 11
Barry, William Taylor, 146-47; death, 189
Barton, Thomas Pennant, spoliation claims, 175, 176-77
Beaumarchais, Caron de, claims, 39-40
Benton, Nathaniel S., 209
Benton, Thomas Hart, 136, 144; supports Jackson's Bank policies, 138-39
Berrien, John McPherson, 103, 156; appointed attorney general, 101; attends anti-tariff convention, 157-60

255

Biddle, Nicholas, 25, 44, 47, 63, 66, 68, 202; friendship with Forsyth, 13-14; requests Bank re-charter, 138; congratulates Forsyth, 169
Biddle, Mrs. Nicholas, 14
Bland, Theodorick, 21
Bonus Bill, 147
Bordeaux, 68, 80; Forsyth visits, 66-67
Branch, John, 136
Brent, Thomas L. L., 44, 46-47, 53, 61, 66-68, 71, 72, 75
Broglie, Achille Leonce V. C. de, spoliation claims, 173-81
Buchanan, James, 169, 178
Burnet, David Gouverneur, 198
Butler, Anthony, efforts to purchase Texas, 194-96, 211
Butler, Reverend Doctor, 218
Butts County, 162

Cadiz, 45, 46, 49-51
Calhoun, John Caldwell, 25, 31, 56, 61, 128, 136; Second Bank of the United States, 22-23; Indian removal, 106, 107; "Crawford letter" incident, 130-34; opposes Van Buren appointment, 134-35; opposes removal of Bank deposits, 141.
Campbell, Duncan G., declines gubernatorial nomination, 83-84; Creek negotiations, 108-09
Canada, northeastern boundary controversy, 202-07; neutrality problems with United States, 207-10, 211, 212, 221; fisheries controversies, 210-11
Canals, Savannah, Ogeechee, and Altamaha, 95-96; Chesapeake and Delaware Company, 147; Louisville and Portland Company, 148; Atlantic-Gulf of Mexico, 148
Caroline, incident, 208-10, 212
Carson, Samuel Price, 198
Cass, Lewis, 181, 187-88, 196-97
Castro, Evaristo Perez de, 68, 70, 74, 75; amicable relations with Forsyth, 62-63
Central Bank of Georgia, 94-95
Centreville, 162
Charleston, 2, 14, 15, 96
Charleston and Hamburg Railroad, 97
Chattahoochee River, 95, 96, 98, 110, 121
Cherokees, 28, 108, 112, 162; removal, 105-07, 110, 113-17, 126; Georgia crim-

inal jurisdiction extended over, 117-18; Creek boundary problem, 118-21; Forsyth's post-gubernatorial interests in, 124-27
Chesapeake and Delaware Canal Company, 147
Chester, New Hampshire, 1
Chevalier, Charles Francis, 3
Cheves, Langdon, 22
Chiclana, 50
Childress, George C., 198-99
Clark, John, 82, 102
Clark, party, 82, 151, 152, 157; opposes Forsyth for governor, 83-86; supports Gilmer, 102-03
Clarke, Elijah, 82
Clay, Henry, 29, 31, 32, 38, 129, 146, 160, 176, 178, 217; South American affairs, 20-21; Second Bank of the United States, 23; opposes Van Buren appointment, 134; opposes removal of Bank deposits, 140-44; 1832 tariff proposal, 153-54; 1833 tariff, 163-65
Clayton, Augustin Smith, 156; attends 1832 party convention, 137; attends anti-tariff convention, 157-58
Cobb, Howell, 11
Cocke, John, 27
Coffee, John, Creek-Cherokee boundary, 120
Collinsworth, James, 199
Columbia Telescope, 152
Compensation Act, 15-16, 25-26
Cook, Daniel Pope, 30
Crawford, Joel, 102
Crawford, William Harris, 5, 16, 35, 38, 44, 56, 61, 67, 85, 128, 129; defended by Forsyth, 29-31; 1824 presidential campaign, 31-33; heads James Jackson party, 81; "Crawford letter" incident, 131-33
Creeks, 28; removal, 105-13; Cherokee boundary problem, 118-21; depredations, 121-24; Forsyth's post-gubernatorial interests in, 124-27
Crowell, John, 108, 109, 110; recall requested, 111; Creek depredations, 121-24
Cumberland River, 148
Cumberland Road, 147
Cumming, William, attends anti-tariff convention, 157
Cuthbert, Alfred, 217-18
Cyrus, 47, 48, 51, 65

Dallas, Alexander James, 21-23
Dallas, George Mifflin, 138
Daveis, Charles Stewart, 204, 205
Democratic party, 151, 163, 205, 211, 218; 1832 convention, 137; selects 1836 candidates, 213; 1840 presidential campaign, 214-16
Dickins, Asbury, 174, 197
Dixon, Mrs., 4
Donelson, Andrew Jackson, 171
Dunlap, Robert Pinckney, 204

Eaton, John Henry, 192; Indian removal, 116; Creek-Cherokee boundary problem, 119; resigns from cabinet, 133; Spanish mission, 190-91, 217
Edwards, Ninian, attacks Crawford, 29-31
Ellicott, Andrew, Georgia-Florida boundary dispute, 98-101
Elliott, John, 16; Indian removal, 106
Erving, George William, 44, 51, 72

Fabius, 69
Fairfield, John, northeastern boundary controversy, 205-07
Febiger, Christopher, 2
Federalist party, 18-19, 81
Fenwick, F. Columbus, 47, 48, 50, 51
Ferdinand VII, King of Spain, 45, 49, 51-53, 54-55, 57, 67; Adams-Onis treaty, 42-43; Forsyth presented to, 51; transfers sovereignty, 62; grants audience to Forsyth, 68; Clara Forsyth presented to, 69; releases United States citizens, 73; Florida claims records, 77; Havana archives, 78; final audience with Forsyth, 79-80
Flint River, 95, 98, 105
Florida, 39, 44, 45, 46, 53, 56, 63, 148; proposed seizure, 37-38; Adams-Onis negotiations, 42-43; claim records, 76-77; Georgia boundary dispute, 97-101; Jackson's expedition into, 129-30, 131
Floyd, John, 29
Foote, Henry Stuart, 11
Forbes, James Grant, seeks Havana archives, 78
Force Bill, 161-63
Forsyth, Anna, daughter of John Forsyth, 6
Forsyth, Clara (Mrs. Murray Mason), daughter of John Forsyth, 6
Forsyth, Clara Meigs (Mrs. John), 7-8, 14; marriage, 5-6; enjoys Madrid, 69

Forsyth, Fanny Johnston Houston (Mrs. Robert), 8; mother of John Forsyth, 2
Forsyth, James, 1
Forsyth, John, 12-13, 63-64, 66, 81, 103-04, 128-29, 148-49, 150, 151, 165-66, 192-93, 194, 211-12, 219-22; ancestry, 1-2; birth, 2; education, 5; marriage, 5-6; early years, 6-9; attorney general of Georgia, 9; 1810 campaign for House of Representatives, 10; elected to House of Representatives (1812), 11; friendship with Biddle, 13-14; moves to Washington, 14; visits Georgia (1818), 14-15; elected to House of Representatives (1814, 1816, 1818), 15-16; appointed to Senate and resignation, 16-17, 45; elected to House of Representatives (1822, 1824, 1826) 17, 79; War of 1812, 17-18; Loan Bill, 18-19; supports Madison and Monroe administrations, 18-21; favors Second Bank of the United States, 21-25; opposes Compensation Act, 25-26; guardian of House integrity, 26-27; Georgia militia claims, 27-29; defends Crawford, 29-31; 1824 presidential campaign, 31-33; attitude toward Negro problem, 33-35; Foreign Relations chairman, 35-41; appointed Minister to Spain, 43-45; instruction, 45-47; voyage to Cadiz, 47-49; Cadiz experiences, 49-51; travels to Madrid, 51, 65; confers with Yurjo, 51-53; confers and corresponds with Salmon, 53-55, 57-59; cabinet discussion and new instructions, 56-57; corresponds with San Fernando, 59-60; criticizes Spanish activities, 60-61; reports Spanish insurrections, 61-62; confers with Jabat, 62; amicable relations with de Castro, 62-63; visits Bordeaux, 66-67; visits United States, 68-69; returns to Spain with family, 69; personal inconveniences, 69-71; seeks liberation of United States citizens, 71-73; protests commercial discriminations, 73-75; seeks recognition of United States consulates, 75-76; efforts to examine Madrid records, 76-77; seeks transmission of Havana archives, 77-79; prepares to depart Spain, 79-80; returns to United States, 80; defends Spanish mission, 80; affiliates with Troup party, 82; gubernatorial cam-

paign and election, 83-86; inauguration, 86-87; Gilmer controversy, 87-
89; denies Lumpkin commission, 89-
90; upholds other state laws, 90;
school funds, 90; advocates law codification, 90-91; recommends improvement of judiciary, 91; r e f o r m s
penitentiary system, 91-92; advocates
sound banking principles, 92-95; favors development of water transportation, 95-96; attitude toward internal
improvements, 96-97; 147-48; Georgia-
Florida boundary dispute, 97-101; re-
fuses second term, 89, 101-02;
appointed to Senate, 103; Indian removal, 105-17; extends criminal jurisdiction over Cherokees, 117-18; Creek-
Cherokee boundary problem 118-21;
Creek depredations, 121-24; post-gubernatorial interest in Indian affairs,
124-27; county named for, 127; critical
of Jackson, 129-30; "Crawford letter"
incident, 130-33; defends Van Buren
appointment, 134-36; attends 1832
party convention, 137; defends Jackson's Bank policies, 137-46; Post Office investigation, 146-47; comments
on tariff of 1816, 151-52; votes against
tariff of 1824, 152; denounces tariff of
1828, 152-53; debates and votes on
tariff of 1832, 153-56; attends anti-
tariff convention, 157-60; supports
Jackson in nullification crisis, 161-63;
votes for 1833 tariff, 163-65; rejects
distribution bill, 165; desires executive position, 167-69; appointed Secretary of State, 169; spoliation claims,
170-81; provoked over Pageot reappointment, 181; reconsiders resignation, 182; involved with slave trade
issues, 182-85; *Amistad* affair, 185-87;
diligence in State Department details,
187-92; difficulties with Butler, 195-
96; Mexican protests over neutrality,
196-98; Texan efforts for recognition
and annexation, 198-202; northeastern
boundary controversy, 202-07; neutrality problems with Canada, 207-
10; fisheries controversies, 210-11; desires vice-presidency, 213-15; 1840
presidential campaign, 215-17; ends
public service, 217; attends Harrison
funeral, 217; aspires to Senate seat,
217-18; death, 218-19

Forsyth, John, Jr., son of John Forsyth, 6; appointed district attorney,
182
Forsyth, Julia (Mrs. Alfred Iverson), 7,
69; daughter of John Forsyth, 6
Forsyth, Julia Hull (Mrs. Robert),
daughter-in-law of John Forsyth, 6
Forsyth, Margaret Hull (Mrs. John, Jr.),
daughter-in-law of John Forsyth, 6
Forsyth, Mary Athenia (Mrs. Arthur
Shaaff), 69; daughter of John Forsyth,
6
Forsyth, Matthew, 1
Forsyth, Robert, father of John Forsyth,
1; in American Revolution, 1-2; post-
war career, 2-4; death, 4-5
Forsyth, Robert, son of John Forsyth, 6
Forsyth, Robert Moriah, brother of
John Forsyth, 2; death, 5
Forsyth, Rosa (Mrs. William P. Aubrey),
daughter of John Forsyth, 6
Forsyth, Virginia (Mrs. George Har-
graves), daughter of John Forsyth, 6
Foster, Thomas Flournoy, attends 1832
convention, 137
Fox, Henry Stephen, 180, 181, 187; slave
trade issues, 183-84; northeastern
boundary controversy, 204-07; neutral-
ity problems with United States, 208-
10, 212
France, Beaumarchais claims, 39-40;
spoliation claims, 170-81, 192; treaties
for suppression of slave trade, 182-83
Franklin College, 6, 9
Fredericksburg, 2, 216; birthplace of
John Forsyth, 1
Frelinghuysen, Theodore, 125
Fulton, Hamilton, 95
Fundy, Bay of, 203

Gaines, Edmund Pendleton, occupies
Nacogdoches, 196-98
Gallatin, Albert, 32, 142
Galphin, Thomas, 7
Gamble, Roger L., attends anti-tariff
convention, 157
General Survey Bill, 147
Georgia Board of Public Works, 95
Gilmer, George Rockingham, contro-
versy with Forsyth, 87-89; announces
candidacy for governorship, 89; elected
governor, 102-03; presides at anti-
tariff convention, 157
Gorostizo, Manuel Eduardo de, protests
United States neutrality, 196-98, 211

Graham, John, 21
Grayson, Peter W., 199
Great Britain, treaty of 1815, 35-36;
West Indian trade, 36; offers mediation, 179-80; slave trade issues, 182-
84; northeastern boundary controversy, 202-07; neutrality problems
with United States, 207-10; fisheries
controversies, 210-11
Grundy, Felix, 185

Hamill, John, 9
Hamilton, James Alexander, "Crawford
letter" incident, 131-33
Hamilton, Robert, 198-99
Hargraves, George, son-in-law of John
Forsyth, 6
Harper, Chancellor William, 160
Harrison, Benjamin, 2
Harrison, William Henry, nominated for
presidency, 214-15; Forsyth comments
on, 216; Georgia votes for, 217, in-
auguration and death, 217
Hartford Convention, 85, 162
Harvey, Sir John, 205, 207
Havana, 46, 63, 184, 185; archives, 78-79
Hawley, Reverend William, 218
Hayne, Robert Young, 135; proposes
tariff amendment, 153-55
Hernandez, Ignacio, 195
Hillsboro, 162
Holabird, William S., Amistad case,
185-87
Horner, John Scott, 188
Hornet, 45, 50, 51, 52, 54, 55, 56; voyage
to Cadiz (1819), 47-49
Hortalez (Rodrique) and Company, 39
Houston, Samuel, 32
Hull, Latham, 6
Hunt, Memucan, 199, 200, 201-02

Indians, 18, 100, 196-98; Georgia militia
claims, 27-29; removal, 105-17, 162,
221; Georgia criminal jurisdiction extended over, 117-18; Creek-Cherokee
boundary problem, 118-21; Creek depredations, 121-24; Forsyth's post-
gubernatorial interests in, 124-27;
Seminoles, 129
Internal improvements, 96-97, 147-48
Iverson, Alfred, son-in-law of John Forsyth, 6

Jabat, Juan, 66, 73; confers with Forsyth, 62

Jackson, Andrew, 18, 85, 123, 128-29, 136,
147, 148-49, 151, 167-69, 192, 194, 196,
211, 213; 1824 presidential campaign,
31-33; Berrien appointment, 101; Indian removal, 116-17, 125; Creek-
Cherokee boundary problem, 119-20;
censured by Cherokees, 126; criticized
by Forsyth, 129-30; "Crawford letter"
incident, 130-33; nominates Van
Buren for Minister, 134; nominated
for re-election, 137; wars on United
States Bank, 137-46; opposes Nullification Ordinance, 161-62; 1833 tariff,
163-64; vetoes distribution measure,
165; spoliation claims, 170-81; accepts
Pageot reappointment, 181; slave trade
policy, 183; confers with Butler, 195-
96; authorizes Nacogdoches occupation, 197; favors Texas recognition,
198-201; northeastern boundary controversy, 203-04
Jackson, James, 5; organizes party, 81-
82
Jefferson, Thomas, 10, 40
Johnson, Richard Mentor, 213, 214, 215
Johnston, Joseph Eggleston, 2
Johnston, Peter, 2
Judiciary system, need for improvement
of, 91

Kendall, Amos, 149, 181, 185, 201
Kent, Edward, 204, 205

La Branche, Alceé, 200
Lacock, Abner, investigates Jackson's
Florida expedition, 129-30
Land system, lotteries and fractional
tracts, 9, 90; distribution bill rejected,
165
Laval, Duke of, 52
Laws, codification of, 90-91
Lee, Henry ("Light-Horse Harry"), 1
Lewis, William Berkeley, 172; "Crawford
letter" incident, 131; accomplishes
Pageot reappointment, 181
Liberia, 34-35
Lincoln, Levi, 28
Livingston, Edward, 168; spoliation
claims, 172-73, 176-77
Loan Bill, 18-19
Louis Philippe, King of France, spolia-
tion claims, 170-72, 174, 180; reap-
points Pageot, 181
Louisville, 7, 8

Louisville and Portland Canal Company, 148

Lucas, Robert, 188

Lumpkin, Wilson, 89, 100

McBride, John, 99-100

McDuffie, George, 142

McIntosh, William, 108

McIntyre, Alexander, dismissed from State Department, 187

McIntyre, Rufus, 205

Mackenzie, William Lyon, 208

McLane, Louis, 134-35; resigns as Secretary of State, 169

McLeod, Alexander, 209-10, 212

Macon, 162

Macon *Telegraph*, opposes Forsyth for governor, 83; pledges cooperation, 86

Madison, James, 18, 19, 22, 23, 25, 37, 40, 142; approves Second Bank of United States, 24

Madrid, 66, Forsyth journeys to, 51; enjoyed by Clara Forsyth, 69; Forsyth departs, 80

Maine, northeastern boundary controversy, 204-07, 211

Martin, J. L., 218

Mason, Murray, son-in-law of John Forsyth, 6

Mason, Stevens Thomson, 188

Mathews, George, 4

Maysville Bill, 148

Maysville, Washington, Paris, and Lexington Turnpike Company, 148

Meade, Richard W., claims, 40-41

Meals, John, 3

Meigs, Henry, 69

Meigs, Josiah, 10, 44; father-in-law of John Forsyth, 6

Meigs, Return Jonathan, 44

Mercer, Jesse, 5

Meriwether, James, Creek negotiations, 108,109

Mexico, 211; boundary dispute, 194; Butler's efforts to purchase Texas, 194-96; protests United States neutrality, 196-98, 221

Middleton, Arthur, 189-90, 191

Middleton, Henry, 44

Milledgeville, 86, 156, 160, 163, 214, 215, 218

Milledgeville *Federal Union*, 156, 214, 216

Milledgeville *Georgia Journal*, 10, 32; supports Forsyth for governor, 83

Milledgeville *Southern Recorder*, 61, 102, 219

Miller, Stephen Decatur, 135

Monroe, James, 5, 18, 19, 30, 31, 35, 36, 40, 43, 44, 45, 46, 47, 59, 85; disapproves East Florida seizure, 37-38; cabinet meeting and instructions to Forsyth, 56-57; disapproves Forsyth's conduct, 61; permits continuation of Forsyth mission, 64; Forsyth visits, 68; Indian removal, 106-09

Monroe Doctrine, 39

Montesquieu, Baron de (Charles Louis), 67

Montez, Pedro, 185

Montgomery, Hugh, 114, 118; Creek-Cherokee boundary problem, 119-20

Moore, Gabriel, 135

Nacogdoches, occupied, 196-97

Napoleon I, Emperor of France, 170

Navy Island, 208

Neches River, 194, 202

Negroes, 3, 192; John Forsyth's views on, 33-35; slave trade issues, 182-85; *Amistad* affair, 185-87

Nelson, Hugh, instructions to, 76, 79

Netherlands, King of, recommends northeastern boundary line, 203, 204

Neuville, Hyde de, 43, 61

New Brunswick, Aroostook War, 205-07

New York *Journal of Commerce*, 177

New York *Star*, 177

New York *Times*, 177

Niagara River, 208

Niles' Register, 45

Noel, John Y., 5

Nova Scotia, 210-11

Nullification, 151, 156, 158, 160, 163, 165-66; crisis of 1832-1833, 161-62, 221

Ogeechee River, 95-96, 105

Ohio-Michigan boundary controversy, 188-89

Onis y Gonzalez, Luis de, 44, 53, 63, 68; Adams-Onis treaty, 42-43

Oregon, Spanish claims abandoned over, 42

Othello, 80

Pageot, Alphonse J. Y., spoliation claims, 172-81; returns to Washington, 181

Palmerston, Viscount, 180, 183, 209, 210, 211; proposes mediation, 179

Panama Congress, 38-39

Paulding, James Kirke, 186
Pelegrin, Don Ramon Lopez, Florida claims records, 77
Penitentiary system, improvements, 91-92
Pinckney, Charles Cotesworth, 85
Pleasonton, S., 191
Poindexter, George, 135, 144-45, 146
Poinsett, Joel Roberts, 14-15, 201, 202, 217
Porter, Peter Buell, 19, 124
Princeton College, 5, 6, 13
Punon Rostro, Count of, 43, 52, 59

Rabun, William, 45
Radal, 48
Railroads, 95; Charleston and Hamburg, 97; Baltimore and Ohio, 148
Randall, Thomas, demands Havana archives, 79
Randolph, Deputy Marshal, 4
Randolph, Thomas Mann, 98-99
Read, George C., 45-48, 50-53, 54, 55, 56
Republican (Jeffersonian) party, 81, 84
Rey, Manuel, quarrels with Forsyth, 70-71
Rhea, John, 19
Rich, Obadiah, 68; Florida claims records, 76-77
Richards, Deputy Marshal, 4
Richmond Academy, 3, 9, 85
Richmond County, 2, 3, 17, 156, 157
Rives, John C., 171
Rives, William Cabell, 143, 188; votes for Force Bill, 162
Roads, Cumberland, 147; Maysville, Washington, Paris, and Lexington Turnpike Company, 148; Washington and Rockville Turnpike Company, 148
Robertson, Thomas Bolling, 19
Rodney, Caesar Augustus, 21
Rosa, Francisco Martinez de la, 75; Havana archives, 78
Ruiz, José, 185

Sabine River, 42, 194, 197, 202
St. John, James, 9
St. John River, 203-04
St. Lawrence River, 203, 210
St. Mary's River, Georgia-Florida boundary dispute, 98-101
Salmon, Manuel Gonzales, 66, 72; confers and corresponds with Forsyth, 53-55, 57-59

San Fernando and Quiroga, Duke of, 66, 72-73; corresponds with Forsyth, 59-60
San Miguel, Don Evaristo, 79-80; corresponds with Forsyth, 70-71; Havana archives, 78-79
Santa Anna, Antonio Lopez de, 195
Savannah, 5, 15, 92, 95, 96-97; conveys land for arsenal, 90
Savannah Georgian, opposes Forsyth for governor, 83
Savannah, Ogeechee, and Altamaha Canal, 95-96
Savannah River, 96-97
Schools, academic and poor school funds, 90
Scott, Winfield, 207, 208, 212
Secession, 151
Seminoles, 129
Serurier, Louis Barbé C., spoliation claims, 170-72
Seville, Forsyth visits, 65
Shaaff, Arthur, son-in-law of John Forsyth, 6
Slave trade, 34, 182-85, 192; Amistad affair, 185-87
Slaves, 3, 192; owned by Forsyth, 33-34; slave trade issues, 182-85; Amistad affair, 185-87
Smith, Mrs. Samuel Harrison (Margaret Bayard), 13, 68
Spain, privateers, 36-37; Meade claims, 40-41; Adams-Onis treaty, 42-43; Amistad affair, 185-87
Spalding, Thomas, 98-99; attends anti-tariff convention, 157
Sparta, 102, 156
Spoliation claims, against France, 170-81, 192
Springer, John, 5
State Rights party, 151
Stephania, 68
Stevenson, Andrew, 183, 209, 210
Summerville, 14

Tait, Charles, 16
Talbot, Matthew, Clarkite gubernatorial candidate, 84, 86; death, 86
Tallmadge, James, Jr., 28
Taney, Roger Brooke, 149; removes Bank deposits, 140-42
Tariff, of 1816, 150, 151-52; of 1820, 150; of 1824, 150, 152, 155; of 1828, 152-53, 155, 161; of 1832, 153-56, 161; (anti-tariff) convention of 1832, 156-

60; of 1833, 163-65; associated with public land policy, 165

Tattnall, Edward Fenwick, 83, 85, 86

Taylor, John, 97

Telfair, Thomas, 11

Temple, Henry John, 179; see also Palmerston, Viscount

Texas, 221; Adams-Onis Treaty, 42; Butler's efforts to purchase, 194-96; efforts for recognition and annexation, 198-202, 211; boundary settlement, 202

Thompson, Wiley, attends 1832 party convention, 137

Tigris, 184

Torrance, Mansfield, investigates Creek depredations, 123-24

Torrance, William H., attends anti-tariff convention, 157

Treaty, of commerce (1815), 35-36; Adams-Onis, 39, 40, 42-43, 45, 63, 194, 202; of San Lorenzo, 98, 100; Indian land cessions, 105; of Indian Springs, 108-11; of Washington (1826), 110-12; of New Echota, 126; with Mexico (1828 and 1831), 194, 196; with Texas, 202; with England (1783), 203, 204; with England (1818), 210

Trist, Nicholas Philip, 184

Troup, George Michael, 17, 85, 99; resigns seat in Senate, 16; heads James Jackson party, 81; vacates governorship, 83; attends Forsyth inauguration, 86; Indian removal, 105-13

Troup party, 82, 85, 86, 89, 102, 151, 152, 156; nominates Forsyth for governor, 83

Tunis, Consul, 49, 50

Tyler, John, 214, 215, 217, 218

Union (Democratic) party, 151, 163; 1840 presidential campaign, 214-16

University of Georgia, 156

Vail, Aaron, 180

Van Buren, Martin, 32, 128-29, 130, 138, 145, 160, 167-69, 185-86, 190-91, 192, 200, 201, 202, 211; appointed to Jackson cabinet 130; "Crawford letter" incident, 131, 133-34; rejected as Minister to Great Britain, 134-35; tours Europe, 136-37; nominated vice-president, 137; spoliation claims, 176-77; retains Forsyth, 182; slave trade policy, 183; northeastern boundary policy, 204-07; 1836 presidential campaign,

213-14; 1840 presidential campaign, 214-17; retires from presidency, 217; informed of Forsyth's death, 218

Van Ness, Cornelius Peter, Spanish mission, 189-90

Van Rensselaer, Stephen, 33

Vargas, Pedro de, 43, 52, 59

Vaughan, Charles Richard, 182-83; northeastern boundary controversy, 203

Verplanck bill, 163-65

Vives, Francisco Dionisio, 60, 63, 73; Havana archives, 79

Wales, Samuel A., Creek-Cherokee boundary problem, 118-19

Walker, Freeman, 61

War of 1812, 11, 17-18, 85, 150

Washington, warship captures Amistad, 185

Washington, D. C., 12-13, 14; during War of 1812, 17-18

Washington, George, 3, 27; Farewell Address, 39; medals affair, 84

Washington, Georgia, 5, 86

Washington and Rockville Turnpike Company, 148

Washington Globe, 139, 171, 172, 179, 198, 215, 216; the "suppressed letter," 175-178

Washington National Intelligencer, 18, 32, 42, 71, 169, 172, 180, 219; the "suppressed letter," 175-78

Washington Republican, 29, 32

Washington United States' Telegraph, 135, 143, 179

Wayne, James Moore, attends 1832 party convention, 137; votes for 1832 tariff, 155-56; votes for Force Bill, 162-63

Waynesboro, 163

Webster, Daniel, 30, 112, 160, 217; opposes Second Bank of United States, 23; opposes Van Buren appointment, 134; opposes removal of Bank deposits, 141

Wharton, William H., 198, 199-201

Whig party, 151, 205; Harrisburg convention, 214-15; 1840 presidential campaign, 215-17; probable disruption, 217

White, Hugh Lawson, 214

Whiting, Henry, 188

Wilde, Richard Henry, 15, 25; interested in Indian affairs, 124

Wilkes County, 2, 5, 17, 82, 86

Williams, Colonel, 12

Williams, Lewis, 26
Williams, Reuel, 205
Wise, Henry Alexander, 217
Woodbury, Levi, 185-86

Wright, James, 98

Yrujo, Marquis of Casa, 66, 72; confers with Forsyth, 51-53; banished, 53

Date Due

PRINTED IN U. S. A.